Mastering Swift 5.3

Sixth Edition

Upgrade your knowledge and become an expert in the latest version of the Swift programming language

Jon Hoffman

BIRMINGHAM - MUMBAI

Mastering Swift 5.3
Sixth Edition

Producer: Tushar Gupta
Acquisition Editor – Peer Reviews: Divya Mudaliar
Content Development Editor: Bhavesh Amin
Technical Editor: Aditya Sawant
Project Editor: Janice Gonsalves
Copy Editor: Safis Editing
Proofreader: Safis Editing
Indexer: Pratik Shirodkar
Presentation Designer: Pranit Padwal

First published: June 2015
Second edition: November 2015
Third Edition: October 2016
Forth Edition: September 2017
Fifth Edition: April 2019
Sixth Edition: November 2020

Production reference: 1191120

Published by Packt Publishing Ltd.
Livery Place
35 Livery Street
Birmingham B3 2PB, UK.

ISBN 978-1-80056-215-8

www.packt.com

packt.com

Subscribe to our online digital library for full access to over 7,000 books and videos, as well as industry leading tools to help you plan your personal development and advance your career. For more information, please visit our website.

Why subscribe?

- Spend less time learning and more time coding with practical eBooks and Videos from over 4,000 industry professionals

- Learn better with Skill Plans built especially for you

- Get a free eBook or video every month

- Fully searchable for easy access to vital information

- Copy and paste, print, and bookmark content

Did you know that Packt offers eBook versions of every book published, with PDF and ePub files available? You can upgrade to the eBook version at www.Packt.com and as a print book customer, you are entitled to a discount on the eBook copy. Get in touch with us at customercare@packtpub.com for more details.

At www.Packt.com, you can also read a collection of free technical articles, sign up for a range of free newsletters, and receive exclusive discounts and offers on Packt books and eBooks.

Contributors

About the author

Jon Hoffman has over 25 years of experience in the information technology field. Over those years, he has worked in the areas of system administration, network administration/security, and application development and architecture. Currently, Jon works as an Enterprise Software Manager for Syntech Systems.

Some of Jon's interests are spending time with his daughters, robotic projects, 3D printing, running/walking, paddle boarding, and playing basketball. Jon also enjoys Tae Kwon Do in which he and his oldest daughter earned their black belts in 2014.

With this being the sixth edition of the *Mastering Swift* book, I would like to thank everyone who has given me encouragement, positive feedback, and constructive criticism through the years. This includes my family, friends, co-workers, and everyone at Packt, but especially three very special people who are my inspiration and make life so wonderful: my two incredible daughters, Kailey and Kara, and Jen, a truly wonderful and amazing woman who I look forward to spending many years with.

About the reviewer

Gianluca Tranchedone has been developing software for over a decade for a number of companies, big and small, focusing mainly on building apps for Apple's operating systems. He adopted Swift in his projects since the first day the language was announced, and has been working with it on both Apple platforms, as well as on the server side, ever since.

Table of Contents

Preface

Swift is a general-purpose programming language, developed by Apple, that takes a very modern development approach. It was first introduced at the **Worldwide Developers Conference (WWDC)** in 2014 and now, six years later, Swift 5.3 has been released.

Over the last six years Swift has gone through many iterations, with each bringing various enhancements and improvements to the language. The last few versions of Swift are no exception, featuring new enhancements like synthesized memberwise initializers and property wrappers.

This book will help anyone master the Swift programming language, because it assumes no prior knowledge of the language. We will start with the very basics of the language and gradually get into more advanced topics, such as adding concurrency to an application, how to add copy-on-write to your custom value types, and how to use various design patterns with Swift.

Who this book is for

This book is for the developer who wants to dive into the newest version of Swift. If you are a developer that learns best by looking at and working with code, then this book is for you.

What this book covers

Chapter 1, Taking the First Steps with Swift, will introduce you to the Swift programming language and discuss what inspired Apple to create Swift. We'll also go over the basic syntax of Swift and how to use playgrounds to experiment and test Swift code.

Chapter 2, Swift Documentation and Installing Swift, will introduce you to the `swift.org` and `swiftdoc.org` sites and how the Swift development process works. We will go through the complete process of building Swift from source and installing it on both Linux and Mac platforms.

Chapter 3, Learning about Variables, Constants, Strings, and Operators, will introduce variables and constants in Swift and explain when to use them. There will be brief overviews of the most common variable types, with examples on how to use them. We'll conclude this chapter with some examples of how to use the most common operators in the Swift language.

Chapter 4, Optional Types, will explain what optional types really are, and the various ways to unwrap them. For a developer who is just learning Swift, optional types can be one of the more confusing concepts to learn.

Chapter 5, Using Swift Collections, will explain Swift's array, set, and dictionary collection types and show examples on how to use them.

Chapter 6, Control Flow, will show you how to use Swift's control flow statements. These include looping, conditional, and control transfer statements.

Chapter 7, Functions, is all about functions in Swift. We will show how to define and properly use them.

Chapter 8, Classes, Structures, and Protocols, is dedicated to Swift's classes, structures, and protocols. We'll look at what makes them similar and how they differ.

Chapter 9, Protocol and Protocol Extensions, will cover both protocols and protocol extensions in detail. Protocols are very important to the Swift language, and having a solid understanding of them will help us write flexible and reusable code.

Chapter 10, Protocol-Oriented Design, will cover the best practices of protocol-oriented design with Swift.

Chapter 11, Generics, will explain how Swift implements generics. Generics allow us to write flexible and reusable code that avoids duplication.

Chapter 12, Error Handling and Availability, will cover error handling in depth as well as the availability feature.

Chapter 13, Custom Subscripting, will discuss how we can use custom subscripts in our classes, structures, and enumerations.

Chapter 14, Working with Closures, will show how to define and use closures in our code. This chapter concludes with a section on how to avoid strong reference cycles with closures.

Chapter 15, Advanced and Custom Operators, will show how to use bitwise and overflow operators. We will also look at how we can create custom operators.

Chapter 16, Concurrency and Parallelism in Swift, will show how to use both Grand Central Dispatch and operation queues to add concurrency and parallelism to our applications.

Chapter 17, Custom Value Types, will cover some advanced techniques that you can use in your applications, like copy-on-write and implementing the Equatable protocol.

Chapter 18, Memory Management, will cover topics like how Automatic Reference Counting (ARC) works, how much faster value types are as compared to reference types, how strong retain cycles work, and how weak and strong references compare.

Chapter 19, Swift Formatting and Style Guide, will define a style guide for the Swift language that can be used as a template for enterprise developers who need to create their own style guide.

Chapter 20, Adopting Design Patterns in Swift, will show you how to implement some of the more common design patterns in Swift. A design pattern identifies a common software development problem and provides a strategy for dealing with it.

To get the most out of this book

This book assumes no knowledge of the Swift programming language or any other language. All code examples have been tested using Xcode 12.01 on a Mac, however they should work using Swift on Linux or Windows as well.

Download the example code files

The code bundle for the book is also hosted on GitHub at `https://github.com/PacktPublishing/Mastering-Swift-5.3_Sixth-Edition`. We also have other code bundles from our rich catalog of books and videos available at `https://github.com/PacktPublishing/`. Check them out!

Download the color images

We also provide a PDF file that has color images of the screenshots/diagrams used in this book. You can download it here: `https://static.packt-cdn.com/downloads/9781800562158_ColorImages.pdf`.

Conventions used

There are a number of text conventions used throughout this book.

CodeInText: Indicates code words in text, database table names, folder names, filenames, file extensions, pathnames, dummy URLs, user input, and Twitter handles. For example; "Once the grade is retrieved, we will use it to set the grade property of the MyValueType instance."

A block of code is set as follows:

```
protocol Occupation {
    var occupationName: String { get set }
    var yearlySalary:Double { get set }
    var experienceYears: Double { get set }
}
```

Any command-line input or output is written as follows:

```
./swift/utils/build-script --preset=buildbot_swiftpm_linux_
platform,tools=RA,stdlib=RA
```

Bold: Indicates a new term, an important word, or words that you see on the screen, for example, in menus or dialog boxes, also appear in the text like this. For example: "Swift is a programming language that was introduced by Apple at the **Worldwide Developers Conference (WWDC) in 2014.**"

 Warnings or important notes appear like this.

 Tips and tricks appear like this.

Get in touch

Feedback from our readers is always welcome.

General feedback: Email `feedback@packtpub.com`, and mention the book's title in the subject of your message. If you have questions about any aspect of this book, please email us at `questions@packtpub.com`.

Errata: Although we have taken every care to ensure the accuracy of our content, mistakes do happen. If you have found a mistake in this book we would be grateful if you would report this to us. Please visit, `http://www.packtpub.com/submit-errata`, selecting your book, clicking on the Errata Submission Form link, and entering the details.

Piracy: If you come across any illegal copies of our works in any form on the Internet, we would be grateful if you would provide us with the location address or website name. Please contact us at `copyright@packtpub.com` with a link to the material.

If you are interested in becoming an author: If there is a topic that you have expertise in and you are interested in either writing or contributing to a book, please visit `http://authors.packtpub.com`.

Reviews

Please leave a review. Once you have read and used this book, why not leave a review on the site that you purchased it from? Potential readers can then see and use your unbiased opinion to make purchase decisions, we at Packt can understand what you think about our products, and our authors can see your feedback on their book. Thank you!

For more information about Packt, please visit `packtpub.com`.

1

Taking the First Steps with Swift

Ever since I was 12 years old and wrote my first program in BASIC, I have been passionate about programming. Even as I became a professional programmer, programming remained more of a passion than a job, but in the years preceding the first release of Swift, that passion had waned. I was unsure why I was losing that passion. I attempted to recapture it with some of my side projects, but nothing really brought back the excitement that I used to have. Then, something amazing happened: Apple announced Swift in 2014. Swift is such an exciting and progressive language that it has brought a lot of that passion back for me and made programming fun again. With official versions of Swift available for the Linux and Windows platforms and an unofficial version for the ARM platform, developing with Swift is becoming available to people outside the Apple ecosystem. There are also some very exciting projects using Swift, such as TensorFlow for machine learning and CoreML for IBM Watson. This is an exciting time to be learning the Swift language.

In this chapter, you will learn about the following topics:

- What is Swift?
- What are some of the features of Swift?
- What are playgrounds?
- How to use playgrounds
- What are the basic syntaxes of the Swift language?

What is Swift?

Swift is a programming language that was introduced by Apple at the **Worldwide Developers Conference (WWDC)** in 2014. Swift was arguably the most significant announcement at WWDC 2014 and very few people, including Apple insiders, were aware of the project's existence prior to it being announced.

It was amazing, even by Apple's standards, that they could keep Swift a secret for as long as they did and that no one suspected they were going to announce a new development language. At WWDC 2015, Apple made another big splash when they announced Swift 2. Swift 2 was a major enhancement to the Swift language. During that conference, Chris Lattner said that a lot of the enhancements were based on direct feedback that Apple received from the development community. It was also announced that Swift would become an open source project. In my opinion, this was the most exciting announcement of WWDC 2015.

In December 2015, Apple officially released Swift as open source with the `https://swift.org/` site, which is dedicated to the open source Swift community. The Swift repository is located on Apple's GitHub page (`http://github.com/apple`). The Swift evolution repository (`https://github.com/apple/swift-evolution`) tracks the evolution of Swift by documenting the proposed changes. A list of which proposals were accepted and rejected can be found in the evolution repository. In addition to these resources, Apple has moved away from using mailing lists as the primary form of communication with the Swift community, and has set up Swift forums (`https://forums.swift.org`).

Swift 3, which was released in 2016, was a major enhancement to the Swift language that was not source-compatible with previous releases of the Swift language. It contained fundamental changes to the language itself and to the Swift standard library. One of the main goals of Swift 3 was to be source-compatible across all platforms, so the code that was written for one platform would be compatible with all other platforms. This means that the code we develop for macOS should work on Linux.

In September 2017, Swift 4 was released. One of the primary goals of the Swift 4 compiler was to be source-compatible with Swift 3. This enables us to compile both Swift 3 and Swift 4 projects with the Swift 4 compiler. Apple has established a community-owned source-compatibility test suite that will be used to regression test changes to the compiler.

Projects that are added to the test suite will be periodically built against the latest development version of Swift to help us understand the impact of the changes being made to Swift. You can find the Swift source compatibility page here: `https://swift.org/source-compatibility/`.

One of the original goals of Swift 4 was to stabilize the Swift **Application Binary Interface (ABI)**. The main benefit of a stable ABI is to allow us to distribute frameworks in a binary format across multiple versions of Swift. If a stable ABI is in place, we can build a framework with the Swift 4 compiler and have it work with applications that were written in future versions of Swift. This feature ended up being deferred to Swift 5.

With the release of Swift 5, the ABI has been declared stable for all Apple platforms. You can read Swift's ABI Stability Manifesto here: `https://github.com/apple/swift/blob/master/docs/ABIStabilityManifesto.md`. As development for Swift on other platforms, such as Linux, matures, the Swift Core team has said that they will evaluate stabilizing the ABI for those platforms as well. A stable ABI means that a library that is compiled for one version of Swift—let's say Swift 5—will theoretically work with future versions of Swift, without having to be recompiled.

Since Swift 5 was released, Apple has released three additional versions: 5.1, 5.2, and 5.3. Each of these releases has added to or improved Swift. Throughout this book, we will see some of these changes and show you how you can use them. However, one of the most exciting changes will not be shown because we do not have a way to actually show it. This change occurred in Swift 5.1 when the Swift community implemented the **Language Server Protocol (LSP)**.

The LSP enables code editors and IDEs to standardize the support for languages. Before LSP, when an editor or IDE wanted to support a particular language, that support had to be built into the tool. With LSP, the language itself provides that functionality, so any editor or IDE that supports LSP can now support Swift with features such as syntax highlighting, autocomplete, and tooltips. This enables support for Swift in any editor that supports LSP, such as VSCode. This is pretty exciting news if you have ever tried to code a Swift application in vi.

One of the most exciting things, with the release of Swift 5.3, was the release of an officially supported Windows 10 port of Swift. This is exciting because we are now able to use our Swift knowledge to develop on the Windows platform. The Windows port is provided by Saleem Abdulrasool, platform champion for the Windows port of Swift.

The development of Swift was started in 2010 by Chris Lattner. He implemented much of the basic language structure when only a few people were aware of its existence. It wasn't until late 2011 that other developers began to contribute to Swift. In July 2013, it became a major focus of the Apple Developer Tools group.

Chris started working at Apple in the summer of 2005. He held several positions within the Developer Tools group and was the director and architect of that group when he left Apple in 2017. On his home page (`http://www.nondot.org/sabre/`), he notes that Xcode's playground (we'll talk more about playgrounds a little later in this chapter) became a personal passion of his because it makes programming more interactive and approachable. If you are using Swift on the Apple platform, you will be using playgrounds a lot as a test and experimentation platform. You can also use Swift Playgrounds on the iPad.

There are a lot of similarities between Swift and Objective-C. Swift adopts the readability of Objective-C's named parameters and dynamic object model. When we refer to Swift as having a dynamic object model, we are referring to the ability of types to change at runtime. This includes adding new (custom) types and changing/extending existing types.

While there are a lot of similarities between Swift and Objective-C, there are significant differences between them as well. Swift's syntax and formatting are a lot closer to Python than Objective-C, but Apple did keep the curly brackets. I know Python people would disagree with me, and that is all right because we all have different opinions, but I like the curly brackets. Swift actually requires the curly brackets for control statements, such as `if` and `while`, which eliminate bugs, such as `goto fail` in Apple's SSL library.

Swift features

When Apple first introduced Swift, it said that *Swift is Objective-C without the C.* This really only tells us half of the story. Objective-C is a superset of C and provides object-oriented capabilities and a dynamic runtime to the C language. This meant that with Objective-C, Apple needed to maintain compatibility with C, which limited the enhancements it could make to the Objective-C language. As an example, Apple could not change how the `switch` statement functioned and has still maintained compatibility with the C language.

Since Swift does not need to maintain the same C compatibility as Objective-C, Apple was free to add any feature/enhancement to the language. This allowed Apple to include the best features from many of today's most popular and modern languages, such as Objective-C, Python, Java, Ruby, C#, and Haskell.

The following table shows a list of some of the most exciting enhancements that Swift offers compared to the Objective-C language:

Swift feature	Description
Type inference	Swift can automatically deduce the type of a variable or constant, based on the initial value.
Generics	Generics allow us to write code once to perform identical tasks for different types of objects.
Collection mutability	Swift does not have separate objects for mutable or non-mutable containers. Instead, you define mutability by defining the container as a constant or variable.
Closure syntax	Closures are self-contained blocks of functionality that can be passed around and used in our code.
Optionals	Optionals define a variable that might not have a value.
`switch` statement	The `switch` statement has been drastically improved. This is one of my favorite improvements.
Tuples	Functions can have multiple return types by using tuples.
Operator overloading	Classes can provide their own implementations of existing operators.
Enumerations with associated values	In Swift, we can do a lot more than just define a group of related values with enumerations.
Protocols and protocol-oriented design	Apple introduced the protocol-oriented programming paradigm with Swift version 2. This is a new way of not only writing applications but also changing how we think about programming. This is discussed in *Chapter 10, Protocol-Oriented Design*.

Table 1.1: Swift features

Before we begin our journey into the wonderful world of Swift development, let's take a detour and visit a place that I have loved ever since I was a kid: the playground.

Playgrounds

When I was a kid, the best part of the school day was going to the playground. It really did not matter what we were playing, as long as we were on the playground. When Apple introduced playgrounds as part of Xcode 6, I was excited just by the name, but I wondered whether Apple would be able to make its playgrounds as fun as the playgrounds of my youth. While Apple's playgrounds might not be as fun as playing kickball when I was 9 years old, it definitely brings a lot of fun back to experimenting and playing with code.

Playgrounds are also available for iPad. While we are not going to cover the iPad version specifically in this section, the iPad version is a great way to experiment with the Swift language and is a great way to get children interested in programming.

Getting started with playgrounds

Playgrounds are interactive work environments that let us write code and see the results immediately as changes are made to the code. This means that playgrounds are a great way to learn and experiment with Swift. Now that we can use Swift Playgrounds on iPad, we do not even need to have a computer in front of us to experiment with Swift.

If you are using Swift on the Linux platform, you will not have playgrounds available, but you can use the **Read-Evaluate-Print-Loop** (**REPL**) shell to experiment with Swift without compiling your code. If you are using Swift on something other than a macOS computer or iPad, you can safely skip this section and go to the *Swift language syntax* section. In *Chapter 2, Swift Documentation and Installing Swift*, we look at additional tools, such as Swift's package manger and the Swift compiler, as alternative ways that we can build and run the sample code in this book.

Playgrounds also make it incredibly easy for us to try out new APIs, prototype new algorithms, and demonstrate how code works. You can use playgrounds throughout this book to see how the sample code works. Therefore, before we really get into Swift development, let's spend some time learning about, and getting comfortable with, playgrounds.

Do not worry if the Swift code does not make a lot of sense right now; as we proceed through this book, the code that we use in the following examples will begin to make sense. We are simply trying to get a feel for playgrounds right now.

A playground can have several sections, but the three that we will be using extensively in this book are:

- **Coding Area**: This is where you enter your Swift code.
- **Results Sidebar**: This is where the results of your code are shown. Each time you type in a new line of code, the results are reevaluated, and the **Results Sidebar** section is updated with the new results.
- **Debug Area**: This area displays the output of the code, and it can be very useful for debugging.

The following screenshot shows how these sections are arranged in a playground:

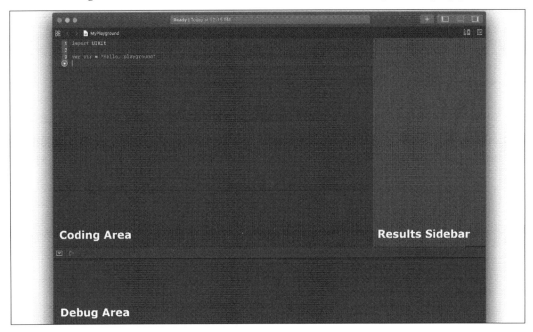

Figure 1.1: Playground layout

Let's start a new playground. The first thing we need to do is start Xcode. Once Xcode has started, we can select the **Get started with a playground** option, as shown in the following screenshot:

Figure 1.2: Starting a new playground

Alternatively, we can navigate to **Playground...** by going to **File** | **New** from the top menu bar, as shown in the following screenshot:

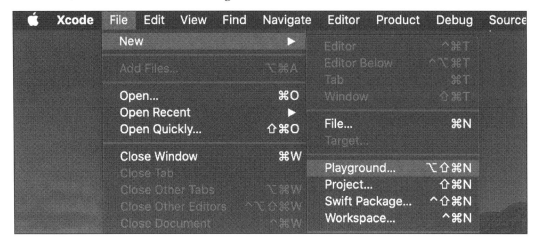

Figure 1.3: Creating a new playground

Next, we should see a screen similar to *Figure 1.4*. This screen lets us name our playground and select whether the playground is an **iOS**, **tvOS**, or **macOS** playground. For most of the examples in this chapter, it is safe to assume that you can select any of the OS options, unless it is otherwise noted. You can also select a template to use. For the examples in this book, we will be using the **Blank** template for all of our code:

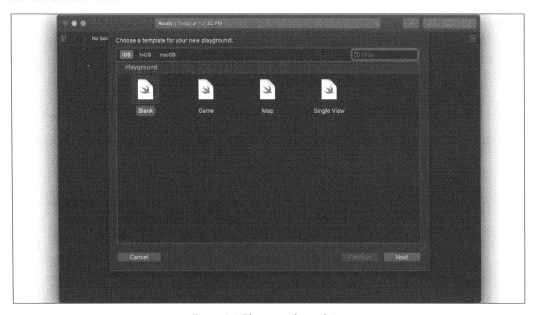

Figure 1.4: Playground templates

Finally, we are asked for the location in which to save our playground. After we select the location, the playground will open and look similar to *Figure 1.5*:

Figure 1.5: Playground screen

In the preceding screenshot, we can see that the coding area of the playground looks similar to the coding area for an Xcode project. What is different here is the sidebar on the right-hand side. This sidebar is where the results of our code are shown. The code in the previous screenshot imports the **Cocoa** framework since it is a macOS playground. If it were an iOS playground, it would import the **UIKit** framework instead.

If your new playground does not open the debug area, you can open it manually by pressing the *shift + command + Y* keys together. Alternatively, you can use the sidebar button at the top-right corner of the playground window. You can also close the debug area by pressing *shift + command + Y* again. Later in this chapter, we will see why the debug area is so useful. Another way to open or close the debug area is to click on the button that looks like an upside-down triangle, in a box that is on the border between the debug area and the coding area.

iOS, tvOS, and macOS playgrounds

When you start a new iOS or tvOS playground, the playground imports the UIKit framework. This gives us access to the UIKit framework, which provides the core infrastructure for iOS and tvOS applications. When we start a new macOS playground, the playground imports the Cocoa framework.

What the last paragraph means is that if we want to experiment with specific features of either UIKit or Cocoa, we need to open the correct playground. As an example, if we have an iOS playground open, and we want to create an object that represents a color, we would use a `UIColor` object. If we had a macOS playground open, we would use an `NSColor` object to represent a color.

Creating and displaying graphs in playgrounds

Creating and displaying graphs is useful when we are prototyping new algorithms. This is because they allow us to see the value of a variable throughout our calculations. To see how graphing works, look at the following playground:

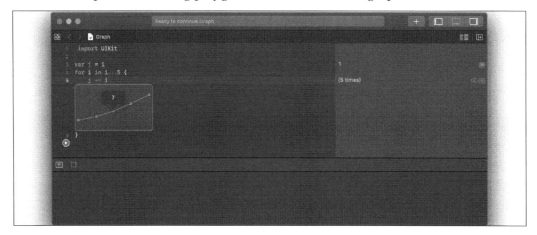

Figure 1.6: Creating a loop

In this playground, we set the j variable to 1. Next, we create a for loop that assigns numbers 1 through 5 to the i variable. At each step in the for loop, we set the value of the j variable to the current value of j plus i. A graph can change the values of the j variable at each step of the for loop, helping us see how the variable changes over time. We will cover for loops in detail later in this book.

To bring up the graph, click on the symbol that is shaped like a circle with a dot in it. We can then move the timeline slider to see the values of the j variable at each step of the for loop. The following playground shows what the graph should look like:

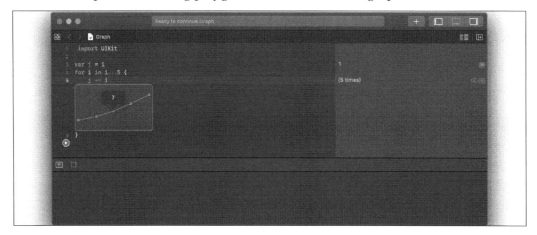

Figure 1.7: Drawing a graph

Graphs can be very helpful when we want to see how variables change over the course of the code's execution.

What playgrounds are not

There is a lot more that we can do with playgrounds, and we have only scratched the surface in our quick introduction here. Before we leave this brief introduction, let's take a look at what playgrounds are not so that we can better understand when not to use playgrounds:

- **Playgrounds should not be used for performance testing**: The performance you see from any code that is run in a playground is not representative of how fast the code will run when it is in your project
- **Playgrounds do not support on-device execution**: You cannot run the code that is present in a playground as an external application or on an external device

Now, let's familiarize ourselves with some basic Swift syntax.

Swift language syntax

If you are an Objective-C developer, and you are not familiar with modern languages such as Python or Ruby, the code in the previous screenshots may have looked pretty strange. The Swift language syntax is a huge departure from Objective-C, which was based largely on Smalltalk and C.

The Swift language uses modern concepts and syntax to create very concise and readable code. There is also a heavy emphasis on eliminating common programming mistakes.

Before we get into the Swift language itself, let's look at some of the basic syntax of the Swift language.

Comments

Writing comments in Swift code is a little different from writing comments in Objective-C code. We can still use double slash (//) for single-line comments and /** and */ for multiline comments; however, if we want to use the comments to also document our code, we need to use the triple slash (///) or multiline comment block.

You can auto-generate a comment template based on your signature of the method/function with Xcode by highlighting it and pushing *command* + *option* + / together.

To document our code, we generally use fields that Xcode recognizes. These fields are as follows:

- **Parameter**: When we start a line with `parameter {param name}:`, Xcode recognizes this as the description of a parameter.

- **Return**: When we start a line with `return:`, Xcode recognizes this as the description of the return value.

- **Throws**: When we start a line with `throws:`, Xcode recognizes this as a description of any errors that this method may throw.

The following playground shows examples of both single-line and multiline comments and how to use the comment fields:

Figure 1.8: Adding comments in a playground

To write good comments, I would recommend using single-line comments within a function to give quick one-line explanations of your code. We then use multiline comments outside functions and classes to explain what the function and class do. The preceding playground shows a good way to use comments. By using proper documentation, as we did in the preceding screenshot, we can use the documentation feature within Xcode. If we hold down the *option* key and then click on the function name anywhere in our code, Xcode will display a popup with a description of the function.

The following screenshot shows what that popup would look like:

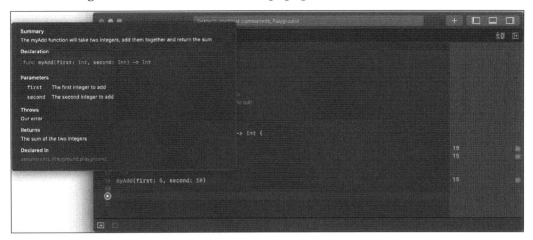

Figure 1.9: Xcode documentation on functions

We can see that the documentation contains five fields. These fields are as follows:

- **Declaration**: This is the function's declaration.
- **Parameters**: This is the description of the function's as they appear in the comments. The parameter descriptions are prefixed with the Parameters: tag in the comment section.
- **Throws**: The throws description is prefixed with the throws tag and describes what errors are thrown by the methods.
- **Returns**: The returns description is prefixed with the returns: tag in the comment section.
- **Declared In**: This is the file that the function is declared in so that we can easily find it.

There are significantly more fields that we can add to our comments. You can find the complete list on Apple's site: https://developer.apple.com/library/content/documentation/Xcode/Reference/xcode_markup_formatting_ref/MarkupFunctionality.html.

 If you are developing for the Linux platform, I would still recommend using Apple's documentation guidelines because, as other Swift IDEs are developed, I believe they will support the same guidelines.

Semicolons

You may have noticed, from the code samples so far, that we are not using semicolons at the end of lines. Semicolons are optional in Swift; therefore, both lines in the following playground are valid in Swift:

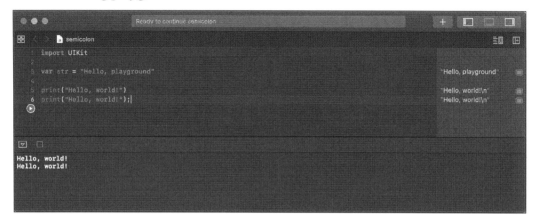

Figure 1.10: The use of semicolons in Swift

For style purposes, it is strongly recommended that you do not use semicolons in your Swift code. If you are really set on using semicolons, be consistent and use them on every line of code; however, there is no warning if you forget them.

 I will stress this again: it is recommended that you do not use semicolons in Swift.

Parentheses

In Swift, parentheses around conditional statements are optional; for example, both if statements in the following playground are valid:

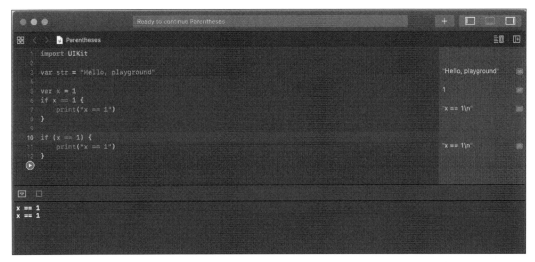

Figure 1.11: Parentheses in Swift

For style purposes, it is recommended that you do not include parentheses in your code unless you have multiple conditional statements on the same line. For readability purposes, it is good practice to put parentheses around individual conditional statements that are on the same line.

Curly brackets

In Swift, unlike most other languages, a curly bracket is required after conditional or loop statements. This is one of the safety features that is built into Swift. Arguably, there have been numerous security bugs that could have been prevented if the developer had used curly brackets. These bugs could have also been prevented by other means, such as unit testing and code reviews, but requiring developers to use curly brackets, in my opinion, is a good security standard.

The following playground shows you the error you get if you forget to include curly brackets:

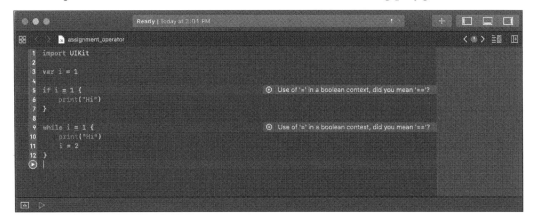

Figure 1.12: Curly brackets in Swift

An assignment operator does not return a value

In most other languages, the following line of code is valid, but it probably isn't what the developer meant to do:

```
if (x = 1) {}
```

In Swift, this statement is not valid. Using an assignment operator (=) in a conditional statement (if, while, and guard) will throw an error. This is another safety feature built into Swift. It prevents the developer from forgetting the second equals sign (=) in a comparison statement. This error is shown in the following playground:

Figure 1.13: Assignment operators in Swift

Spaces are optional in conditional and assignment statements

For both conditional (`if` and `while`) and assignment (`=`) statements, the white spaces are optional. Therefore, in the following playground, both the i and j blocks of code are valid:

Figure 1.14: Spaces in Swift

For style purposes, I recommend adding the white spaces as the j block shows (for readability), but as long as you pick one style and are consistent, either style is acceptable.

Hello World

All good computer books that are written to teach a computer language have a section that shows the user how to write a Hello World application. This book is no exception. In this section, we will show you how to write two different Hello World applications.

Our first Hello World application will be a traditional Hello World application that simply prints Hello World to the console. Let's begin by creating a new playground and naming it `Chapter_1_Hello_World`.

In Swift, to print a message to the console, we use the `print()` function. In its most basic form, we would use the `print()` function to print out a single message, as shown in the following code:

```
print("Hello World")
```

Usually, when we use the `print()` function, we want to print more than just static text. We can include the value of variables and/or constants by using string interpolation or by separating the values within the `print()` function with commas. String interpolation uses a special sequence of characters, \( ), to include the values of variables and/or constants in the string. The following code shows how to do this:

```
let name = "Jon"
let language = "Swift"
var message1 = " Welcome to the wonderful world of "
var message2 = "\(name), Welcome to the wonderful world of \
(language)!"
print(message2)
print(name, message1, language, "!")
```

We can also define two parameters in the `print()` function that change how the message is displayed in the console. These parameters are the `separator` and `terminator` parameters. The `separator` parameter defines a string that is used to separate the values of the variables/constants in the `print()` function. By default, the `print()` function separates each variable/constant with a space. The `terminator` parameter defines what character is put at the end of the line. By default, the newline character is added at the end of the line.

The following code shows how we would create a comma-separated list that does not have a newline character at the end:

```
let name1 = "Jon"
let name2 = "Kailey"
let name3 = "Kara"
print(name1, name2, name3, separator:", ", terminator:"")
```

There is one other parameter that we can add to our `print()` function: the `to:` parameter. This parameter will let us redirect the output of the `print()` function. In the following example, we redirect the output to a variable named `line`:

```
let name1 = "Jon"
let name2 = "Kailey"
let name3 = "Kara"
var line = ""
```

```
print(name1, name2, name3, separator:", ", terminator:"", to:&line)
print(line)
```

Previously, the print() function was simply a useful tool for basic debugging, but now, with the new, enhanced print() function, we can use it for a lot more.

The output from the previous two examples is a comma-separated list of Jon, Kailey, Kara.

Summary

We began this chapter with a discussion on the Swift language and gave a brief history of it. We also mentioned some of the changes that are present in the newer versions of Swift. We then showed you how to start and use playgrounds to experiment with Swift programming. We also covered the basic Swift language syntax and discussed proper language styles. This chapter concluded with two Hello World examples.

In the next chapter, we will look at the documentation offered by Apple and the Swift community. We will then see how we can build Swift from source and use the Swift compiler.

2
Swift Documentation and Installing Swift

I spent a lot of my career working as a Linux System Administrator and Network Security Administrator. These positions required me to compile and install packages from source. There are a lot of advantages to building packages from source rather than downloading prebuilt binaries. The biggest advantage, in my opinion, is that you can get the latest version without having to wait for someone else to build it. This allows me to patch my systems with the latest security updates without delay. With Swift, we are also able to download the latest code and compile ourselves without having to wait for someone else to build it.

In this chapter, you will learn:

- About the swift.org website and what it offers
- How to find the latest documentation on Swift
- Ways to install Swift
- How to build Swift from source with its full toolchain and package manager

In the previous chapter, we mentioned that Apple has released Swift as an open source project with the swift.org site dedicated to the Swift community. This means we can download the source code for the Swift language, examine it, and build Swift ourselves. Before we really dive into the Swift language and develop with it, let's look at how we can build Swift from source and the resources that Apple has made available to us. We will start by looking at the swift.org site.

Swift.org

On December 3, 2015, Apple officially released the Swift language, supporting libraries, the debugger, and the package manager to the open source community under the Apache 2.0 license. At that time, the `swift.org` site was created as the community's gateway to the project. This site has a wealth of information and should be your primary site to find out what is happening in the Swift community and the language itself. The blog posts will keep you up to date with new releases of Swift, new Swift open source libraries, changes to the standard library, and other Swift news.

You can also download pre-built binaries for several flavors of Linux. At the time this book is being written, we can download pre-built binaries for Ubuntu 16.04, Ubuntu 18.04, Ubuntu 20.04, CentOS 8, and Amazon Linux 2. The getting started page provides a list of dependencies for the previously mentioned flavors of Linux and instructions on how to install the binaries.

The website also includes the official Swift documentation, which includes things like the language guide, a Swift introduction, and an API design guideline. Understanding the API design guideline is essential to ensuring that your code meets the recommended coding standards. In *Chapter 18, Swift Formatting and Style Guide*, we provide recommendations for coding standards in Swift, which go hand in hand with Apple's recommendations.

You will also find information on how to contribute to the Swift community, where the Swift source code can be downloaded, and there is even a section on recommended Google Summer of Code projects with Swift. If you really want to get into Swift development, whether it be server-side, Mac, or iOS development, I would recommend making regular visits to the `swift.org` site to keep up to date with what is happening in the Swift community.

Apple and the Swift community also have a number of documentation resources that you can use for reference.

Swift documentation

Apple and the Swift community, as a whole, have released a number of resources to help developers program in Swift. Apple's official documentation, which can be found at `https://developer.apple.com/documentation/`, includes API documentation for Swift as well as all of Apple's frameworks. Only a small portion of Apple's frameworks are open source and work across all platforms; however if you are looking to get started on one of Apple's frameworks this is definitely the place to start. However it can be hard to find documentation on specific Swift APIs.

To quickly find documentation on Swift's API, my favorite site is `https://swiftdoc.org`. This site is incredibly easy to navigate and has autogenerated documentation for all types, protocols, operators, and global functions that make up the Swift language. I have noticed that this site does not always stay up to date; however, it is a great reference for any Swift developer. The code that generates this site is open source as well and can be found on GitHub here: `https://github.com/SwiftDocOrg/swift-doc`. The GitHub page gives directions on how you can generate your own offline documentation.

The final site that I am going to mention here is one that I recently discovered on one of my favorite Swift sites. It is the Swift knowledge base on the Hacking with Swift site located here: `https://www.hackingwithswift.com/example-code/`. Once you learn Swift and need to know how to do something like parsing JSON, extracting a PDF, or any other specific function, there is a good chance you can find what you need here.

Now that we know where to look for documentation on Swift, let's see the different ways that we can install Swift.

Installing Swift from swift.org

If you are developing on and for the Apple platform, I strongly suggest that you stick with the version of Swift that comes with Xcode. Apple will not approve an app that was compiled using a version of Swift that is different than the one that came with the version of Xcode that you are using. This may seem a little extreme, but it ensures that the apps are compiled with a stable version of Swift and one that has been fully vetted to work with your version of Xcode.

If you are using one of the flavors of Linux that has pre-built binaries on the `swift.org` site, it is recommended that you use those. They are the easiest and quickest path to getting Swift up and running. You can also find complete installation instructions with a list of dependencies on the `swift.org` site under the *Getting Started* section.

If pre-built binaries are not provided for your flavor of Linux, if you want to try the latest version of Swift, or if you just want to see what it is like to build Swift from source, you can do that as well.

Building Swift and the Swift toolchain from source

There are a number of sites that show you how to build Swift from source, but unfortunately most of these sites give directions for building just the Swift language itself without the toolchain. I find that not very useful, unless you are only writing very simple applications. In my opinion, building Swift for Linux without the entire toolchain and the package manager is more of an exercise of *"Can I do it"* rather than building something you can use long term.

 While using the latest build of Swift is not recommended for production systems, it does enable us to use the latest features of the language and also verify that changes introduced in our application are compatible with future versions of the Swift language.

In this chapter, we will look at how we can build Swift, its entire toolchain, and the Swift package manager from source. Since each flavor of Linux and macOS are somewhat different, I need to pick one platform to write these instructions on; therefore I am using Ubuntu 18.04 and the current Swift 5.3 development release at the time of writing this book. For other flavors or versions of Linux, you may have to make changes to the dependencies that are installed or how they are installed. The command to build Swift itself will be the same across all platforms.

 Some of these commands can be quite large to type. All of the commands are in text files that you can cut and paste from in the downloadable code for this book.

Now let's start building Swift by installing the dependencies.

Installing dependencies

The first thing we need to do is to make sure we have all of the dependencies required. The following command includes dependencies I have needed to install on different flavors of Linux.

You may find that your distribution already has some of these preinstalled but to make sure you have everything, run the following command:

```
sudo apt-get install git cmake ninja-build clang python uuid-dev
libicu-dev icu-devtools libedit-dev libxml2-dev libsqlite3-dev swig
libpython-dev python-six libncurses5-dev pkg-config libcurl4-openssl-
dev systemtap-sdt-dev tzdata rsync
```

One thing to note is dependencies can change and if you attempt to compile from source and you receive an error that something is missing, add it with the `apt-get install` command or the package manager on your system. Now that we have all of the dependencies installed, we need to download the Swift source code.

Swift source

To download the Swift source code, we will want to create a new directory that we can download the code to, change to that directory, and then run the `git` command to retrieve the source. The following commands will download the Swift source to a directory named `swift-source`:

```
mkdir swift-source
cd swift-source
git clone https://github.com/apple/swift.git
./swift/utils/update-checkout --clone
```

Now that we have the source and have cloned what we need, let's build Swift.

Building Swift

Before you begin building Swift, you will need to understand that this will take hours to build depending on your system or virtual machine setup. If you are using a virtual machine, like VirtualBox, I would strongly recommend that you allocate multiple cores to your virtual machine; it will dramatically shorten the build time. The following command will build Swift, its toolchain, and the package manager:

```
./swift/utils/build-script --preset=buildbot_swiftpm_linux_
platform,tools=RA,stdlib=RA
```

Once this has built everything, we need to install it somewhere and put the binaries in our path.

Installing Swift

Now that we have built Swift and its toolchain, we are ready to install it. I like to install Swift under the /opt directory, others prefer installing it under the /usr/ local/share directory. What directory you put it under is totally up to you. I will walk you through installing it under the /opt directory, if you would like to put it someplace else then simply replace the /opt in the paths with the directory that you wish to install it to.

Let's start the installation by changing to the /opt directory and creating a new directory named swift. We need to change the permissions for this directory so that we can read, write, and execute files. The following commands will do this:

```
cd /opt
sudo mkdir swift
sudo chmod 777 swift
```

The command chmod 777 swift adds read, write, and execute permissions for all users of this computer. I like to use this mode because then any user on the system can use Swift; however, this can be considered a security issue because it also means anyone can modify the files. Use this at your own risk and for production systems, I would really look at who needs permissions for this directly and lock it down more.

Next we need to move the Swift binaries that we built to the swift directory. To do this we will change to the swift directory, create a new directory for our build, change to the directory, and copy the files over. The following commands will do this:

```
cd swift
mkdir swift-5.3-dev
cd swift-5.3-dev
cp -R ~/swift-source/build/buildbot_incremental/toolchain-
linux-x86_64/* ./
```

Now we want to make a symlink to this directory called swift-current. The reason for this is it enables us to add an entry to our PATH environmental variable so that the operating system can find the Swift executables without us needing to enter the full path. If we set up this entry using the swift-current path rather than the swift.5.3-dev path, it enables us, when we install new versions of Swift, to simply change where the swift-current symlink points to and have everything work. We can do this with the following command from the /opt/swift directory:

```
sudo ln -s /opt/swift/swift-5.3-dev swift-current
```

Now we need to create the entry in our PATH variable. To do this we add the /opt/swift/swift-current/usr/bin/ directory to the PATH variable in our .profile file located in your home directory. Then update the environment. The following commands do this:

```
cd ~
echo 'PATH=$PATH:/opt/swift/swift-current/usr/bin/' >> .profile
source ~/.profile
```

We should now have Swift installed and ready to go. The last thing we want to do is to test our installation.

Testing the installation

The last thing we need to do is to verify that Swift has been successfully installed. To do this, we can run the following command:

```
swift --version
```

The output should look something like this but with the version of Swift that you installed:

```
Apple Swift version 5.3-dev (LLVM a60975d8a4, Swift afe134eb2e)
Target: x86_64-unknown-linux-gnu
```

If the output looks similar to this, then congratulations, Swift has been successfully installed on your system. If there is an issue, and your system is unable to find the swift command, then the issue probably lies within the path. The first thing you will want to do is to echo your PATH variable to verify that /opt/swift/swift-current/usr/bin/ is in your path. The following command will do this:

```
echo $PATH
```

If /opt/swift/swift-current/usr/bin/ is not in your path, you can attempt to run the PATH=$PATH:/opt/swift/swift-current/usr/bin/ command manually rather than adding it to your .profile file.

Finally let's verify that the package manager was also properly installed. To do this, we want to create a `swift-code` directory under your home directory and create a new package as the following commands show:

```
cd ~
mkdir swift-code
cd swift-code/
mkdir test
cd test
swift package init --type=executable
```

The output should look something like this:

```
Creating executable package: test
Creating Package.swift
Creating README.md
Creating .gitignore
Creating Sources/
Creating Sources/test/main.swift
Creating Tests/
Creating Tests/LinuxMain.swift
Creating Tests/testTests/
Creating Tests/testTests/testTests.swift
Creating Tests/testTests/XCTestManifests.swift
```

We are now ready to use Swift and the package manager.

Using the Swift package manager

There is a lot that you can do with the package manager that makes it a necessity for creating complex applications on the Linux platform. It helps with adding dependencies to projects and enables us to break our code up into multiple files and create library projects. You can use the package manager on the Mac platform as well, but I do find it easier to use Xcode.

For the examples in this book, we will not need to add dependencies or use multiple files. Let's see how we can simply build and run an executable project in the package manager so you can use it to run the examples from this book if you would like. Keep in mind you are able to use the package manager on the Apple platform as well. When the package manager created `main.swift` in the `Sources/test/` directory it added the following code to it:

```
print("Hello, world!")
```

This code gives us the basic `Hello World` application. You can replace this code with examples from this book as you are going through it. To see how we would build and run an application using the package manager, let's leave the code as is for now and run the following commands:

```
swift build
swift run
```

You should see the following output:

```
Hello, world!
```

The `swift build` command compiled our application, and the `swift run` command ran the executable that was built with the previous command. Most of the code in this book doesn't need the package manager to run, and it may be easier to simply use the compiler. Just keep in mind that for anything larger than a simple example, you will want to use the package manager or Xcode.

Next, let's see how to use the Swift compiler.

Using the Swift compiler

The Swift compiler is the basic utility to build Swift code and it is used by the package manager, Xcode, and any other utility that builds Swift code into executables. We can also call it ourselves. To see how to call it ourselves, create a file named `hello.swift` and add the `print("Hello, world!")` code to it as shown with the following code:

```
echo `print("Hello, world!")` >> hello.swift
```

Now we can compile this code with the following command, which calls the Swift compiler:

```
swiftc hello.swift
```

Finally we can execute the newly created application like we would any other executable:

```
./hello
```

And we will be greeted with our `Hello, world!` message.

Summary

In this chapter, we looked at some of the different documentation that Apple and the Swift community offer. This documentation can be essential as you are learning Swift and also for reference once you have mastered the language itself. We also looked at how we can build and install Swift and its full toolchain. While using the latest build of Swift is not recommended for production systems, I usually keep a virtual machine or my desktop setup with a recent build. This enables me to use the latest features of the language and also run my code against it to make sure I am not introducing changes that are not compatible with future versions of the language.

In the next chapter, we will start to get into the language itself and we will see how to use variables and constants in Swift. We will also look at the various data types and how to use operators in Swift.

3

Learning about Variables, Constants, Strings, and Operators

The first program I ever wrote was written in BASIC and was the typical Hello World application. This application was exciting at first, but the excitement of printing static text wore off pretty quickly. For my second application, I used BASIC's input command to ask the user for a name and then printed out a custom "hello" message with the name they entered. At the age of 12, it was pretty cool to display `Hello Han Solo`. This application led me to create numerous Mad Libs-style applications that prompted the user for various words, and then put those words into a story that was displayed after the user had entered all the required words. These applications introduced me to, and taught me, the importance of variables. Every useful application I've created since then has used variables.

In this chapter, we will cover the following topics:

- What are variables and constants?
- What is the difference between explicit and inferred typing?
- What are numeric, string, and Boolean types?
- Explaining how enumerations work in Swift
- Explaining how Swift's operators work

We recognize that Swift is becoming very popular on platforms outside of the Apple eco-system. Therefore, starting with this chapter, in the downloadable code samples, we will be including both a Swift playground and a `.swift` code file for all the sample code. This will enable you to easily try the samples on whichever platform you wish. This is a new feature starting with the *Mastering Swift 5.3, Sixth Edition* book. Let's start our tour of the Swift language by understanding what constants and variables are.

Constants and variables

Constants and variables associate an identifier (such as `myName` or `currentTemperature`) with a value of a particular type (such as the `String` or `Integer` type), where the identifier can be used to retrieve the value. The difference between a constant and a variable is that a variable can be updated or changed, while a constant cannot be changed once a value is assigned to it.

Constants are good for defining values that you know will never change, like the temperature that water freezes at or the speed of light. Constants are also good for defining a value that we use many times throughout our application, such as a standard font size or the maximum number of characters in a buffer. There will be numerous examples of constants throughout this book, and it is recommended that we use constants rather than variables whenever possible.

Variables tend to be more common in software development than constants. This is mainly because developers tend to prefer variables over constants. In Swift, the compiler will warn us if we declare a variable whose value never changes. We can make useful applications without using constants (although it is good practice to use them); however, it is almost impossible to create a useful application without variables.

 The use of constants is encouraged in Swift. If we do not expect or want a value to change, we should declare it as a constant. This adds a very important safety constraint to our code that ensures that the value never changes.

You can use almost any character in the naming/identifier of a variable or constant (even Unicode characters); however, there are a few rules that you must follow:

- An identifier must not contain any whitespace.
- It must not contain any mathematical symbols or arrows.
- An identifier must not contain private-use or invalid Unicode characters.

- It must not contain line or box-drawing characters.
- It must not start with a number, but it can contain numbers.
- Using a Swift keyword as an identifier is strongly discouraged but if you do, surround it with backticks.

Keywords are words that are used by the Swift programming language. Some examples of keywords that you will see in this chapter are var and let. You should avoid using Swift keywords as identifiers to avoid confusion when reading your code.

Defining constants and variables

Constants and variables must be defined prior to using them. To define a constant, you use the let keyword, and to define a variable, you use the var keyword. The following code shows how to define both constants and variables:

```
// Constants
let freezingTemperatureOfWaterCelsius = 0
let speedOfLightKmSec = 300000

// Variables
var currentTemperature = 22
var currentSpeed = 55
```

We can declare multiple constants or variables in a single line by separating them with a comma. For example, we could shrink the preceding four lines of code down to two lines, as shown here:

```
// Constants
let freezingTemperatureOfWaterCelsius = 0, speedOfLightKmSec = 300000

// Variables
var currentTemperature = 22, currentSpeed = 55
```

We can change the value of a variable to another value of a compatible type; however, as we noted earlier, we cannot change the value of a constant. Let's look at the following playground. Can you tell what is wrong with the code from the error message?

Figure 3.1: Error thrown as a constant cannot be changed

Did you figure out what was wrong with the code? Any physicist can tell you that we cannot change the speed of light, and in our code, `speedOfLightKmSec` is a constant, so we cannot change it here either. When we attempted to change the `speedOfLightKmSec` constant, an error was thrown. We can change the value of `highTemperature` without an error because it is a variable. We have mentioned the difference between variables and constants a couple of times because it is a very important concept to grasp, especially when we move on to define mutable and immutable collection types in *Chapter 5, Using Swift Collections*.

> When something is mutable, that means we are able to change it, and when we say something is immutable, that means we are unable to change it.

Type safety

Swift is a type-safe language, which means we are required to define the types of the values we are going to store in a variable. We will get an error if we attempt to assign a value to a variable that is of the wrong type. The following playground shows what happens if we attempt to put a string value into a variable that expects integer values:

We will go over the most popular types later in this chapter.

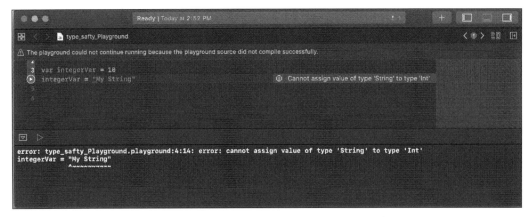

Figure 3.2: Type-safety error in a Swift playground

Swift performs a type check when it compiles code, and so it will flag any mismatched types with an error. The error message in this playground explains quite clearly that we are trying to insert a string value into an integer variable.

How does Swift know that the constant `integerVar` is of the integer type? Swift uses type inference to figure out the appropriate type. Let's look at what type inference is.

Type inference

Type inference allows us to omit the variable type when the variable is defined with an initial value. The compiler will infer the type based on that initial value. For example, in Objective-C, we would define an integer like this:

```
int myInt = 1
```

This tells the compiler that the `myInt` variable is of the `Int` type, and that the initial value is the number 1. In Swift, we would define the same integer as this:

```
var myInt = 1
```

Swift infers that the variable type is an integer because the initial value is an integer. Let's look at a couple more examples:

```
var x = 3.14   // Double type
var y = "Hello"  // String type
var z = true    // Boolean type
```

In the preceding example, the compiler will correctly infer that variable x is a Double, variable y is a String, and variable z is a Boolean, based on their initial values. We are able to explicitly define a variable type. However, it is recommended that we only do this if we are not assigning an initial value to a variable.

Explicit types

Type inference is a very nice feature in Swift and is one that you will probably get used to very quickly. However, there are times when we would like to explicitly define a variable's type. For example, in the preceding example, the variable x is inferred to be Double, but what if we wanted the variable type to be Float? We can explicitly define a variable type like this:

```
var x:Float = 3.14
```

Notice the Float declaration (the colon and the word Float) after the variable identifier. This tells the compiler to define this variable to be of the Float type and gives it an initial value of 3.14. When we define a variable in this manner, we need to make sure that the initial value is the same type as what we defined the variable to be. If we try to give a variable an initial value that is a different type than what we defined the variable as, then we receive an error. As an example, the following line will throw an error because we are explicitly defining the variable to be that of the Float type, while we are trying to put a String value in it:

```
var x: Float = "My str"
```

We will need to explicitly define the variable type if we are not setting an initial value. For example, the following line of code is invalid because the compiler does not know what type to set the variable x to:

```
var x
```

If we use this code in our application, we will receive a **Type annotation missing in pattern** error. If we are not setting an initial value for a variable, we are required to define the variable type, as shown in the following example:

```
var x: Int
```

Now that we have seen how to explicitly define a variable type, let's look at some of the most commonly used types.

Numeric types

Swift contains many of the standard numeric types that are suitable for storing various integer and floating-point values. Let's start by looking at the integer type.

Integer types

An integer is a whole number and can be either signed (positive, negative, or zero) or unsigned (positive or zero). Swift provides several **Integer** types of different sizes. *Table 3.1* shows the value ranges for the different integer types on a 64-bit system:

Type	Minimum	Maximum
Int8	-128	127
Int16	-32,768	32,767
Int32	-2,147,483,648	2,147,483,647
Int64	- 9,223,372,036,854,775,808	9,223,372,036,854,775,807
Int	- 9,223,372,036,854,775,808	9,223,372,036,854,775,807
UInt8	0	255
UInt16	0	65,535
UInt32	0	4,294,967,295
UInt64	0	18,446,744,073,709,551,615
UInt	0	18,446,744,073,709,551,615

Table 3.1: Different Integer types available on Swift

You may notice from the chart that unsigned integers begin with a U (UInt, UInt8...), while signed integers do not (Int, Int8).

Unless there is a specific reason to define the size of an integer, I would recommend using the standard Int or UInt types. This will save you from needing to convert between different types of integers later.

In Swift, the `Integer` type and other numerical types are actually named types and are implemented in the Swift standard library using structures. This gives us a consistent mechanism for the memory management of all the data types, as well as properties that we can access. For the preceding chart, I retrieved the minimum and maximum values of each `Integer` type using the `min` and `max` properties of the `Integer` types. Look at the following playground to see how these values were retrieved:

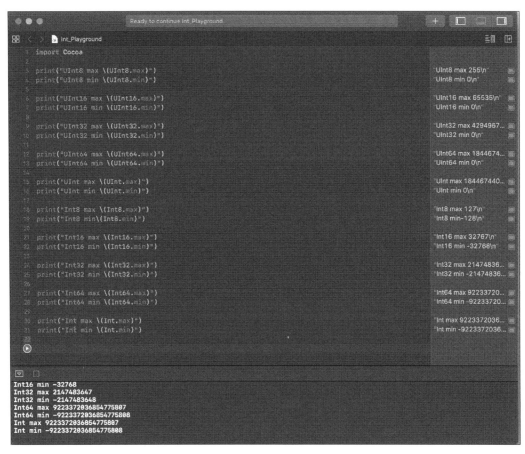

Figure 3.3: Ranges of different numerical types

Integers can also be represented as binary, octal, and hexadecimal numbers. We just need to add a prefix to the number to tell the compiler which base the number should be in. The prefix takes the form of a zero, followed by the base specifier. *Table 3.2* shows the prefix for each numerical base:

Base	Prefix
Decimal	None
Binary	0b
Octal	0o
Hexadecimal	0x

Table 3.2: Prefixes for each numerical base

The following playground shows how the number 95 is represented in each of the numerical bases:

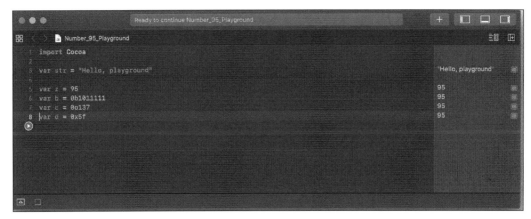

Figure 3.4: Defining values with different numerical bases

Swift also allows us to insert arbitrary underscores in our numeric literals. This can improve the readability of our code without changing the underlying value. As an example, if we were defining the speed of light, which is constant, we could define it like this:

```
let speedOfLightKmSec = 300_000
```

The Swift compiler will ignore these underscores and interpret this value as if the underscores were not there.

The `Integer` type in Swift has a method named `isMultiple(of:)`, which can be very useful. This method allows us to check if one number is the multiple of another number. Prior to this method, we would have used the following code:

```
let number = 4

if number % 2 == 0 {
    print("Even")
} else {
    print("Odd")
}
```

Now, we can use the `isMultiple(of:)` method like this:

```
let number = 4

if number.isMultiple(of: 2) {
    print("Even")
} else {
    print("Odd")
}
```

While this new method really doesn't eliminate a lot of code, it does make our code much easier to read and understand. Now, let's look at floating-point and `Double` types.

Floating-point and Double values

A floating-point number is a number with a decimal component. There are two standard floating-point types in Swift: `Float` and `Double`. The `Float` type represents a 32-bit floating-point number, while the `Double` type represents a 64-bit floating-point number. While the `Float` type is a 32-bit floating-point number, Swift actually supports four floating-point types. These are `Float16`, `Float32`, `Float64`, and `Float80`. Remember, when the `Float` type is used, it is a 32-bit floating-point number; if you want to use the other precisions, you will need to define it.

Swift 5.3, with Swift Evolution SE-0277, added the `Float16` type to the Swift language because it is commonly used in graphics programming and also machine learning.

It is recommended that we use the Double type over the Float type unless there is a specific reason to use the latter. The Double type has a precision of at least 15 decimal digits, while the Float type's precision can be as small as six decimal digits. Let's look at an example of how this can affect our application without us knowing. *Figure 3.5* shows the results of what happens if we add two decimal numbers together using both a Float type and a Double type:

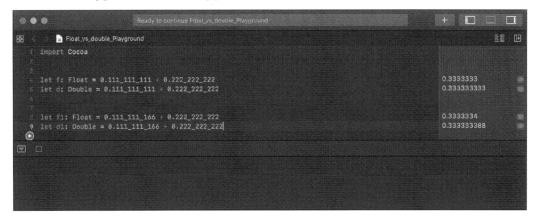

Figure 3.5: Calculations in Float and Double

As we can see from the preceding screenshot, the first two decimal numbers that we are adding contain nine digits past the decimal point; however, the results in the Float type only contain seven digits, while the results in the Double type contain the full nine digits. This loss of precision can cause issues if we are working with currency or other numbers that need accurate calculations, as we can see when we compare the results in the second set of numbers.

Note that when you use type inference for a decimal number, Swift will default to a Double type rather than a Float type.

What if we have two variables, where one is an integer and the other is a double? Do you think we can add them as the following code shows?

```
var a: Int = 3
var b: Double = 0.14
var c = a + b
```

If we put the preceding code into a playground, we would receive the following error:

```
operator '+' cannot be applied to operands of type Int and Double
```

This error lets us know that we are trying to add two different types of numbers, which is not allowed. To add an `Int` and a `Double` type together, we need to convert the integer value into a double value. The following code shows how to do this:

```
var a: Int = 3
var b: Double = 0.14
var c = Double(a) + b
```

Notice how we use the `Double()` function to initialize a `Double` value with the `Int` value. All numeric types in Swift have an initializer to do these types of conversion. These initializers are called **convenience initializers**, similar to the `Double()` function shown in the preceding code sample. For example, the following code shows how you can initialize a `Float` or `uint16` value with an integer value:

```
var intVar = 32
var floatVar = Float(intVar)
var uint16Var = UInt16(intVar)
```

Generally, when we are adding two different types together, we will want to convert the number with the least floating-point precision, like an integer or float, to the type with the highest precision, like a double.

The Boolean type

Boolean values are often referred to as logical values because they can be either `true` or `false`. Swift has a built-in `Boolean` type that accepts one of the two built-in Boolean constants: `true` and `false`.

Boolean constants and variables can be defined like this:

```
let swiftIsCool = true
var itIsRaining = false
```

Boolean values are especially useful when working with conditional statements, such as the `if`, `while`, and `guard` statements. For example, what do you think this code would do?

```
let isSwiftCool = true
var isItRaining = false
if isSwiftCool {
    print("YEA, I cannot wait to learn it")
}
if isItRaining {
```

```
    print("Get a rain coat")
}
```

If you answered that this code would print out YEA, I cannot wait to learn it, then you would be correct. This line is printed out because the isSwiftCool Boolean type is set to true, while the isItRaining variable is set to false; therefore, the Get a rain coat message is not printed.

In most languages, if we wanted to toggle the value of a Boolean variable, we would have to do something like this:

```
isItRaining = !isItRaining
```

In Swift, the Boolean type has a method called toggle() that lets us toggle the value of the variable. This is used if we do not know the value that's stored in the variable. For example, if the isItRaining constant was a variable instead and we wanted to change the value, but we did not know what it actually was, we could use the following line of code to change it:

```
isItRaining.toggle()
```

As with the Integer's isMultiple(of:) method, this makes our code much easier to read and understand. Now, let's look at the String type.

The String type

A **string** is an ordered collection of characters, such as Hello or Swift, and is represented by the String type. We have seen several examples of strings in this book, and therefore the following code should look familiar. This code shows how to define two strings:

```
var stringOne = "Hello"
var stringTwo = "World"
```

We can also create a string using a multiline string literal. The following code shows how we can do that:

```
var multiLine = """
This is a multiline string literal.
This shows how we can create a string over multiple lines.
"""
```

Notice that we put three double quotes around the multiline string. We can use quotes in our multiline string to quote specific text. The following code shows how to do this:

```
var multiLine = """
This is a multiline string literal.
This shows how we can create a string over multiple lines.
Jon says, "multiline string literals are cool"
"""
```

Since a string is an ordered collection of characters, we can iterate through each character of a string. The following code shows how to do this:

```
var stringOne = "Hello"
for char in stringOne {
    print(char)
}
```

The preceding code will display the results that are shown in the following screenshot:

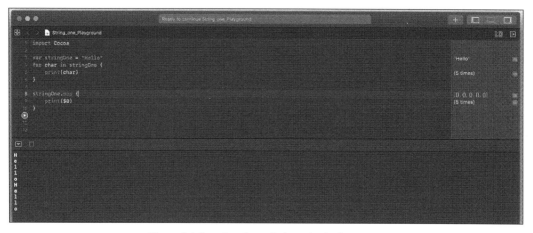

Figure 3.6: Iterating through the string's characters

We can also use the map() function, as shown in *Figure 3.6*, of the String type to retrieve each character, as shown in the following code:

```
stringOne.map {
    print($0)
}
```

We will look at the map() method and how it works later on in this book.

There are two ways in which we can add one string to another. We can concatenate them or include them in-line. To concatenate two strings, we can use the + or += operators. The following code shows both ways in which we can concatenate two strings. The first example appends stringB to the end of stringA, and the results are put into the new stringC variable. The second example appends string directly to the end of stringA, without creating a new string:

```
var stringC = stringA + stringB
stringA += string
```

To include a string in-line with another string, we use a special sequence of characters: \(). The following code shows how to include a string interpolation with another string:

```
var stringA = "Jon"
var stringB = "Hello \(stringA)"
```

In the previous example, stringB will contain the message Hello Jon, because Swift will replace the \(stringA) sequence of characters with the value of the stringA variable.

Starting with Swift 5, we have the ability to create raw strings. In previous versions of Swift, if we wanted to include quotes or backslashes in a string, we had to *escape* it out using a backslash, as shown in the following code:

```
let str = "The main character said \"hello\""
```

With a raw string, the double quotes and backslashes are treated as part of the string literal, and so do not need to escape them. The following example shows how to do this:

```
let str1 = #"The main character said "hello""#
```

Notice the hashtag and double quotes at the start and end of the string. That tells Swift that this is a raw string. This makes it much easier to read what the string actually contains. If we wanted to append another string in-line, as we did previously, we would use the \#() character sequence. The following code illustrates this:

```
let ans = 42
var str2 = #"The answer is \#(ans)"#
```

The result of this code would be a str2 variable containing the following string: **The answer is 42**.

In Swift, we define the mutability of variables and collections by using the var and let keywords. If we define a string as a variable using var, the string is mutable, meaning that we can change and edit the value. If we define a string as a constant using let, the string is immutable, meaning that we cannot change or edit the value once it is set. The following code shows the difference between a mutable and an immutable string:

```
var x = "Hello"
let y = "HI"
var z = " World"

//This is valid because x is mutable
x += z

//This is invalid because y is not mutable.
y += z
```

Strings in Swift have two methods that can convert the case of the string. These methods are lowercased() and uppercased(). The following example demonstrates these methods:

```
var stringOne = "hElLo"
print("Lowercase String: \(stringOne.lowercased())")
print("Uppercase String: \(stringOne.uppercased())")
```

If we run this code, the results will be as follows:

```
Lowercase String: hello
Uppercase String: HELLO
```

Swift provides four ways to compare a string; these are string equality, prefix equality, suffix equality, and isEmpty. The following example demonstrates these:

Figure 3.7: String comparison methods in Swift

The isEmpty() method checks to see if the string contains any characters or not. The string equality (==) checks to see if the characters (which are case-sensitive) in the two strings are the same. The prefix and suffix equality checks to see if the string starts with or ends with a specific string. The prefix and suffix equality is case-sensitive as well.

We can replace all the occurrences of a target string with another string, which is done with the replacingOccurrances(of:) method. The following code demonstrates this:

```
var stringOne = "one,to,three,four"
var stringTwo = stringOne.replacingOccurrences(of: "to", with: "two")
print(stringTwo)
```

The preceding example will print one, two, three, four to the screen because we are replacing all the occurrences of to with two in the stringOne variable.

 Note that the replacingOccurrences(of:) method is only available on Apple platforms and is not available for other platforms.

We can also retrieve substrings and individual characters from our strings; however, when we retrieve a substring from a string, that substring is an instance of the Substring type and not the String type. The Substring type contains most of the same methods as the String type, so you can use them in a similar way. Unlike String types, however, they are meant to be used only for short periods of time, only while we are working with the value. If you need to use a Substring type for a long period of time, you should convert it into a String type. The following example shows how we can work with substrings:

```
var path = "/one/two/three/four"

//Create start and end indexes
let startIndex = path.index(path.startIndex, offsetBy: 4)
let endIndex = path.index(path.startIndex, offsetBy: 14)

let sPath = path[startIndex ..< endIndex] //returns the "/two/three"
//convert the substring to a string
let newStr = String(sPath)

path[..<startIndex]      //returns the "/one"
path[endIndex...]        //returns the "/four"

path.last
path.first
```

In the preceding example, we used the subscript path to retrieve the substring between a start and end index. The indices are created with the index(_: offsetBy:) function. The first property in the index(_: offsetBy:) function gives the index of where we wish to start, and the offsetBy property tells us how much to increase the index by.

The path[..<startIndex] line creates a substring from the beginning of the string to the index, while the path[endIndex...] line creates a substring from the index to the end of the string. We then use the last property to get the last character of the string and the first property to get the first character.

 The ..< operator that we saw in the previous example is known as a **half-open range operator**. We will look at the different range operators at the end of this chapter.

We can retrieve the number of characters in a string by using the count property. The following example shows how you can use this function:

```
var path = "/one/two/three/four"
var length = path.count
```

This completes our whirlwind tour of strings. We went through these properties and functions very quickly, but we will be using strings extensively throughout this book, so there will be a lot of code to help you get familiar with them.

Tuples

Tuples group multiple values into a single compound type. These values are not required to be of the same type.

The following example shows how to define a tuple:

```
var team = ("Boston", "Red Sox", 97, 65, 59.9)
```

In the preceding example, an unnamed tuple was created that contains two strings, two integers, and one double. The values of the tuple can be decomposed into a set of variables, as shown in the following example:

```
var team = ("Boston", "Red Sox", 97, 65, 59.9)
var (city, name, wins, losses, percent) = team
```

In the preceding code, the `city` variable will contain `Boston`, the `name` variable will contain `Red Sox`, the `wins` variable will contain `97`, the `losses` variable will contain `65`, and finally the `percent` variable will contain `59.9`.

The values of the tuple can also be retrieved by specifying the location of the value. The following example shows how we can retrieve values by their location:

```
var team = ("Boston", "Red Sox", 97, 65, 59.9)
var city = team.0
var name = team.1
var wins = team.2
var losses = team.3
var percent = team.4
```

Naming tuples, known as **named tuples**, allows us to avoid the decomposition step. A named tuple associates a name (key) with each element of the tuple. The following example shows how to create a named tuple:

```
var team = (city:"Boston", name:"Red Sox", wins:97, losses:65,
percent:59.9)
```

Values from a named tuple can be accessed using the dot syntax. In the preceding code, we can access the `city` element of the tuple like this: `team.city`. In the preceding code, the `team.city` element will contain `Boston`.

Tuples are incredibly useful and can be used for all sorts of purposes. I have found that they are very useful for replacing classes and structures that are designed to simply store data and do not contain any methods. They are also very useful for returning multiple values, of different types, from a function. Now, let's look at enumerations.

Enumerations

Enumerations (also known as **enums**) are a special data type that enables us to group related types together and use them in a type-safe manner. Enumerations in Swift are not tied to integer values as they are in other languages, such as C or Java. In Swift, we are able to define an enumeration with a type (string, character, integer, or floating-point value) and then define its actual value (known as the **raw value**). Enumerations also support features that are traditionally only supported by classes, such as computed properties and instance methods. We will discuss these advanced features in depth in *Chapter 7, Classes, Structures, and Protocols*. In this section, we will look at the traditional features of enumerations.

We will define an enumeration that contains a list of `Planets`, like this:

```
enum Planets {
    case mercury
    case venus
    case earth
    case mars
    case Jupiter
    case Saturn
    case Uranus
    case neptune
}
```

 Note: When defining the enumeration type, the name of the enumeration should be uppercase, like other types. The member values can be uppercase or lowercase; however, it should be preferred to use lowercase.

The values defined in an enumeration are considered to be the member values (or simply the members) of the enumeration. In most cases, you will see the member values defined like they are in the preceding example because it is easy to read; however, there is a shorter version. This shorter version lets us define multiple members in a single line, separated by commas, as the following example shows:

```
enum Planets {
case mercury, venus, earth, mars, jupiter
case saturn, uranus, neptune
}
```

We can then use the `Planets` enumeration like this:

```
var planetWeLiveOn = Planets.earth
var furthestPlanet = Planets.neptune
```

The type for the `planetWeLiveOn` and `furthestPlanet` variables is inferred when we initialize the variable with one of the member values of the `Planets` enumeration. Once the variable type is inferred, we can then assign a new value without the `Planets` prefix, as shown here:

```
planetWeLiveOn = .mars
```

We can compare an enumeration value using the traditional equals (`==`) operator or by using a `switch` statement.

Note: We will learn about the Swift `switch` statement in *Chapter 6, Control Flow*, later in this book. For now, we wanted to illustrate its use with the enumeration type.

The following example shows how to use the equals operator and the `switch` statement with an enum:

```
// Using the traditional == operator
if planetWeLiveOn == .earth {
    print("Earth it is")
}

// Using the switch statement
switch planetWeLiveOn {

case .mercury:
```

```
    print("We live on Mercury, it is very hot!")
case .venus:
    print("We live on Venus, it is very hot!")
case .earth:
    print("We live on Earth, just right")
case .mars:
    print("We live on Mars, a little cold")
default:
    print("Where do we live?")
}
```

Enumerations can come prepopulated with raw values, which are required to be of the same type. The following example shows how to define an enumeration with string values:

```
enum Devices: String {
    case MusicPlayer = "iPod"
    case Phone = "iPhone"
    case Tablet = "iPad"
}

print("We are using an \(Devices.Tablet.rawValue)")
```

The preceding example creates an enumeration with three types of devices. We then use the rawValue property to retrieve the stored value for the Tablet member of the Devices enumeration. This example will print a message saying, We are using an iPad.

Let's create another Planets enumeration, but this time, we'll assign numbers to the members, as follows:

```
enum Planets: Int {
    case Mercury = 1
    case Venus
    case Warth
    case Mars
    case Jupiter
    case Saturn
    case Uranus
    case Neptune
}
print("Earth is planet number \(Planets.earth.rawValue)")
```

The big difference between these last two enumeration examples is that in the second example, we only assign a value to the first member (mercury). If integers are used for the raw values of an enumeration, then we do not have to assign a value to each member. If no value is present, the raw values will be auto-incremented.

In Swift, enumerations can also have associated values. Associated values allow us to store additional information, along with member values. This additional information can vary each time we use the member. It can also be of any type, and the types can be different for each member. Let's look at how we might use associate types by defining a Product enumeration, which contains two types of products:

```swift
enum Product {
    case Book(Double, Int, Int)
    case Puzzle(Double, Int)
}

var masterSwift = Product.Book(49.99, 2017, 310)
var worldPuzzle = Product.Puzzle(9.99, 200)

switch masterSwift {
case .Book(let price, let year, let pages):
    print("Mastering Swift was published in \(year) for the price of \
(price) and has \(pages) pages")
case .Puzzle(let price, let pieces):
    print("Mastering Swift is a puzzle with \(pieces) and sells for \
(price)")
}

switch worldPuzzle {
case .Book(let price, let year, let pages):
    print("World Puzzle was published in \(year) for the price of \
(price) and has \(pages) pages")
case .Puzzle(let price, let pieces):
    print("World Puzzle is a puzzle with \(pieces) and sells for \
(price)")
}
```

In the preceding example, we begin by defining a `Product` enumeration with two members: `Book` and `Puzzle`. The `Book` member has associated values of the `Double`, `Int`, and `Int` types, while the `Puzzle` member has associated values of the `Double` and `Int` types. Notice that we are using named associated types, where we assign a name for each associated type. We then create two products, `masterSwift` and `worldPuzzle`. We assign the `masterSwift` variable a value of `Product.Book` with the associated values of `49.99`, `2017`, and `310`. We then assign the `worldPuzzle` variable a value of `Product.Puzzle` with the associated values of `9.99` and `200`.

We can then check the `Product` enumeration using a `switch` statement, as we did in an earlier example. We then extract the associated values within the `switch` statement. In this example, we extracted the associated values as constants with the `let` keyword, but you can also extract the associated values as variables with the `var` keyword.

If you put the previous code into a playground, the following results will be displayed:

```
"Master Swift was published in 2017 for the price of 49.99 and has 310
pages"
"World Puzzle is a puzzle with 200 and sells for 9.99"
```

We are able to opt into the conformance of the `Comparable` protocols with our enumerations that have no associated values or associated values, which themselves conform to the `Comparable` protocol. By conforming to the `Comparable` protocol, we are able to compare cases of the same enum using the `<` and `>` operators. Let's see how this works:

 Don't worry if you do not understand what protocols are or how a type can conform to them at this point. We will be going over protocols in *Chapter 9, Protocols and Protocol Extensions*.

```
enum Grades: Comparable {
    case f
    case d
    case c
    case b
    case a
}
let acceptableGrade = Grades.c
let testOneGrade = Grades.b
```

```
if  testOneGrade < acceptableGrade {
    print("Grade is unacceptable")
}
else {
    Print("Grade is acceptable")
}
```

In the previous code, we defined an enumeration that defined the different grade levels. By adding : Comparable after the enumeration declaration, we are adding conformance to the Comparable protocol. We then created a constant that defined what our acceptable grade level was. We are now able to compare any variable that contains a Grades value with the acceptableGrade constant to make sure it contains an acceptable grade, as shown in our example.

Synthesized Comparable conformance for enumerations was added to Swift in version 5.3 with Swift Evolution SE-0266 and is one of the features I am most excited about. It allows us to conform to the Comparable protocol with our enumerations, without having to write the code, to conform to the protocol ourselves.

In future chapters in this book, we will look at additional features of enumerations and see why they can be so powerful. So far in this book, we have used operators in a number of examples. Let's take a closer look at them.

Operators

An operator is a symbol or combination of symbols that we can use to check, change, or combine values. We have used operators in most of the examples so far in this book, but we did not specifically call them operators. In this section, we will show you how to use most of the basic operators that Swift supports.

Swift supports most standard C operators and also improves on some of them to eliminate several common coding errors. For example, the assignment operator does not return a value, which prevents it from being used where we are meant to use the equality operator, which is two equal signs (==).

Let's look at the operators in Swift.

The assignment operator

The assignment operator initializes or updates a variable. Here is a prototype:

```
var A = var B
```

Here is an example:

```
let x = 1
var y = "Hello"
a = b
```

Comparison operators

The comparison operators return a Boolean value of true if the statement is true or a Boolean value of false if the statement is not true.

Here are some prototypes:

```
Equality:  varA == varB
Not equal:  varA != varB
Greater than:  varA > varB
Less than:  varA < varB
Greater than or equal to: varA >= varB
Less than or equal to: varA <= varB
```

Here are some examples:

```
2 == 1 //false, 2 does not equal 1
2 != 1 //true, 2 does not equal 1
2 > 1 //true, 2 is greater than 1
2 < 1 //false, 2 is not less than 1
2 >= 1 //true, 2 is greater or equal to 1
2 <= 1 //false, 2 is not less or equal to 1
```

Arithmetic operators

The arithmetic operators perform the four basic mathematical operations. Here are some prototypes:

```
Addition: varA + varB
Subtraction: varA - varB
Multiplication: varA * varB
Division: varA / varB
```

Here are some examples:

```
var x = 4 + 2  //x will equal 6
var x = 4 - 2  //x will equal 2
```

```
var x = 4 * 2  //x will equal 8
var x = 4 / 2  //x will equal 2
var x = "Hello " + "world"  //x will equal "Hello World"
```

The remainder operator

The remainder operator calculates the remainder if the first operand is divided by the second operand. In other languages, this is sometimes referred to as the modulo or modulus operator.

Here is a prototype:

```
varA % varB
```

Here is an example:

```
var x = 10 % 3  //x will equal 1
var x = 10 % 6  //x will equal 4
```

Compound assignment operators

The compound assignment operators combine an arithmetic operator with an assignment operator.

Here are some prototypes:

```
varA += varB
varA -= varB
varA *= varB
varA /= varB
```

Here are some examples:

```
var x = 6
x += 2  //x now is 8
x -= 2  //x now is 4
x *= 2  //x now is 12
x /= 2  //x now is 3
```

The closed range operator

The closed range operator defines a range that runs from the first number to the second number. The numbers are separated by three dots.

Here is a prototype:

```
(a...b)
```

Here is an example. Note that we will cover the for loop in *Chapter 6, Control Flow*:

```
for i in 1...3 {
    print("Number: \(i)")
}
```

This example would print out the following:

```
Number: 1
Number: 2
Number: 3
```

The half-open range operator

The half-open range operator defines a range that runs from the first number to one, minus the second number. The numbers are separated by two dots and the less than sign.

Here is a prototype:

```
(a..<b)
```

Here is an example:

```
for i in 1..<3 {
    print("Number: \(i)")
}
```

This example would print out the following:

```
Number: 1
Number: 2
```

Notice that in the closed range operator, the line `Number:  3` was printed out, but with the half open range operator, it wasn't.

There are also one-side range operators that we use with arrays. We will look at those in *Chapter 5, Using Swift Collections*.

The ternary conditional operator

The ternary conditional operator assigns a value to a variable based on the evaluation of a comparison operator or `Boolean` value.

Here is a prototype:

```
(boolValue ? valueA : valueB)
```

Here is an example:

```
var x = 2
var y = 3
var z = (y >x ? "Y is greater" : "X is greater")  //z equals "Y is
greater"
```

The logical NOT operator

The logical `NOT` operator inverts a `Boolean` value. Here is a prototype:

```
varA = !varB
```

Here is an example:

```
var x = true
var y = !x    //y equals false
```

The logical AND operator

The logical `AND` operator returns `true` if both operands are `true`; otherwise, it returns `false`.

Here is a prototype:

```
varA && varB
```

Here is an example:

```
var x = true
var y = false
var z = x && y   //z equals false
```

The logical OR operator

The logical OR operator returns true if either of the operands are true. Here is a prototype:

```
varA || varB
```

Here is an example:

```
var x = true
var y = false
var z = x|| y  //z is true
```

For those who are familiar with C or similar languages, these operators should look pretty familiar. For those of you who aren't that familiar with the C operators, rest assured that, once you begin using them frequently, they will become second nature.

Summary

In this chapter, we covered topics ranging from variables and constants to data types and operators. The items in this chapter will act as the foundation for every application that you write; therefore, it is important to understand the concepts we discussed here.

In this chapter, we have seen that we should prefer constants to variables when the value is not going to change. Swift will give you a compile-time warning if you set but never change a variable's value. We also saw that we should prefer type inference over declaring a type.

Numeric and string types, which are implemented as primitives in other languages, are named types that are implemented with structures in Swift. In future chapters, you will see why this is important. One of the most important things to remember from this chapter is that, if a variable contains a nil value, you must declare it as an optional.

In the next chapter, we will look at Swift optional types. The optional type in Swift can be one of the hardest concepts to grasp if you are used to languages that don't use them.

4
Optional Types

When I first started using Swift, the concept that I had the most trouble understanding was optional types. Coming from an Objective-C, C, Java, and Python background, I was able to relate most of Swift's features to how things worked in one of the other languages that I knew, but optionals were different. When Swift was first announced, there was really nothing like optionals in the other languages that I used, so it took a lot of reading to fully understand them.

In this chapter, we will cover the following topics:

- What are optional types?
- Why do we need optional types in Swift?
- How to unwrap an optional
- What is optional binding?
- What is optional chaining?

Introducing optionals

When we declare variables in Swift, they are by default non-optional, which means that they must contain a valid, non-nil value. If we try to set a non-optional variable to nil, it will result in an error.

For example, the following code will throw an error when we attempt to set the message variable to nil because it is a non-optional type:

```
var message: String = "My String"
message = nil
```

It is very important to understand that `nil` in Swift is very different from `nil` in Objective-C or other C-based languages. In these languages, `nil` is a pointer to a non-existent object; however, in Swift, a `nil` value is the absence of a value. Grasping this concept is very important in order to fully understand optionals in Swift.

A variable defined as an optional can contain a valid value, or it can indicate the absence of a value. We indicate the absence of a value by assigning it a special `nil` value. Optionals of any type can be set to `nil`, whereas in Objective-C, only objects can be set to `nil`.

To really understand the concept behind optionals, let's look at a line of code that defines an optional:

```
var myString: String?
```

The question mark at the end indicates that the `myString` variable is an optional. We read this line of code as saying that the `myString` variable is an optional type, which may contain a value of the `string` type or may contain no value. How this line is written is very important in understanding how optionals work.

Optionals are a special type in Swift. When we defined the `myString` variable, we actually defined it as an optional type. To understand this, let's look at some more code:

```
var myString1: String?
var myString2: Optional<String>
```

These two declarations are equivalent. Both lines declare an optional type that may contain a`sstring` type or may lack a value. In Swift, we can think of the absence of a value as being set to nil, but always remember that this is different than setting something to nil in Objective-C. In this book, when we refer to nil, we are referring to how Swift uses nil and not how Objective-C uses nil.

The optional type is an enumeration with two possible values, `None` and `Some(T)`, where `T` is the generic associated value of the appropriate type. We will discuss generics in *Chapter 11*, *Generics*. If we set the optional to `nil`, it will have a value of `None`, and if we set a value, the optional will have a value of `Some` with an associated value of the appropriate type. In *Chapter 3*, *Learning about Variables, Constants, Strings, and Operators*, we explained that an enumeration in Swift might have associated values. Associated values allow us to store additional information along with the enumeration's member values.

Internally, an optional is defined as follows:

```
enum Optional<T>
{
    case None
    case Some(T)
}
```

Here, T is the type to associate with the optional. The T symbol is used to define a generic and can be used to represent any type.

The need for optional types in Swift

Now, the burning question: why does Swift need optionals? To understand this question, we should examine what problems optionals are designed to solve.

In most languages, it is possible to create a variable without giving it an initialized value. For example, in Objective-C, both of these lines of code are valid:

```
int i;
MyObject *m;
```

Now, let's say that the MyObject class, written in Objective-C, has the following method:

```
-(int)myMethodWithValue:(int)i {
    return i*2;
}
```

This method takes the value passed in from the i parameter, multiplies it by two, and returns the results. Let's try to call this method using the following code:

```
MyObject *m;
NSLog(@"Value: %d",[m myMethodWithValue:5]);
```

Our first thought might be that this code would display Value: 10, since we are pass athe value of 5 to a method that doubles the value passed in; however, this would be incorrect. In reality, this code would display Value: 0 because we did not initialize the m object prior to using it.

When we forget to initialize an object or set a value for a variable, we can get unexpected results at runtime, as we just demonstrated. The unexpected results can be, at times, very difficult to track down.

With optionals, Swift is able to detect problems such as this at compile time and alert us before it becomes a runtime issue. If we expect a variable or object to always contain a value prior to using it, we will declare the variable as a non-optional (this is the default declaration). Then we will receive an error if we try to use it prior to initializing it. Let's look at an example of this. The following code would display an error because we are attempting to use a non-optional variable prior to initializing it:

```
var myString: String
print(myString)
```

If a variable is declared as an optional, it is good programming practice to verify that it contains a valid value before attempting to use it. We should only declare a variable as an optional if there is a valid reason for the variable to contain no value. This is the reason Swift declares variables as non-optional by default.

Now that we have a better understanding of what optionals are and what types of problems they are designed to solve, let's look at how to use them.

Defining an optional

One thing to keep in mind is that the type we define in the variable's declaration is actually the associated value in the optional enumeration. The following code shows us how we would typically declare an optional:

```
var myOptional: String?
```

This code declares an optional variable that might contain a string or might contain no value. When a variable such as this is declared, by default it is set to nil. Now that we have seen how to define an optional, let's look at how we can use it.

Using optionals

The key to using optionals is to always verify that they contain a valid value prior to accessing them. The reason for this is if we attempt to use an optional value without verifying that it contains a valid value, we may encounter a runtime error, causing our application to crash. We use the term unwrapping to refer to the process of retrieving a value from an optional. We are going to introduce two methods for retrieving the values of an optional; please keep in mind that using optional binding is preferred.

Forced unwrapping of an optional

To unwrap or retrieve the value of an optional, we place an exclamation mark (!) after the variable name. This is called forced unwrapping. Forced unwrapping, in this manner, is very dangerous and should be used only if we are certain that the variable contains a non-nil value. Otherwise, if it does contain a nil value, we will get a runtime error and the application will crash.

When we use the exclamation point to unwrap an optional, we are telling the compiler that we know the optional contains a value, so go ahead and give it to us. Let's look at how to do this:

```
var myString1: String?
myString1 = "test"
var test: String = myString1!
```

This code will work as we expect it to, where the test variable will contain the "test" string; however, if the line that set the myString1 optional to test was removed, we would receive a runtime error when the application is run. Note that the compiler will not alert us to an issue because we are using the exclamation point to unwrap the optional; therefore, the compiler assumes that we know what we are doing and will happily compile the code for us. We should verify that the myString1 optional contains a valid value before unwrapping it. The following example is one way to do this:

```
var myString1: String?
myString1 = "test"
if myString1 != nil {
    var test = myString1!
}
```

Now, if the line that sets the myString1 optional to test were removed, we would not receive a runtime error because we only unwrap the myString1 optional if it contains a valid (non-nil) value.

Unwrapping optionals, as we just described, is not optimal, and it is not recommended that optionals be unwrapped in this manner. We can combine verification and unwrapping in one step, called optional binding.

Optional binding

Optional binding is the recommended way to unwrap an optional. With optional binding, we perform a check to see whether the optional contains a valid value and, if so, unwrap it into a temporary variable or constant. This is all performed in one step.

Optional binding is performed with `if` or `while` conditional statements. It takes the following format if we want to put the value of the optional in a constant:

```
if let constantName = optional {
    statements
}
```

If we need to put the value in a variable, instead of a constant, we can use the `var` keyword, as shown in the following example:

```
if var variableName = optional {
    statements
}
```

The following example shows how to perform optional binding:

```
var myString3: String?
myString3 = "Space, the final frontier"
if let tempVar = myString3 {
    print(tempVar)
} else {
    print("No value")
}
```

In the example, we define the `myString3` variable as an optional type. If the `myString3` optional contains a valid value, the new variable, named `tempvar`, is set to that value and is printed to the console. If the `myString3` optional does not contain a value, No value is printed to the console.

We are able to use optional binding to unwrap multiple optionals within the same optional binding line. For example, if we had three optionals named `optional1`, `optional2`, and `optional3`, we could use the following code to attempt to unwrap all three at once:

```
if let tmp1 = optional1, let tmp2 = optional2, let tmp3 = optional3 {
}
```

If any of the three optionals are `nil`, the whole optional binding statement fails. It is also perfectly acceptable with optional binding to assign the value to a variable of the same name. The following code illustrates this:

```
if let myOptional = myOptional {
    print(myOptional)
} else {
    print("myOptional was nil")
}
```

One thing to note is that the temporary variable is scoped only for the conditional block and cannot be used outside it. To illustrate the scope of the temporary variable, let's take a look at the following code:

```
var myOptional: String?
myOptional = "test"
if var tmp = myOptional {
    print("Inside:\(tmp)")
}
// This next line will cause a compile time error
print("Outside: \(tmp)")
```

This code would not compile because the `tmp` variable is only valid within the conditional block and we are attempting to use it outside the block.

Using optional binding is a lot cleaner and easier than manually verifying that the optional has a value and using forced unwrapping to retrieve the value of the optional. There are different ways that we can use optional typeswith tuples;, let's look at these.

Optional types with tuples

We can define a whole tuple as an optional or any of the elements within a tuple as an optional. It is especially useful to use optionals with tuples when we return a tuple from a function or method. This allows us to return part (or all) of the tuple as `nil`. The following example shows how to define a tuple as an optional, and also how to define individual elements of a tuple as optional types:

```
var tuple1: (one: String, two: Int)?
var tuple2: (one: String, two: Int?)
```

The first line defines the whole tuple as an optional type. The second line defines the second value within the tuple as an optional, while the first value is a non-optional.

Optional chaining

Optional chaining allows us to call properties, methods, and subscripts on an optional that might be nil. If any of the chained values return nil, the return value will be nil. The following code gives an example of optional chaining using a fictitious car object. In this example, if either the `car` or `tires` optional variables are nil, the `tireSize` variable will be nil, otherwise the `tireSize` variable will be equal to the `tireSize` property:

```
var tireSize = car?.tires?.tireSize
```

We will look at optional chaining again in *Chapter 8*, *Classes, Structures, and Protocols.*

The nil coalescing operator

The nil coalescing operator is similar to the ternary operator that we discussed in *Chapter 3*, *Learning about Variables, Constants, Strings, and Operators*. The ternary operator assigns a value to a variable, based on the evaluation of a comparison operator or a Boolean value. The nil coalescing operator attempts to unwrap an optional, and if it contains a value, it will return that value, or a default value if the optional is nil, as shown in the following code.

Let's look at a prototype for the nil coalescing operator:

```
optionalA ?? defaultValue
```

In this example, we demonstrate the `nil` coalescing operator when the optional is set to nil and also when it contains a value:

```
var defaultName = "Jon"
var optionalA: String?
var optionalB: String?
optionalB = "Buddy"
var nameA = optionalA ?? defaultName
var nameB = optionalB ?? defaultName
```

In this example, we begin by initializing our `defaultName` variable to `Jon`. We then define two optionals, named `optionalA` and `optionalB`. The `optionalA` variable is set to `nil`, while the `optionalB` variable is set to `Buddy`.

The nil coalescing operator is used in the final two lines. Since the `optionalA` variable contains nil, the `nameA` variable will be set to the value of the `defaultName` variable, which is `Jon`. The `nameB` variable will be set to the value of the `optionalB` variable since it contains a value.

The nil coalescing operator is shorthand for using the ternary operator as follows:

```
var nameC = optionalA != nil ? optionalA! : defaultName
```

As we can see, the nil coalescing operator is much cleaner and easier to read than the equivalent ternary operator.

Summary

In this chapter, we described what optionals actually are and how they are defined internally in the Swift language. It is important to understand this concept because optionals are used a lot in Swift, and knowing how they work internally will help you to use them properly. While the concept of optional types, as used in the Swift language, might seem a little confusing at first, the more you use them, the more they will make sense. One of the biggest advantages of optional types is the additional compile-time checks that alert us if we forget to initialize non-optionals prior to using them. We will see additional examples of optionals later in this book.

In the next chapter, we will look at how to use collections.

5
Using Swift Collections

Once I got past the basic Hello, World! beginner applications, I quickly began to realize the shortcomings of variables, especially with the Mad Libs-style applications that I was starting to write. These applications requested that the user enter numerous strings, which resulted in the creation of separate variables for each input field that the user entered.

Having all these separate variables quickly became cumbersome. I remember talking to a friend about this, and he asked me why I was not using arrays. At that time, I was not familiar with arrays, so I asked him to show me what they were. Even though he had a TI-99/4A and I had a Commodore Vic-20, the concept of arrays was the same. Even today, the arrays found in modern development languages have the same basic concepts as the arrays I used on my Commodore Vic-20. While it is definitely possible to create a useful application without using collections, such as arrays, when used properly, collections make application development significantly easier.

In this chapter, we will cover the following topics:

- What an array is in Swift and how to use it
- What a dictionary is in Swift and how to use it
- What a set is in Swift and how to use it

Swift collection types

A collection groups multiple items into a single unit. Swift provides three native collection types. These collection types are arrays, dictionaries, and sets. *Arrays* store data in an ordered collection, *dictionaries* are unordered collections of key-value pairs, and *sets* are unordered collections of unique values. In an array, we access the data by the location or index within the array, whereas in a set we usually iterate through the collection, and dictionaries are accessed using a unique key.

The data stored in a Swift collection must be of the same type. This means, as an example, that we are unable to store a string value in an array of integers. Since Swift does not allow us to mismatch data types in a collection, we can be certain of the data type when we retrieve elements from a collection. This is another feature that, on the surface, might seem like a shortcoming, but actually helps eliminate common programming mistakes.

Let's start off by looking at mutability with collections.

Mutability

For those who are familiar with Objective-C, you will know that there are different classes for mutable and immutable collections. For example, to define a mutable array, we use the NSMutableArray class, and to define an immutable array, we use the NSArray class. Swift is a little different because it does not contain separate classes for mutable and immutable collections. Instead, we define whether a collection is constant (immutable) or variable (mutable) by using the let and var keywords. This should seem familiar since we define constants with the let keyword and variables with the var keyword.

 It is a good practice to create immutable collections unless there is a specific need to change the objects within the collection. This allows the compiler to optimize performance.

Let's begin our tour of collections by looking at the most common collection type: the array type.

Arrays

Arrays can be found in virtually all modern programming languages. In Swift, an array is an ordered list of objects of the same type.

When an array is created, we must declare the type of data that can be stored in it by explicit type declaration or through type inference. Typically, we only explicitly declare the data type of an array when we are creating an empty array. If we initialize an array with data, the compiler uses type inference to infer the data type for the array.

Each object in an array is called an **element**. Each of these elements is stored in a set order and can be accessed by searching for its location (index) in the array.

Creating and initializing arrays

We can initialize an array with an array literal. An array literal is a set of values that prepopulates the array. The following example shows how to define an immutable array of integers using the `let` keyword:

```
let arrayOne = [1,2,3]
```

If we need to create a mutable array, we would use the `var` keyword to define the array, as we did with standard variables. The following example shows how to define a mutable array:

```
var arrayTwo = [4,5,6]
```

In the preceding two examples, the compiler inferred the type of values stored in the array by looking at the type of values stored in the array literal. If we want to create an empty array, we need to explicitly declare the type of values to store in the array. There are two ways to declare null arrays in Swift. The following examples show how to declare an empty mutable array that can be used to store integers:

```
var arrayThree = [Int]()
var arrayThree: [Int] = []
```

In the preceding examples, we created arrays with integer values, and the majority of the array examples in this chapter will also use integer values; however, we can create arrays in Swift with any type. The only rule is that, once an array is defined as containing a particular type, all the elements in the array must be of that type. The following example shows how we can create arrays of various data types:

```
var arrayOne = [String]()
var arrayTwo = [Double]()
var arrayThree = [MyObject]()
```

Swift provides special type aliases for working with nonspecific types. These aliases are AnyObject and Any. We can use these aliases to define arrays whose elements are of different types as follows:

```
var myArray: [Any] = [1,"Two"]
```

The AnyObject aliases can represent an instance of any class type, while the Any aliases can represent an instance of any type, including function types. We should use the Any and AnyObject aliases only when there is an explicit need for this behavior. It is always better to be specific about the types of data our collections contain.

 If there is a need to mix types in a single collection, we could consider using a tuple.

An array can also be initialized to a certain size with all the elements set to a predefined value. This can be very useful if we want to create an array and prepopulate it with default values. The following example defines an array with 7 elements, with each element containing the number 3:

```
var arrayFour = [Int](repeating: 3, count: 7)
```

 Starting in Swift 5.1, with SE-0245, we have the ability to create an uninitialized array. With this feature, we would not populate the array with a default value and instead could provide what is known as a **closure to populate the array** as needed. We will show this feature in *Chapter 14, Working with Closures.*

While the most common arrays are one-dimensional arrays, multidimensional arrays can also be created. A multidimensional array is really nothing more than an array of arrays. For example, a two-dimensional array is an array of arrays, while a three-dimensional array is an array of arrays of arrays. The following examples show the two ways to create a two-dimensional array in Swift:

```
var multiArrayOne = [[1,2],[3,4],[5,6]]
var multiArrayTwo = [[Int]]()
```

Now that we have seen how to initialize an array, let's look at how we can access the elements of an array.

Accessing the array element

The subscript syntax is used to retrieve values from an array. Subscript syntax, for an array, is where a number appears between two square brackets, and that number specifies the location (index) within the array of the element we wish to retrieve. The following example shows how to retrieve elements from an array using the subscript syntax:

```
let arrayOne = [1,2,3,4,5,6]
print(arrayOne[0]) //Displays '1'
print(arrayOne[3]) //Displays '4'
```

In the preceding code, we create an array of integers that contains six numbers. We then print out the value at indexes 0 and 3.

 One important fact to note is that indices in Swift arrays start with the number zero. This means that the first item in an array has an index of 0. The second item in an array has an index of 1.

If we want to retrieve an individual value within a multidimensional array, we need to provide a subscript for each dimension of the array. If we do not provide a subscript for each dimension, we will retrieve an array rather than an individual value within the array. The following example shows how we can define a two-dimensional array and retrieve an individual value within the two dimensions:

```
let multiArray = [[1,2],[3,4],[5,6]]
let arr = multiArray[0]    //arr contains the array [1,2]
let value = multiArray[0][1]   //value contains 2
```

In the preceding code, we begin by defining a two-dimensional array. When we retrieve the value at index 0 of the first dimension (`multiArray[0]`), we retrieve the array [1,2]. When we retrieve the value at index 0 of the first dimension and index 1 of the second dimension (`multiArray[0][1]`), we retrieve the integer 2.

We can retrieve the first and last elements of an array using the `first` and `last` properties. The `first` and `last` properties return an optional value, since the values may be nil if the array is empty. The following example shows how to use these properties to retrieve the first and last elements of both a one-dimensional and a multidimensional array:

```
let arrayOne = [1,2,3,4,5,6]
let first = arrayOne.first    //first contains
let last = arrayOne.last    //last contains 6


let multiArray = [[1,2],[3,4],[5,6]]
let arrFirst1 = multiArray[0].first     //arrFirst1 contains 1
let arrFirst2 = multiArray.first     //arrFirst2 contains[1,2]
let arrLast1 = multiArray[0].last     //arrLast1 contains 2
let arrLast2 = multiArray.last     //arrLast2 contains [5,6]
```

Now let's see how we can count the elements of an array.

Counting the elements of an array

At times, it is essential to know the number of elements in an array. The array type in Swift contains a read-only count property. The following example shows how to use this property to retrieve the number of elements in both single-dimensional and multidimensional arrays:

```
let arrayOne = [1,2,3]
let multiArrayOne = [[3,4],[5,6],[7,8]]

print(arrayOne.count)     //Displays 3
print(multiArrayOne.count)     //Displays 3 for the three array
print(multiArrayOne[0].count)     //Displays 2 for the two elements
```

The value that is returned by the count property is the number of elements in the array, and not the largest valid index of the array. For non-empty arrays, the largest valid index is the number of elements in the array minus 1. This is because the first element of the array has an index number of 0. As an example, if an array has two elements, the valid indexes are 0 and 1, while the count property would return 2. This is illustrated in the following code:

```
let arrayOne = [0,1]
print(arrayOne[0])     //Displays 0
print(arrayOne[1])     //Displays 1
print(arrayOne.count)     //Displays 2
```

If we attempt to retrieve an element from an array that is outside the range of the array, the application will throw an **array index out of range** error. Therefore, if we are unsure of the size of an array, it is a good practice to verify that the index is not outside the range of the array. The following examples illustrate this concept:

```
//This example will throw an array index out of range error
let arrayOne = [1,2,3,4]
print(arrayOne[6])

//This example will not throw an array index out of range error
let arrayTwo = [1,2,3,4]
if (arrayTwo.count > 6) {
    print(arrayTwo[6])
}
```

In the preceding code, the first block would throw an **array index out of range** error because we are attempting to access the value from the arrayOne array at index 6; however, there are only four elements in the array. The second example would not throw the error because we are checking whether the arrayTwo array contains more than six elements before trying to access the element at the sixth index.

Is the array empty?

To check whether an array is empty (that is, it does not contain any elements), we use the isEmpty property. This property will return true if the array is empty and false if it is not. The following example shows how to check whether an array is empty:

```
var arrayOne = [1,2]
var arrayTwo = [Int]()
arrayOne.isEmpty  //Returns false because the array is not empty
arrayTwo.isEmpty  //Returns true because the array is empty
```

Now let's see how we can shuffle an array.

Shuffling an array

An array can be very easily shuffled using the shuffle() and shuffled() methods. This can be very useful if we are creating a game, such as a card game, where the array contains the 52 cards in the deck. To shuffle the array in place, the shuffle() method can be used; to put the shuffled results in a new array, leaving the original array untouched, the shuffled() method would be used. The following examples show this:

```
var arrayOne = [1,2,3,4,5,6]
arrayOne.shuffle()
let shuffledArray = arrayOne.shuffled()
```

Now let's look at how we can append data to an array.

Appending to an array

A static array is somewhat useful but having the ability to add elements dynamically is what makes arrays really useful. To add an item to the end of an array, we can use the append method. The following example shows how to append an item to the end of an array:

```
var arrayOne = [1,2]
arrayOne.append(3)  //arrayOne will now contain 1, 2 and 3
```

Swift also allows us to use the addition assignment operator (+=) to append an array to another array. The following example shows how to use the addition assignment operator to append an array to the end of another array:

```
var arrayOne = [1,2]
arrayOne += [3,4]    //arrayOne will now contain 1, 2, 3 and 4
```

The way you append an element to the end of an array is really up to you. Personally, I prefer the assignment operator because, to me, it is a bit easier to read, but we will be using both in this book.

Inserting a value into an array

We can insert a value into an array by using the insert method. The insert method will move all the items up one spot, starting at the specified index, to make room for the new element, and then insert the value into the specified index. The following example shows how to use this method to insert a new value into an array:

```
var arrayOne = [1,2,3,4,5]
arrayOne.insert(10, at: 3)    //arrayOne now contains 1, 2, 3, 10, 4
and 5
```

Now that we have seen how to insert a value, let's see how we can replace an element within an array.

Replacing elements in an array

We use the subscript syntax to replace elements in an array. Using the subscript, we pick the element of the array we wish to update and then use the assignment operator to assign a new value. The following example shows how we will replace a value in an array:

```
var arrayOne = [1,2,3]
arrayOne[1] = 10     //arrayOne now contains 1,10,3
```

 You cannot update a value that is outside the current range of the array. Attempting to do so will throw the same **index out of range** exception that was thrown when we tried to insert a value outside the range of the array.

Now let's look at how we can remove elements from an array.

Removing elements from an array

There are three methods that we can use to remove one or all of the elements in an array. These methods are removeLast(), remove(at:), and removeAll(). The following example shows how to use the three methods to remove elements from an array:

```
var arrayOne = [1,2,3,4,5]
arrayOne.removeLast()     //arrayOne now contains 1, 2, 3 and 4
arrayOne.remove(at:2)     //arrayOne now contains 1, 2 and 4
arrayOne.removeAll()      //arrayOne is now empty
```

The removeLast() and remove(at:) methods will also return the value of the element being removed. Therefore, if we want to know the value of the item that was removed, we can rewrite the remove(at:) and removeLast() lines to capture the value, as shown in the following example:

```
var arrayOne = [1,2,3,4,5]
var removed1 = arrayOne.removeLast()  //removed1 contains the value 5
var removed = arrayOne.remove(at: 2)  //removed contains the value 3
```

Merging two arrays

To create a new array by adding two arrays together, we use the addition (+) operator. The following example shows how to use the addition (+) operator to create a new array that contains all the elements of two other arrays:

```
let arrayOne = [1,2] let arrayTwo = [3,4]
var combined = arrayOne + arrayTwo   //combine contains 1, 2, 3 and 4
```

In the preceding code, arrayOne and arrayTwo are left unchanged, while the combined array contains the elements from arrayOne, followed by the elements from arrayTwo.

Retrieving a subarray from an array

We can retrieve a subarray from an existing array by using the subscript syntax with a range operator. The following example shows how to retrieve a range of elements from an existing array:

```
let arrayOne = [1,2,3,4,5]
var subArray = arrayOne[2...4]     //subArray contains 3, 4 and 5
```

The operator (three periods) is known as a **two-sided range operator**. The range operator in the preceding code says that we want all the elements from 2 to 4 inclusively (elements 2 and 4 as well as what is between them). There is another two-sided range operator, ..<, known as the **half-open range operator**. The half-open range operator functions the same as the previous range operator; however, it excludes the last element. The following example shows how to use the ..< operator:

```
let arrayOne = [1,2,3,4,5]
var subArray = arrayOne[2..<4]     //subArray contains 3 and 4
```

In the preceding example, the subarray contains two elements: 3 and 4. A two-sided range operator has numbers on either side of the operator. In Swift, we are not limited to two-sided range operators; we can also use one-sided range operators. The following examples show how we can use one-sided range operators:

```
let arrayOne = [1,2,3,4,5]
var a = arrayOne[..<3]     //subArray contains 1, 2 and 3
var b = arrayOne[...3]     //subArray contains 1, 2, 3 and 4
var c = arrayOne[2...]     //subArray contains 3, 4 and 5
```

The one-sided range operators were added in version 4 of the Swift language. The previous range operators enable us to access a contiguous range of elements from an array.

SE-0270 enables us to fetch elements that are not contiguous, which means the elements may not be next to each other. This update to the Swift standard library introduced a new RangeSet type, which is a subrange of indexes that are non-contiguous. Let's see how this works with the following code:

```
var numbers = [1,2,3,4,5,6,7,8,9,10]
let evenNum = numbers.subranges(where: { $0.isMultiple(of: 2) })
print(numbers[evenNum].count)

//numbers[evenNum] contains 2,4,6,8,10
```

In this code, we define an array that contains the numbers 1 through 10. We then use the `subranges(where:)` method to retrieve the even elements. This method takes a closure as the argument, which hasn't been discussed yet. For now, we just need to know that we are able to retrieve non-contiguous subarrays and we will look at this again in *Chapter 14, Working with Closures*.

Making bulk changes to an array

We can use the subscript syntax with a range operator to change the values of multiple elements. The following example shows how to do this:

```
arrayOne[1...2] = [12,13]  //arrayOne contains 1,12,13,4 and 5
```

In the preceding code, the elements at indices 1 and 2 will be changed to the numbers 12 and 13; therefore, arrayOne will contain 1, 12, 13, 4, and 5.

The number of elements that you are changing in the range operator does not need to match the number of values that you are passing in. Swift makes bulk changes by first removing the elements defined by the range operator and then inserting the new values. The following example demonstrates this concept:

```
var arrayOne = [1,2,3,4,5]
arrayOne[1...3] = [12,13]  //arrayOne now contains 1, 12, 13 and 5
```

In the preceding code, the arrayOne array starts with five elements. We then replace the range of elements 1 to 3 inclusively. This causes elements 1 through 3 (that is, three elements) to be removed from the array first. After those three elements are removed, then the two new elements (12 and 13) are added to the array, starting at index 1. After this is complete, arrayOne will contain four elements: 1, 12, 13, and 5. Using the same logic, we can also add more elements than we remove. The following example illustrates this:

```
var arrayOne = [1,2,3,4,5]
arrayOne[1...3] = [12,13,14,15]
//arrayOne now contains 1, 12, 13, 14, 15 and 5 (six elements)
```

In the preceding code, arrayOne starts with five elements. We then say that we want to replace the range of elements 1 through 3 inclusively. As in the previous example, this causes elements 1 through 3 (three elements) to be removed from the array. We then add four elements (12, 13, 14, and 15) to the array, starting at index 1. After this is complete, arrayOne will contain six elements: 1, 12, 13, 14, 15, and 5.

Algorithms for arrays

Swift arrays have several methods that take a closure as their argument. These methods transform the array in a way defined by the code in the closure. Closures are self-contained blocks of code that can be passed around, and are similar to blocks in Objective-C and lambdas in other languages. We will discuss closures in depth in *Chapter 14, Working with Closures*. For now, the goal is to become familiar with how the algorithms work in Swift.

Sort

The **sort** algorithm sorts an array in place. This means that, when the sort() method is used, the original array is replaced with the sorted one. The closure takes two arguments (represented by $0 and $1), and it should return a Boolean value that indicates whether the first element should be placed before the second element. The following code shows how to use the sort algorithm:

```
var arrayOne = [9,3,6,2,8,5]
arrayOne.sort(){ $0 < $1 }
//arrayOne contains 2,3,5,6,8 and 9
```

The preceding code will sort the array in ascending order. We know this because the rule will return true if the first number ($0) is less than the second number ($1). Therefore, when the sort algorithm begins, it compares the first two numbers (9 and 3) and returns true if the first number (9) is less than the second number (3). In our case, the rule returns false, so the numbers are reversed. The algorithm continues sorting in this manner until all of the numbers are sorted in the correct order.

To sort an array in ascending order, we can actually use the sort() method by itself without using a closure as shown in the following code:

```
var arrayOne = [9,3,6,2,8,5]
arrayOne.sort()
```

The preceding examples sorted the array in a numerically-increasing order; if we wanted to reverse the order, we would reverse the arguments in the closure. The following code shows how to reverse the sort order:

```
var arrayOne = [9,3,6,2,8,5]
arrayOne.sort(){ $1 < $0 }
//arrayOne contains 9,8,6,5,3 and 2
```

When we run this code, arrayOne will contain the elements 9, 8, 6, 5, 3, and 2.

The preceding code can be simplified by using the sort(by:) method and passing in a greater-than or less-than operator, as shown in the following code:

```
var arrayTwo = [9,3,6,2,8,5]
arrayTwo.sort(by: <)
```

In the preceding code, by using the less-than operator, the array is sorted in ascending order. If we'd used the greater-than operator, the array would have been sorted in descending order.

Sorted

While the sort algorithm sorts the array in place (that is, it replaces the original array), the **sorted** algorithm does not change the original array; it instead creates a new array with the sorted elements from the original array. The following example shows how to use the sorted algorithm:

```
var arrayOne = [9,3,6,2,8,5]
let sorted = arrayOne.sorted(){ $0 < $1 }
//sorted contains 2,3,5,6,8 and 9
//arrayOne contains 9,3,6,2,8 and 5
```

After we run this code, arrayOne will contain the original unsorted array (9, 3, 6, 2, 8, and 5) and the sorted array will contain the new sorted array (2, 3, 5, 6, 8, and 9).

Filter

The **filter** algorithm will return a new array by filtering the original array. This is one of the most powerful array algorithms and may end up being the one you use the most. If you need to retrieve a subset of an array based on a set of rules, I recommend using this algorithm rather than trying to write your own method to filter the array.

The closure takes one argument, and it should return a Boolean true if the element should be included in the new array, as shown in the following code:

```
var arrayOne = [1,2,3,4,5,6,7,8,9]
let filtered = arrayOne.filter{$0 > 3 && $0 < 7}
//filtered contains 4,5 and 6
```

In the preceding code, the rule that we are passing to the algorithm returns true if the number is greater than 3 and less than 7; therefore, any number that is greater than 3 and less than 7 is included in the new filtered array.

This next example shows how we can retrieve a subset of cities that contain the letter o in their name:

```
var city = ["Boston", "London", "Chicago", "Atlanta"]
let filteredCity = city.filter{$0.range(of:"o") != nil}
//filtered contains "Boston", "London" and "Chicago"
```

In the preceding code, we use the `range(of:)` method to return `true` if the string contains the letter o. If the method returns `true`, the string is included in the `filtered` array.

Map

While the filter algorithm is used to select only certain elements of an array, **map** is used to apply logic to all elements in the array. The following example shows how to use the map algorithm to divide each number by 10:

```
var arrayOne = [10, 20, 30, 40]
let applied = arrayOne.map{ $0 / 10}
//applied contains 1,2,3 and 4
```

In the preceding code, the new array contains the numbers 1, 2, 3, and 4, which is the result of dividing each element of the original array by 10.

The new array created by the map algorithm is not required to contain the same element types as the original array; however, all the elements in the new array must be of the same type. In the following example, the original array contains integer values, but the new array created by the map algorithm contains string elements:

```
var arrayTwo = [1, 2, 3, 4]
let applied = arrayTwo.map{ "num:\($0)"}
//applied contains "num:1", "num:2", "num:3" and "num:4"
```

In the preceding code, we created an array of strings that appends the numbers from the original array to the `num:` string.

Count

We can combine the filter algorithm with the `count` method to count the number of items in an array that match a rule. For example, if we had an array that contained the grades from a test, we could use the **count** algorithm to count how many of the grades were greater than or equal to 90, like this:

```
let arrayOne = [95, 90, 75, 80,60]
let count = arrayOne.filter{ $0 >= 90 }.count
```

As we did with the filter algorithm, we can use methods from the array type, such as the range(of:) method from the string type. For example, rather than returning a subset of cities that contain the letter o in their name, as we did in the filter algorithm, we can count the cities like this:

```
var city = ["Boston", "London", "Chicago", "Atlanta"]
let count1 = city.filter{$0.range(of:"o") != nil}.count
```

In the preceding count, the count1 constant contains 3.

Diff

In Swift 5.1 with SE-0240, the **Diff** algorithm was introduced. This addition to the Swift language enables support for diff and patching of ordered collections like arrays. To really see the power of this change we need to understand how switch statements work, which is introduced in *Chapter 6, Control Flow*; therefore, we will briefly show how the Diff algorithm works here with the applying method. We will look at this algorithm more when we cover the switch statement in *Chapter 6, Control Flow*.

Let's look at the following code:

```
var scores1 = [100, 81, 95, 98, 99, 65, 87]
var scores2 = [100, 98, 95, 91, 83, 88, 72]

let diff2 = scores2.difference(from: scores1)
var newArray = scores1.applying(diff2) ?? []
```

In the preceding code, we started off by creating two arrays. We then used the difference(from:) method, which returns the difference between the two arrays. This new array would now contain the values: 100, 98, 95, 91, 83, 88, and 72. The return value is a collection of enumerations that tell us how we can produce a collection, from one collection, that will contain the same elements as another collection. This might not make a whole lot of sense right now, but as we dive into more of this, it will become clear.

The last line uses the applying() method to apply the changes to the scores1 array and returns an array that has the same elements as the scores2 array; therefore, after this method is called, the newArray array contains the same elements as the scores2 array.

forEach

We can use the forEach algorithm to iterate over a sequence. The following example shows how we would do this:

```
var arrayOne = [10, 20, 30, 40]
arrayOne.forEach{ print($0) }
```

This example will print the following results to the console:

```
10
20
30
40
```

While using the forEach algorithm is very easy, it does have some limitations. The recommended way to iterate over an array is to use the for-in loop, which we will see in the next section.

Iterating over an array

We can iterate over all elements of an array, in order, with a for-in loop. The for-in loop will execute one or more statements for each element of the array. We will discuss the for-in loop in greater detail in *Chapter 6, Control Flow*. The following example shows how we would iterate over the elements of an array:

```
var arrayOne = ["one", "two", "three"]
for item in arrayOne {
    print(item)
}
```

In the preceding example, the for-in loop iterates over the array and executes the print(item) line for each element in the array. If we run this code, it will display the following results in the console:

```
one
two
three
```

There are times when we would like to iterate over an array, as we did in the preceding example, but we would also like to know the index, as well as the value of an element. To do this, we can use the enumerated method of an array, which returns a tuple for each item in the array that contains both the index and value of the element. The following example shows how to use this function:

```
var arrayOne = ["one", "two", "three"]
for (index,value) in arrayOne.enumerated() {
    print("\(index) \(value)")
}
```

The preceding code will display the following results in the console:

```
one
two
three
```

Now that we have introduced arrays in Swift, let's move on to dictionaries.

Dictionaries

While dictionaries are not as commonly used as arrays, they have additional functionality that makes them incredibly powerful. A dictionary is a container that stores multiple key-value pairs, where all the keys are of the same type and all the values are of the same type. The key is used as a unique identifier for the value. A dictionary does not guarantee the order in which the key-value pairs are stored since we look up the values by key rather than by the index of the value.

Dictionaries are good for storing items that map to unique identifiers, where the unique identifier should be used to retrieve the item. Countries with their abbreviations are a good example of items that can be stored in a dictionary. In the following table, we show countries with their abbreviations as key-value pairs:

Key	Value
US	United States
IN	India
UK	United Kingdom

Table 5.1: Countries and their abbreviations

Creating and initializing dictionaries

We can initialize a dictionary using a dictionary literal, similarly to how we initialized an array with the array literal. The following example shows how to create a dictionary using the key-value pairs in the preceding chart:

```
let countries = ["US":"UnitedStates","IN":"India","UK":"UnitedKingdom"]
```

The preceding code creates an immutable dictionary that contains each of the key-value pairs in the chart we saw before. Just like the array, to create a mutable dictionary we will need to use the var keyword in place of let. The following example shows how to create a mutable dictionary that contains the countries:

```
var countries = ["US":"UnitedStates","IN":"India","UK":"UnitedKingdom"]
```

In the preceding two examples, we created a dictionary where the key and value were both strings. The compiler inferred that the key and value were strings because that was the type of the keys and values used to initiate the dictionary. If we wanted to create an empty dictionary, we would need to tell the compiler what the key and value types are. The following examples create various dictionaries with different key-value types:

```
var dic1 = [String:String]()
var dic2 = [Int:String]()
var dic3 = [String:MyObject]()
var dic4: [String:String] = [:]
var dic5: [Int:String] = [:]
```

 If we want to use a custom object as the key in a dictionary, we will need to make the custom object conform to the **Hashable** protocol from Swift's standard library. We will discuss protocols extensively later in this book, but for now just understand that it is possible to use custom objects as a key in a dictionary.

Now let's see how we can access the values of a dictionary.

Accessing dictionary values

We use the subscript syntax to retrieve the value for a particular key. If the dictionary does not contain the key we are looking for, the dictionary will return nil; therefore, the variable returned from this lookup is an optional variable. The following example shows how to retrieve a value from a dictionary using its key in the subscript syntax:

```
let countries = ["US":"United States", "IN":"India","UK":"UnitedKingd
om"]
var name = countries["US"]
```

In the preceding code, the name variable contains the United States string.

Counting the keys or values in a dictionary

We use the `count` property of the dictionary to get the number of key-value pairs in the dictionary. The following example shows how to use this property:

```
let countries = ["US":"United States", "IN":"India","UK":"United
Kingdom"]
var cnt = countries.count     //cnt contains 3
```

In the preceding code, the `cnt` variable will contain the number 3 since there are three key-value pairs in the dictionary.

Is the dictionary empty?

To test whether a dictionary contains any key-value pairs, we can use the `isEmpty` property. This property will return `false` if the dictionary contains one or more key-value pairs and `true` if it is empty. The following example shows us how to use this property to determine whether our dictionary contains any key-value pairs:

```
let countries = ["US":"United States", "IN":"India","UK":"United
Kingdom"]
var empty = countries.isEmpty
```

In the preceding code, the `isEmpty` property returned `false` as there are three key-value pairs in the dictionary.

Updating the value of a key

To update the value of a key in a dictionary, we can use either the subscript syntax or the `updateValue(_: ,forKey:)` method. The `updateValue(_:, forKey:)` method has an additional feature that the subscript syntax doesn't: it returns the original value associated with the key prior to changing the value. The following example shows how to use both the subscript syntax and the `updateValue(_:, forKey:)` method to update the value of a key:

```
var countries = ["US":"United States", "IN":"India","UK":"United
Kingdom"]

countries["UK"] = "Great Britain"
//The value of UK is now set to "Great Britain"

var orig = countries.updateValue("Britain", forKey: "UK")
//The value of UK is now set to "Britain"
//The orig variable equals "Great Britain"
```

In the preceding code, we use the subscript syntax to change the value associated with the UK key from United Kingdom to Great Britain. The original value of United Kingdom was not saved prior to replacing it. We then used the updateValue(_:, forKey:) method to change the value associated with the UK key from Great Britain to Britain. With the updateValue(_:, forKey:) method, the original value of Great Britain is assigned to the orig variable prior to changing the value in the dictionary.

Adding a key-value pair

To add a new key-value pair to a dictionary, we can use the subscript syntax or the same updateValue(_:, forKey:) method that we used to update the value of a key. If we use the updateValue(_:, forKey:) method and the key is not currently present in the dictionary, this method will add a new key-value pair and return nil. The following example shows how to use both the subscript syntax and the updateValue(_:, forKey:) method to add a new key-value pair to a dictionary:

```
var countries = ["US":"United States", "IN":"India","UK":"United
Kingdom"]
countries["FR"] = "France" //The value of "FR" is set to"France"

var orig = countries.updateValue("Germany", forKey: "DE")
//The value of "DE" is set to "Germany" and orig is nil
```

In the preceding code, the countries dictionary starts with three key-value pairs and we then add a fourth key-value pair (FR/France) to the dictionary using the subscript syntax. We use the updateValue(_:,forKey:) method to add a fifth key-value pair (DE/Germany) to the dictionary. The orig variable is set to nil because the countries dictionary did not contain a value associated with the DE key.

Removing a key-value pair

There may be times when we need to remove values from a dictionary. There are three ways to achieve this: the subscript syntax, the removeValue(forKey:) method, or the removeAll() method. The removeValue(forKey:) method returns the value of the key prior to removing it. The removeAll() method removes all the elements from the dictionary. The following example shows how to use all three methods to remove key-value pairs from a dictionary:

```
var countries = ["US":"UnitedStates","IN":"India","UK":"United Kingdom"]
countries["IN"] = nil //The "IN" key/value pair is removed

var orig = countries.removeValue(forKey:"UK")
//The "UK" key value pair is removed and orig contains "United Kingdom"
```

```
countries.removeAll()
//Removes all key/value pairs from the countries dictionary
```

In the preceding code, the `countries` dictionary starts off with three key-value pairs. We then set the value associated with the `IN` key to `nil`, which removes the key-value pair from the dictionary. We use the `removeValue(forKey:)` method to remove the key associated with the `UK` key. Prior to removing the value associated with the `UK` key, the `removeValue(forKey:)` method saves the value in the `orig` variable. Finally, we use the `removeAll()` method to remove all the remaining key-value pairs in the `countries` dictionary.

Now let's look at the set type.

Set

The set type is a generic collection that is similar to the array type. While the array type is an ordered collection that may contain duplicate items, the set type is an unordered collection where each item must be unique.

Like the key in a dictionary, the type stored in an array must conform to the **Hashable** protocol. This means that the type must provide a way to compute a hash value for itself. All of Swift's basic types, such as `String`, `Double`, `Int`, and `Bool`, conform to this protocol and can be used in a set by default.

Let's look at how we would use the set type.

Initializing a set

There are a couple of ways to initialize a set. Just like the array and dictionary types, Swift needs to know what type of data is going to be stored in it. This means that we must either tell Swift the type of data to store in the set or initialize it with some data so that it can infer the data type.

Just like the array and dictionary types, we use the `var` and `let` keywords to declare whether the set is mutable:

```
//Initializes an empty set of the String type
var mySet = Set<String>()

//Initializes a mutable set of the String type with initial values
var mySet = Set(["one", "two", "three"])

//Creates an immutable set of the String type.
let mySet = Set(["one", "two", "three"])
```

Inserting items into a set

We use the `insert` method to insert an item into a set. If we attempt to insert an item that is already in the set, the item will be ignored. Here are some examples of inserting items into a set:

```
var mySet = Set<String>()
mySet.insert("One")
mySet.insert("Two")
mySet.insert("Three")
```

The `insert()` method returns a tuple that we can use to verify that the value was successfully added to the set. The following example shows how to check the returned value to see whether it was added successfully:

```
var mySet = Set<String>()
mySet.insert("One")
mySet.insert("Two")
var results = mySet.insert("One")
if results.inserted {
    print("Success")
} else {
    print("Failed")
  }
```

In this example, `Failed` would be printed to the console since we are attempting to add the `One` value to the set when it is already in the set.

Determining the number of items in a set

We can use the `count` property to determine the number of items in a set. Here is an example of how to use this method:

```
var mySet = Set<String>()
mySet.insert("One")
mySet.insert("Two")
mySet.insert("Three")
print("\(mySet.count) items")
```

When executed, this code will print the message 3 `items` to the console because the set contains three items.

Checking whether a set contains an item

We can verify whether a set contains an item by using the contains() method, as shown here:

```
var mySet = Set<String>()
mySet.insert("One")
mySet.insert("Two")
mySet.insert("Three")
var contain = mySet.contains("Two")
```

In the preceding example, the contain variable is set to true because the set contains a string with a value of Two.

Iterating over a set

We can use the for-in statement to iterate over the items in a set as we did with arrays. The following example shows how we would iterate through the items in a set:

```
for item in mySet {
    print(item)
}
```

The preceding example will print out each item in the set to the console.

Removing items in a set

We can remove a single item or all the items in a set. To remove a single item, we would use the remove() method and, to remove all the items, we would use the removeAll() method. The following example shows how to remove items from a set:

```
//The remove method will return and remove an item from a set
var item = mySet.remove("Two")

//The removeAll method will remove all items from a set
mySet.removeAll()
```

Set operations

Apple has provided four methods that we can use to construct a set from two other sets. These operations can be performed in place, on one of the sets, or used to create a new set. These operations are as follows:

- union and formUnion: These create a set with all the unique values from both sets and can be thought of as removing the duplicates.

- subtracting and subtract: These create a set with values from the first set that are not in the second set.

- intersection and formIntersection: These create a set with values that are common to both sets.

- symmetricDifference and formSymmetricDifference: These create a new set with values that are in either set, but not in both sets.

Let's look at some examples and see the results that can be obtained from each of these operations. For all the examples of set operations, we will be using the following two sets:

```
var mySet1 = Set(["One", "Two", "Three", "abc"])
var mySet2 = Set(["abc","def","ghi", "One"])
```

The first example uses the union method. This method takes the unique values from both sets to make another set:

```
var newSetUnion = mySet1.union(mySet2)
```

The newSetUnion variable will contain the following values: One, Two, Three, abc, def, and ghi. We can use the formUnion method to perform the union function in place without creating a new set:

```
mySet1.formUnion(mySet2)
```

In this example, the mySet1set set will contain all the unique values from the mySet1 and mySet2 sets.

Now let's look at the subtract and subtracting methods. These methods will create a set with the values from the first set that are not in the second set:

```
var newSetSubtract = mySet1.subtracting(mySet2)
```

In this example, the newSetSubtract variable will contain the Two and Three values because those are the only two values that are not also in the second set.

We use the subtract method to perform the subtraction function in place without creating a new set:

```
mySet1.subtract(mySet2)
```

In this example, the mySet1 set will contain the Two and Three values because those are the only two values that are not in the mySet2 set.

Now let's look at the intersection method, which creates a new set from the values that are common between the two sets:

```
var newSetIntersect = mySet1.intersection(mySet2)
```

In this example, the newSetIntersect variable will contain the One and abc values since they are the values that are common between the two sets.

We can use the formIntersection() method to perform the intersection function in place without creating a new set:

```
mySet1.formIntersection(mySet2)
```

In this example, the mySet1 set will contain the One and abc values since they are the values that are common between the two sets.

Finally, let's look at the symmetricDifference() methods. These methods will create a new set with values that are in either set, but not in both:

```
var newSetExclusiveOr = mySet1.symmetricDifference(mySet2)
```

In this example, the newSetExclusiveOr variable will contain the Two, Three, def, and ghi values.

To perform this method in place, we use the fromSymmetricDifference() method:

```
mySet1.formSymmetricDifference(mySet2)
```

These four operations (union, subtraction, intersection, and symmetric difference) add functionality that is not present with arrays. Combined with faster lookup speeds, as compared to an array, the set type can be a very useful alternative when the order of the collection is not important and the instances in the collection must be unique.

Summary

In this chapter, we covered Swift collections. Having a good understanding of the native collection types of Swift is essential to architecting and developing applications in Swift since all but the most basic applications use them.

The three Swift collection types are arrays, sets, and dictionaries. Arrays store data as an ordered collection. Sets store data as an unordered collection of unique values. Dictionaries store data in an unordered collection of key-value pairs.

In the next chapter, we will look at how to use Swift's control flow statements.

6
Control Flow

When I was a teen, every month while I was learning BASIC programming on my Commodore Vic-20, I would read several of the early computer magazines, such as *Byte Magazine*. I remember one particular review for a game called *Zork*. While Zork was not a game that was available for my Vic-20, the concept of the game fascinated me because I was really into sci-fi and fantasy. I remember thinking how cool it would be to write a game like that, so I decided to figure out how to do it. One of the biggest concepts that I had to grasp at that time was how to control the flow of the application depending on the user's actions.

In this chapter, we will cover the following topics:

- What conditional statements are and how to use them
- What loops are and how to use them
- What control transfer statements are and how to use them

What have we learned so far?

Up to this point, we have been laying the foundation for writing applications with Swift. While it is possible to write a very basic application with what we have learned so far, it would be difficult to write a useful application using only what we've covered in the first five chapters.

Starting with this chapter, we will begin to move away from the foundations of the Swift language and begin to learn the building blocks of application development with Swift. In this chapter, we will go over control flow statements. To become a master of the Swift programming language, it is important that you fully understand and comprehend the concepts that are discussed in this chapter.

Before we cover control flow and functions, let's take a look at how curly brackets and parentheses are used in Swift.

Curly brackets

In Swift, unlike other C-like languages, curly brackets are required for conditional statements and loops. In other C-like languages, if there is only one statement to execute for a conditional statement or a loop, curly brackets around that line are optional. This has led to numerous errors and bugs, such as Apple's goto fail bug. When Apple was designing Swift, they decided to introduce the use of curly brackets, even when there was only one line of code to execute. Let's take a look at some code that illustrates this requirement. This first example is not valid in Swift because it is missing the curly brackets; however, it will be valid in most other languages:

```
if (x > y)
    x=0
```

In Swift, you are required to have curly brackets as illustrated in the following example:

```
if (x > y) {
    x=0
}
```

Parentheses

Unlike other C-like languages, the parentheses around conditional expressions in Swift are optional. In the preceding example, we put parentheses around the conditional expression, but they are not required. The following example will be valid in Swift, but not valid in most C-like languages:

```
if x > y {
    x=0
}
```

Control flow

Control flow, also known as the flow of control, refers to the order in which statements, instructions, and functions are executed within an application. Swift supports most of the familiar control flow statements that are used in C-like languages.

These include loops (such as `while`), conditional statements (including `if`, `switch`, and `guard`), and the transfer of control statements (including `break` and `continue`). It is worth noting that Swift does not include the traditional C `for` loop and, rather than the traditional `do-while` loop, Swift has the `repeat-while` loop.

In addition to the standard C control flow statements, Swift has also included statements such as the `for-in` loop and enhanced some of the existing statements, such as the `switch` statement.

Let's begin by looking at conditional statements in Swift.

Conditional statements

A conditional statement checks a condition and executes a block of code only if the condition is `true`. Swift provides both the `if` and `if...else` conditional statements. Let's take a look at how to use these conditional statements to execute blocks of code if a specified condition is `true`.

The if statement

The `if` statement will check a conditional statement and, if it is `true`, it will execute the block of code. This statement takes the following format:

```
if condition {
    block of code
}
```

Now, let's take a look at how to use the `if` statement:

```
let teamOneScore = 7
let teamTwoScore = 6
if teamOneScore > teamTwoScore {
    print("Team One Won")
}
```

In the preceding example, we begin by setting the `teamOneScore` and `teamTwoScore` constants. We then use the `if` statement to check whether the value of `teamOneScore` is greater than the value of `teamTwoScore`. If the value is greater, we print Team One Won to the console. When this code is run, we will indeed see that Team One Won is printed to the console, but if the value of `teamTwoScore` is greater than the value of `teamOneScore`, nothing will be printed. This is not the best way to write an application, as we want the user to know which team has actually won. The `if...else` statement can help us with this problem.

Conditional code execution with the if...else statement

The `if...else` statement checks a conditional statement and, if it is `true`, it executes a block of code. If the conditional statement is not `true`, it executes a separate block of code; this statement takes the following format:

```
if condition {
    block of code if true
} else {
    block of code if not true
}
```

Let's now modify the preceding example to use the `if...else` statement to tell the user which team has won:

```
let teamOneScore = 7
let teamTwoScore = 6
if teamOneScore > teamTwoScore{
    print("Team One Won")
} else {
    print("Team Two Won")
}
```

This new version will print out Team One Won if the value of `teamOneScore` is greater than the value of `teamTwoScore`; otherwise, it will print out the message, Team Two Won.

This fixes one problem with our code, but what do you think the code will do if the value of `teamOneScore` is equal to the value of `teamTwoScore`? In the real world, we would see a tie, but in the preceding code, we would print out Team Two Won, which would not be fair to team one. In cases like this, we can use multiple `else if` statements and an `else` statement at the end to act as the default path if no conditional statements are met.

This is illustrated in the following code sample:

```
let teamOneScore = 7
let teamTwoScore = 6
if teamOneScore > teamTwoScore {
```

```
    print("Team One Won")
} else if teamTwoScore > teamOneScore {
    print("Team Two Won")
} else {
    print("We have a tie")
}
```

In the preceding code, if the value of teamOneScore is greater than the value of teamTwoScore, we print Team One Won to the console. We then have an else if statement, which means that the conditional statement is only checked if the first if statement returns false. Finally, if both of the if statements return false, the code in the else block is called and We have a tie is printed to the console.

This is a good time to point out that it is not good practice to have numerous else if statements stacked up, as demonstrated in the previous example. It is better to use the switch statement, which we will explore later in this chapter.

The guard statement

In Swift, and most modern languages, our conditional statements tend to focus on testing whether a condition is true. As an example, the following code tests whether the x variable is greater than 10 and, if so, then we perform some kind of function. If the condition is false, we handle the following error condition:

```
var x = 9
if x > 10 {
// Functional code here
} else {
// Do error condition
}
```

This type of code embeds our functional code within our checks and tucks the error conditions away at the end of our functions, but what if that is not what we really want? Sometimes (actually a lot of times), it might be better to take care of our error conditions at the beginning of the function. In our simple example, we can easily check whether x is less than or equal to 10 and, if so, then we perform the error condition. Not all conditional statements are that easy to rewrite, especially items such as optional binding.

In Swift, we have the guard statement. This statement focuses on performing a function if a condition is `false`; this allows us to trap errors and perform the error conditions early in our functions. We can rewrite our previous example using the guard statement, as follows:

```
var x = 9
guard x > 10 else {
    // Do error condition
    return
}
//Functional code here
```

In this new example, we check to see whether the x variable is greater than 10, and if not, we perform the error condition. If the variable is greater than 10, the application continues to the functional part of our code. You will notice that we have a return statement embedded within the guard condition. The code within the guard statement must contain a transfer of control statement; this is what prevents the rest of the code from executing. If we forget the transfer of control statement, Swift will show a compile-time error. We will look at transfer of control statements a little later in this chapter.

Let's take a look at some more examples of the guard statement. The following example shows how we can use the guard statement to verify that an optional contains a valid value:

```
func guardFunction(str: String?) {
    guard let goodStr = str else {
        print("Input was nil")
        return
    }
    print("Input was \(goodStr)")
}
```

Functions have not been covered yet but they will be covered in *Chapter 7, Functions.*

In this example, we create a function named guardFunction() that accepts an optional that contains a string or nil value. We then use the guard statement with optional binding to verify that the string optional is not nil. If it does contain nil, then the code within the guard statement is executed and the return statement is used to exit the function. The great thing about using the guard statement with optional binding is that the new variable is within the scope of the rest of the function, rather than just within the scope of the optional binding statement.

A conditional statement checks the condition once and, if the condition is met, it executes the block of code. However, what if we wanted to continuously execute the block of code until a condition is met? For this, we use loop statements.

The switch statement

The switch statement takes a value, compares it to several possible matches, and executes the appropriate block of code based on the first successful match. The switch statement is an alternative to using multiple else if statements when there could be several possible matches. The switch statement takes the following format:

```
switch value {
    case match1:
        block of code
    case match2:
        block of code
        //as many cases as needed
    default:
        block of code
}
```

Unlike most other languages, in Swift, the switch statement does not fall through to the next case statement; therefore, we do not need to use a break statement to prevent this fall-through. This is another safety feature that has been built into Swift, as one of the most common programming mistakes regarding the switch statement made by beginner programmers is to forget the break statement at the end of the case statement. Let's take a look at how to use the switch statement:

```
var speed = 300000000
switch speed {
    case 300000000:
        print("Speed of light")
    case 340:
        print("Speed of sound")
    default:
        print("Unknown speed")
}
```

In the preceding example, the switch statement took the value of the speed variable and compared it to the two case statements. If the value of speed matches either case, the code prints the speed. If it does not find a match, it prints the Unknown speed message.

Every switch statement must have a match for all the possible values. This means that, unless we are matching against an enumeration that has a defined number of values, each switch statement must have a default case. Let's take a look at a case where we do not have a default case:

```
var num = 5
switch num {
    case 1 :
        print("number is one")
    case 2 :
        print("Number is two")
    case 3 :
        print("Number is three")
}
```

If we put the preceding code into a Playground and attempt to compile the code, we will receive a Switch must be exhaustive error. This is a compile-time error, and therefore, we will not be notified until we attempt to compile the code.

It is possible to include multiple items in a single case. To do this, we need to separate the items with a comma. Let's take a look at how we use the switch statement to tell us whether a character is a vowel or a consonant:

```
var char : Character = "e"
switch char {
    case "a", "e", "i", "o", "u":
        print("letter is a vowel")
    case "b", "c", "d", "f", "g", "h", "j", "k", "l", "m", "n", "p",
"q", "r", "s", "t", "v", "w","x", "y", "z":
        print("letter is a consonant")
    default:
        print("unknown letter")
}
```

We can see in the preceding example that each case has multiple items. Commas separate these items and the switch statement attempts to match the char variable to each item listed in the case statements.

It is also possible to check the value of a switch statement to see whether it is included in a range. To do this, we use one of the range operators in the case statement, as shown in the following example:

```
var grade = 93
switch grade {
```

```
    case 90...100: print("Grade is an A")
    case 80...89: print("Grade is a B")
    case 70...79: print("Grade is an C")
    case 60...69: print("Grade is a D")
    case 0...59: print("Grade is a F")
    default:
        print("Unknown Grade")
}
```

In the preceding example, the `switch` statement took the grade variable, compared it with the ranges in each `case` statement, and printed out the appropriate grade.

In Swift, any `case` statement can contain an optional `where` clause, which provides an additional condition that needs validating. Let's say that, in our preceding example, we have students who are receiving special assistance in class and we wanted to define a grade of D for them as a range from 55 to 69. The following example shows how we can do this:

```
var studentId = 4
var grade = 57
switch grade {
    case 90...100:
        print("Grade is an A")
    case 80...89:
        print("Grade is a B")
    case 70...79:
        print("Grade is an C")
    case 55...69 where studentId == 4:
        print("Grade is a D for student 4")
    case 60...69:
        print("Grade is a D")
    case 0...59:
        print("Grade is a F")
    default:
        print("Unknown Grade")
}
```

One thing to bear in mind with the `where` expression is that Swift will attempt to match the value, starting with the first `case` statement and working its way down, checking each `case` statement in order. This means that, if we put the `case` statement with the `where` expression after the grade F `case` statement, then the `case` statement with the `where` expression will never be reached. This is illustrated in the following example:

```
var studentId = 4
var grade = 57
switch grade {
    case 90...100:
        print("Grade is an A")
    case 80...89:
        print("Grade is a B")
    case 70...79:
        print("Grade is an C")
    case 60...69:
        print("Grade is a D")
    case 0...59:
        print("Grade is a F")
        //The following case statement would never be reached because
        //the grades would always match one of the previous two
    case 55...69 where studentId == 4:
        print("Grade is a D for student 4")

    default:
        print("Unknown Grade")
}
```

 If you are using the where clause, a good rule of thumb is to always put the case statements with the where clause before any similar case statements withou the where clause.

sSwitch statements are also extremely useful for evaluating enumerations. Since an enumeration has a finite number of values, if we provide a case statement for all the values in the enumeration, we would not need to provide a default case. The following example demonstrates how we can use a switch statement to evaluate an enumeration:

```
enum Product {
    case Book(String, Double, Int)
    case Puzzle(String, Double)
}
var order = Product.Book("Mastering Swift 4", 49.99, 2017)
switch order {
    case .Book(let name, let price, let year):
        print("You ordered the book \(name): \(year) for \(price)")
    case .Puzzle(let name, let price):
```

```
        print("You ordered the Puzzle \(name) for \(price)")
    }
```

In this example, we began by defining an enumeration named Product with two values, each with associated values. We then created an order variable of Product type and used the switch statement to evaluate it.

When using a switch statement with enumerations, we must have a case statement for all possible values or a default statement. Let's take a look at some additional code that illustrates this:

```
enum Planets {
    case Mercury, Venus, Earth, Mars, Jupiter
    case Saturn, Uranus, Neptune
}
var planetWeLiveOn = Planets.Earth
// Using the switch statement
switch planetWeLiveOn {
    case .Mercury:
        print("We live on Mercury, it is very hot!")
    case .Venus:
        print("We live on Venus, it is very hot!")
    case .Earth:
        print("We live on Earth, just right")
    case .Mars:
        print("We live on Mars, a little cold")
    case .Jupiter, .Saturn, .Uranus, .Neptune:
        print("Where do we live?")
}
```

In this sample code, we have a case statement that handles each planet in the Planets enumeration. We can also add a default statement to handle any additional planets if they are added in later. However, it is recommended that if a switch statement uses a default case with an enumeration, then we should use the @unknown attribute, as follows:

```
switch planetWeLiveOn {
    case .Mercury:
        print("We live on Mercury, it is very hot!")
    case .Venus:
        print("We live on Venus, it is very hot!")
    case .Earth:
        print("We live on Earth, just right")
```

```
    case .Mars:
        print("We live on Mars, a little cold")
    case .Jupiter, .Saturn, .Uranus, .Neptune:
        print("Where do we live?")
    @unknown default:
        print("Unknown planet")
}
```

This will always throw a warning to remind us that if we add a new planet to the Planet enumeration, then we need to handle that new planet in this part of the code.

In *Chapter 5*, *Using Swift Collections*, we briefly covered the Diff algorithm. At that time we mentioned that we couldn't see the power of this algorithm until we understood the switch statement. Now that we understand the switch statement, let's see what we can do with this algorithm:

```
var cities1 = ["London", "Paris", "Seattle", "Boston", "Moscow"]
var cities2 = ["London", "Paris", "Tulsa", "Boston", "Tokyo"]

let diff = cities2.difference(from: cities1)

for change in diff {
    switch change {
    case .remove(let offset, let element, _ ):
        cities2.remove(at: offset)
    case .insert(let offset, let element, _):
        cities2.insert(element, at: offset)
}
```

In the preceding code, we start by creating two arrays of strings that each contain a list of cities. We then run the difference(from:) method, which we covered in the previous chapter. The difference(from:) method returns a collection containing instances of the Change enumeration. The Change enumeration is defined like this:

```
public enum Change {
    case insert(offset: Int, element: ChangeElement, associatedWith:
Int?)
    case remove(offset: Int, element: ChangeElement, associatedWith:
Int?)
}
```

This enumeration contains two possible values. The insert value tells us if we need to insert a value because the array is missing an element from the other array. The remove value tells us we need to remove an element because the array has an element that is not in the other array. In our code, we are handling both the insert and remove values, which means that after the code is executed, the cities2 array will have the same elements and in the same order as the cities1 array. This isn't too exciting but let's say that we want to remove any elements from the cities2 array that do not appear in the cities1 array. We could change our code to the following:

```
var cities1 = ["London", "Paris", "Seattle", "Boston", "Moscow"]
var cities2 = ["London", "Paris", "Tulsa", "Boston", "Tokyo"]

for change in diff {
    switch change {
    case .remove(let offset, let element, _ ):
        cities2.remove(at: offset)
    default:
        break
    }
}
```

When this code is executed, the cities2 array would contain the three elements of London, Paris, and Boston. If we just handled the insert conditions then the cities2 array would contain any elements that were part of either array. sSwitch on tuples

We can also use the switch statement with tuples; let's take a look at how to do this:

```
let myDog = ("Maple", 4)

switch myDog {
    case ("Lily", let age):
        print("Lily is my dog and is \(age)")
    case ("Maple", let age):
        print("Maple is my dog and is \(age)")
    case ("Dash", let age):
        print("Dash is my dog and is \(age)")
    default:
        print("unknown dog")
}
```

In this code, we created a tuple named `myDog` that contained the name of my dog and her age. We then used the `switch` statement to match the name (the first element of the tuple) and a `let` statement to retrieve the age. In this example, the message, `Maple is my dog and is 4`, will be printed to the screen.

We can also use the underscore (wildcard) and range operators with tuples in the `case` statement, as shown in the following example:

```
switch myDog {
    case(_, 0...1):
        print("Your dog is a puppy")
    case(_, 2...7):
        print("Your dog is middle aged")
    case(_, 8...):
        print("Your dog is getting old")
    default:
        print("Unknown")
}
```

In this example, the underscore will match any name, while the range operators will look for the age of the dog. In this example, since Maple is four years old, the message `Your dog is middle aged` will be printed on the screen.

Match on wildcard

In Swift, we can also combine the underscore (wildcard) with the `where` statement. This is illustrated in the following example:

```
let myNumber = 10
switch myNumber {
    case _ where myNumber.isMultiple(of: 2):
        print("Multiple of 2")
    case _ where myNumber.isMultiple(of: 3):
        print("Multiple of 3")
    default:
        print("No Match")
}
```

In this example, we create an integer variable named `myNumber` and use the `switch` statement to determine whether the value of the variable is a multiple of 2 or 3. Notice the `case` statement is proceeded by an underscore followed by the `where` statement. The underscore will match all the values of the variable, and then the `where` statement is called to see if the item we are switching on matches the rule defined within it.

Loops

Loop statements enable us to continuously execute a block of code until a condition is met. They also enable us to iterate over elements of a collection. Let's look at how we would use the `for-in` loop to iterate over the elements of a collection.

The for-in loop

While Swift does not offer the standard C-based `for` loop, it does have the `for-in` loop. The standard C-based `for` loop was removed from the Swift language in Swift 3 because it was rarely used. You can read the full proposal to remove this loop on the Swift evolution site at `https://github.com/apple/swift-evolution/blob/master/proposals/7-remove- c-style-for-loops.md`. The `for-in` statement is used to execute a block of code for each item in a range, collection, or sequence.

Using the for-in loop

The `for-in` loop iterates over a collection of items or a range of numbers, and executes a block of code for each item in the collection or range. The format for the `for-in` statement is as follows:

```
for variable in collection/range {
    block of code
}
```

As we can see in the preceding code, the `for-in` loop has twos:

- `variable`: This variable will change each time the loop executes and will hold the current item from the collection or range
- `collection/range`: This is the collection or range to iterate through

Let's take a look at how to use the `for-in` loop to iterate through a range of numbers:

```
for index in 1...5 {
    print(index)
}
```

In the preceding example, we iterated over a range of numbers from 1 to 5 and printed each of the numbers to the console. This loop used the closed range operator (`...`) to give the loop a range to iterate through. Swift also provides the half-open range operator (`..>`) and the one-sided range operators that we saw in the previous chapter.

Now, let's take a look at how to iterate over an array with the for-in loop:

```
var countries = ["USA","UK", "IN"]
for item in countries {
    print(item)
}
```

In the preceding example, we iterated through the countries array and printed each element of the array to the console. As you can see, iterating through an array with the for-in loop is safer, cleaner, and a lot easier than using the standard C-based for loop. Using the for-in loop prevents us from making common mistakes, such as using the less than or equal to (<=) operator rather than the less than (<) operator in our conditional statement.

Let's take a look at how to iterate over a dictionary with the for-in loop:

```
var dic = ["USA": "United States", "UK": "United Kingdom","IN":"India"]

for (abbr, name) in dic {
    print("\(abbr) --\(name)")
}
```

In the preceding example, we used the for-in loop to iterate through each key-value pair of the dictionary. In this example, each item in the dictionary is returned as a (key,value) tuple. We can decompose (key,value) tuple members as named constants within the body of the loop. One thing to note is that since a dictionary does not guarantee the order that items are stored in, the order that they are iterated through may not be the same as the order in which they were inserted.

Now, let's take a look at another type of loop, the while loop.

The while loop

The while loop executes a block of code until a condition is met. Swift provides two forms of the while loop; these are the while and repeat-while loops. In Swift 2.0, Apple replaced the do-while loop with the repeat-while loop. The repeat-while loop functions in the same way as the do-while loop did. Swift uses the do statement for error handling. A while loop is used when you want to run a loop zero or more times, while a repeat-while loop is used when you want to run the loop one or more times.

We use while loops when the number of iterations to be performed is not known and is usually dependent on some business logic. This could be something like looping through a collection until a certain value is found or a condition is met.

Using the while loop

The while loop starts by evaluating a conditional statement and then repeatedly executes a block of code while the conditional statement is true. The format for the while statement is as follows:

```
while condition {
    block of code
}
```

Let's take a look at how to use a while loop. In the following example, the while loop will continue to execute the block of code while the randomly-generated number is less than 7. In this example, we are using the Int.random() function to generate a random number between 0 and 9:

```
var ran = 0 while ran < 7 {
    ran = Int.random(in: 1..<20)
}
```

In the preceding example, we began by initializing the ran variable to 0. The while loop then checks this variable and, if the value is less than 7, a new random number between 0 and 19 is generated. The while loop will continue to loop while the randomly-generated number is less than 7. Once the randomly-generated number is equal to or greater than 7, the loop will exit.

In the preceding example, the while loop checked the conditional statement prior to generating a new random number. But what if we don't want to check the conditional statement prior to generating a random number? We could generate a random number when we first initialize the variable, but that means we need to duplicate the code that generates the random numbers, and duplicating code is never an ideal solution. It is preferable to use the repeat-while loop instead.

Using the repeat-while loop

The difference between the while and repat-while loops is that the while loop checks the conditional statement prior to executing the block of code for the first time; therefore, all the variables in the conditional statements need to be initialized prior to executing the while loop.

The repeat-while loop will run through the loop block prior to checking the conditional statement for the first time. This means that we can initialize the variables in the conditional block of code. The use of the repeat-while loop is preferred when the conditional statement is dependent on the code in the loop block. The repeat-while loop takes the following format:

```
repeat {
    block of code
} while condition
```

Let's look at this specific example by creating a repeat-while loop where we initialize the variable that we are checking within the loop block:

```
var ran: Int repeat {
    ran = Int.random(in: 1..>20)
} while ran < 4
```

In the preceding example, we defined the ran variable as an integer; however, we did not initialize it until we entered the loop block and generated a random number. If this is attempted with the while loop (leaving the ran variable uninitialized), we will receive the variable used before being initialized exception.

Earlier, we mentioned that the switch statement is preferred over using multiple else if blocks. Let's see how we can use the switch statement.

Using case and where statements with conditional statements and loops

As we saw with switch statements, the case and where statements within a switch statement can be very powerful. Using case and where statements within our conditional statements can also make our code much smaller and easier to read. Conditional statements and loops, such as if, for, and while, can also make use of the where and case keywords. Let's take a look at some examples, starting off with using the where statement to filter the results in a for-in loop.

Filtering with the where statement

In this example, we take an array of integers and print out only multiples of 3. However, before we look at how to filter the results with the where statement, let's take a look at how to do this without the where statement:

```
for number in 1...30 {
    if number % 3 == 0 {
        print(number)
    }
}
```

In this example, we use a `for-in` loop to cycle through the numbers 1 to 30. Within the `for-in` loop, we use an `if` conditional statement to filter out multiples of 3. In this simple example, the code is relatively easy to read, but let's examine how we can use the `where` statement to use fewer lines of code and make them easier to read:

```
for number in 1...30 where number % 3 == 0 {
    print(number)
}
```

We still have the same `for-in` loop as in the previous example. However, we have now put the `where` statement at the end; therefore, we only loop through numbers that are multiples of 3. Using the `where` statement shortens our example by two lines and makes it easier to read, because the `where` clause is on the same line as the `for-in` loop, rather than being embedded in the loop itself.

Now, let's look at how we could filter with the `for-case` statement.

Filtering with the for-case statement

In this next example, we will use the `for-case` statement to filter through an array of tuples and print out only the results that match our criteria. The `for-case` example is very similar to using the `where` statement where it is designed to eliminate the need for an `if` statement within a loop to filter the results. In this example, we will use the `for-case` statement to filter through a list of World Series winners and print out the year(s) that a particular team won the World Series:

```
var worldSeriesWinners = [
    ("Red Sox", 2004),
    ("White Sox", 2005),
    ("Cardinals", 2006),
    ("Red Sox", 2007),
    ("Phillies", 2008),
    ("Yankees", 2009),
    ("Giants", 2010),
    ("Cardinals", 2011),
    ("Giants", 2012),
    ("Red Sox", 2013),
    ("Giants", 2014),
    ("Royals", 2015)
]
for case let ("Red Sox", year) in worldSeriesWinners {
    print(year)
}
```

In this example, we created an array of tuples named worldSeriesWinners, where each tuple in the array contained the name of the team and the year that they won the World Series. We then use the for-case statement to filter through the array and only print out the years that the Red Sox won the World   Series. The filtering is done within the case statement, where ("Red Sox", year) states that we want all the results that have the Red Sox string in the first item of the tuple, and the value of the second item in the year constant. The for-in loop then loops through the results of the case statement, printing out the value of the year constant.

The for-case-in statement also makes it very easy to filter out the nil values in an array of optionals; let's look at an example of this:

```
let myNumbers: [Int?] = [1, 2, nil, 4, 5, nil, 6]
for case let .some(num) in myNumbers {
    print(num)
}
```

In this example, we created an array of optionals named myNumbers that could contain either an integer value or nil. As we saw in *Chapter 4, Optional Types*, an optional is internally defined as an enumeration, as shown in the following code:

```
enum Optional < Wrapped > {
    case none,
    case some(Wrapped)
}
```

If an optional is set to nil, it will have a value of none, but if it is not nil, it will have a value of some, with an associated type of the actual value. In our example, when we filter for .some(num), we are looking for any optional that has a non-nil value. As a shorthand for .some(), we could use the question mark (?) symbol, as we will see in the following example. This example also combines the for-case-in statement with a where statement to perform additional filtering:

```
let myNumbers: [Int?] = [1, 2, nil, 4, 5, nil, 6]
for case let num? in myNumbers where num < 3 {
    print(num)
}
```

This example is the same as the previous example, except that we have put the additional filtering in the where statement. In the previous example, we looped through all of the non-nil values; however, in this example, we have looped through the non-nil values that are greater than 3. Let's examine how we can do this same filtering without the case or where statements:

```
let myNumbers: [Int?] = [1, 2, nil, 4, 5, nil, 6]

for num in myNumbers {
    if let num = num {
        if num < 3 {
            print(num)
        }
    }
}
```

Using the `for-case-in` and `where` statements can greatly reduce the number of lines that are needed. It also makes our code much easier to read because all the filtering statements are on the same line.

Let's take a look at one more filtering example. This time, we will look at the `if-case` statement.

Using the if-case statement

Using the `if-case` statement is very similar to using the `switch` statement. Most of the time, the `switch` statement is preferred when we have over two cases that we are trying to match, but there are instances where the `if-case` statement is needed. One of those times is when we are only looking for one or two possible matches, and we do not want to handle all the possible matches; let's take a look at an example of this:

```
enum Identifier {
    case Name(String)
    case Number(Int)
    case NoIdentifier
}
var playerIdentifier = Identifier.Number(2)
if case let .Number(num) = playerIdentifier {
    print("Player's number is \(num)")
}
```

In this example, we created an enumeration named `Identifier` that contains three possible values: `Name`, `Number`, and `NoIdentifier`. We then created an instance of the `Identifier` enumeration named `playerIdentifier`, with a value of `Number` and an associated value of 2. We then used the `if-case` statement to see if the `playerIdentifier` had a value for `Number` and if so, we printed a message to the console.

Just like the `for-case` statement, we can perform additional filtering with the `where` statement. The following example uses the same `Identifier` enumeration that we used in the previous example:

```
var playerIdentifier = Identifier.Number(2)

if case let .Number(num) = playerIdentifier, num == 2 {
    print("Player is either XanderBogarts or Derek Jeter")
}
```

In this example, we have used the `if-case` statement to see whether the `playerIdentifier` had a value of `Number`, but we also added the `where` statement to see if the associated value was equal to 2. If so, we identified the player as either `XanderBogarts` or `Derek Jeter`.

As we saw in our examples, using the `case` and `where` statements with our conditional statements can reduce the number of lines that are needed to perform certain types of filtering. It can also make our code easier to read. Now let's take a look at control transfer statements.

Control transfer statements

Control transfer statements are used to transfer control to another part of the code. Swift offers six control transfer statements; these are `continue`, `break`, `fallthrough`, `guard`, `throws`, and `return`. We will look at the `return` statement in *Chapter 7, Functions*, and will discuss the `throws` statement in *Chapter 12, Availability and Error Handling*. The remaining control transfer statements will be discussed in this section.

The continue statement

The `continue` statement tells a loop to stop executing the code block and to go to the next iteration of the loop. The following example shows how we can use this statement to print out only the odd numbers in a range:

```
for i in 1...10 {
    if i % 2 == 0 {

        continue
    }
    print("\(i) is odd")
}
```

In the preceding example, we looped through a range from 1 to 10. For each iteration of the for-in loop, we used the remainder (%) operator to see whether the number was odd or even. If the number is even, the continue statement tells the loop to immediately go to the next iteration of the loop. If the number is odd, we print that the number is odd and then move on. The output of the preceding code is as follows:

```
1 is odd
3 is odd
5 is odd
7 is odd
9 is odd
```

Now let's take a look at the break statement.

The break statement

The break statement immediately ends the execution of a code block within the control flow. The following example demonstrates how to break out of a for-in loop when we encounter the first even number:

```
for i in 1...10 {
    if i % 2 == 0 {
        break
    }

    print("\(i) is odd")
}
```

In the preceding example, we loop through the range from 1 to 10. For each iteration of the for-in loop, we use the remainder (%) operator to see whether the number is odd or even. If the number is even, we use the break statement to immediately exit the loop. If the number is odd, we print out that the number is odd, and then go to the next iteration of the loop. The preceding code has the following output:

```
1 is odd
```

The fallthrough statement

In Swift, the switch statement does not fall through like other languages; however, we can use the fallthrough statement to force them to fall through. The fallthrough statement can be very dangerous because, once a match is found, the next case defaults to true and that code block is executed.

This is illustrated in the following example:

```
var name = "Jon"
var sport = "Baseball"
switch sport {
    case "Baseball":
        print("\name) plays Baseball")
        fallthrough
    case "Basketball":
        print("\(name) plays Basketball")
        fallthrough
    default:
        print("Unknown sport")
}
```

When this code is run, the following results are printed to the console:

```
Jon plays Baseball
Jon plays Basketball
Unknown sport
```

I recommend that you be very careful about using the fallthrough statement. Apple purposely disabled falling through on the case statement to avoid the common errors that programmers make. By using the fallthrough statement, you could introduce these errors back into your code.

Summary

In this chapter, we covered control flow and functions in Swift. It is essential that you understand the concepts in this chapter before moving ahead. Every application that we write, beyond the simple Hello World applications, will rely very heavily on control flow statements and functions.

Control flow statements are used to make decisions within our application, and functions, which we will be discussing in the next chapter, are used to group our code into sections that are reusable and organized.

7
Functions

When I first learned to program with BASIC, my first few programs were written in one long block of code. I quickly realized that I was repeating the same code over and over. I thought that there must be a better way to do this, which was when I learned about subroutines and functions. Functions are one of the key concepts that you need to understand to write good code.

In this chapter, we will cover the following topics:

- What are functions?
- How to return values from a function
- How to use parameters in a function
- What are variadic parameters?
- What are inout parameters?

In Swift, a function is a self-contained block of code that performs a specific task. Functions are generally used to logically break our code into reusable named blocks. The function's name is used to call the function.

When we define a function, we can also optionally define one or more parameters. Parameters are named values that are passed into the function by the code that calls it. These parameters are generally used within the function to perform the task of the function. We can also define default values for the parameters to simplify how the function is called.

Every Swift function has a type associated with it. This type is referred to as the return type and it defines the types of data returned from the function to the code that called it. If a value is not returned from a function, the return type is Void.

Let's look at how to define functions in Swift.

Using a single-parameter function

The syntax that's used to define a function in Swift is very flexible. This flexibility makes it easy for us to define simple C-style functions, or more complex functions with local and external parameter names, which we will see later in this chapter. Let's look at some examples of how to define functions. The following example accepts one parameter and does not return any value to the code that called it:

```
func sayHello(name: String) ->    Void {
    let retString = "Hello " + name
    print(retString)
}
```

In the preceding example, we defined a function named sayHello() that accepted one parameter, named name. Inside the function, we printed out a greeting to the person. Once the code within the function is executed, the function exits, and control is returned to the code that called it. Rather than printing out the greeting, we could return it to the code that called it by adding a return type, as follows:

```
func sayHello2(name: String) ->String {
    let retString = "Hello " + name
    return retString
}
```

The -> string defines the return type associated with the function as a string. This means that the function must return an instance of the String type to the code that calls it. Inside the function, we build a string constant, named retString, with the greeting message and then return it using the return statement.

Calling a Swift function is a similar process to calling functions or methods in other languages, such as C or Java. The following example shows how to call the sayHello(name:) function, which prints the greeting message to the screen:

```
sayHello(name:"Jon")
```

Now, let's look at how to call the sayHello2(name:) function, which returns a
value to the code that called it:

```
var message = sayHello2(name:"Jon")
print(message)
```

In the preceding example, we called the sayHello2(name:) function and inputted the
value that was returned in the message variable. If a function defines a return type as
the sayHello2(name:) function does, it must return a value of that type to the code
that called it. Therefore, every possible conditional path within the function must
end by returning a value of the specified type. This does not mean that the code that
called the function is required to retrieve the returned value. As an example, both
lines in the following snippet are valid:

```
sayHello2(name:"Jon")
var message = sayHello2(name:"Jon")
```

If you do not specify a variable for the return value to go into, the value is dropped.
When the code is compiled, you will receive a warning if a function returns a value
and you do not put it into a variable or a constant. You can avoid this warning by
using an underscore, as shown in the following example:

```
_ = sayHello2(name:"Jon")
```

The underscore tells the compiler that you are aware of the return value, but you do
not want to use it. Using the @discardableResult attribute when declaring a function
will also silence the warning. This attribute is used as follows:

```
@discardableResult func sayHello2(name: String) ->String {
    let retString = "Hello " + name
    return retString
}
```

With SE-0255 in Swift 5.1, we can omit the return statement in single expression
functions. Let's look at the following code as an example of what this would look
like:

```
func sayHello4(name: String) -> String {
    "Hello " + name
}
```

This function is defined similarly to the previous hello functions with a `String` return type; however, you will notice that there is no return statement in the function. With SE-0255, if we have a function with a single expression, like the `sayHello4(name:)` function, the value of the expression can be returned without the need of the `return` statement. If we called the function like this:

```
Let message = sayHello4(name:"Kara")
```

The `message` constant would contain the string `"Hello Kara"`.

Let's look at how we would define multiple parameters for our functions.

Using a multi-parameter function

We are not limited to just one parameter with our functions; we can also define multiple parameters. To create a multi-parameter function, we list the parameters in parentheses and separate the parameter definitions with commas. Let's look at how to define multiple parameters in a function:

```
func sayHello(name: String, greeting: String) {
    print("\(greeting) \(name)")
}
```

In the preceding example, the function accepts two arguments: `name` and `greeting`. We then print a greeting to the console using both parameters.

Calling a multi-parameter function is a little different from calling a single-parameter function. When calling a multi-parameter function, we separate the parameters with commas. We also need to include the parameter name for all the parameters. The following example shows how to call a multi-parameter function:

```
sayHello(name:"Jon", greeting:"Bonjour")
```

We do not need to supply an argument for each parameter of the function if we define default values. Let's look at how to configure default values for our parameters.

Defining a parameter's default values

We can define default values for any parameter by using the equal to operator (=) within the function definition when we declare the parameters. The following example shows how to declare a function with a parameter's default values:

```
func sayHello(name: String, greeting: String = "Bonjour") {
    print("\(greeting) \(name)")
}
```

In the function declaration, we have defined one parameter without a default value (name:String) and one parameter with a default value (greeting: String = "Bonjour"). When a parameter has a default value declared, we can call the function with or without setting a value for that parameter. The following example shows how to call the sayHello() function without setting the greeting parameter, and also how to call it when you do set the greeting parameter:

```
sayHello(name:"Jon")
sayHello(name:"Jon", greeting: "Hello")
```

In the sayHello(name:"Jon") line, the function will print out the message Bonjour Jon since it uses the default value for the greeting parameter. In the sayHello(name:"Jon", greeting: "Hello") line, the function will print out the message Hello Jon since we have overridden the default value for the greeting parameter.

We can declare multiple parameters with default values and override only the ones we want by using the parameter names. The following example shows how we would do this by overriding one of the default values when we call it:

```
func sayHello(name: String = "Test", name2: String = "Kailey",
greeting: String = "Bonjour") {
    print("\(greeting) \(name) and \(name2)")
}

sayHello(name:"Jon",greeting: "Hello")
```

In the preceding example, we declared a function with three parameters, each with a default value. We then called the function, leaving the name2 parameter with its default value, while overriding the default values for the remaining two parameters.

The preceding example will print out the message Hello Jon and Kailey.

Now, let's see how we can return multiple values from a function.

Returning multiple values from a function

There are a couple of ways to return multiple values from a Swift function. One of the most common ways is to put the values into a collection type (an array or dictionary) and then return the collection.

The following example shows how to return a collection type from a Swift function:

```
func getNames() -> [String] {
    var retArray = ["Jon", "Kailey", "Kara"]
    return retArray
}

var names = getNames()
```

In the preceding example, we declared the getNames() function with no parameters and a return type of [String]. The return type of [String] specifies the return type to be an array of string types.

In the preceding example, our array could only return string types. If we needed to return numbers with our strings, we could return an array of the Any type and then use typecasting to specify the object type. However, this would not be a good design for our application, as it would be prone to errors. A better way to return values of different types would be to use a tuple type.

When we return a tuple from a function, it is recommended that we use a named tuple to allow us to use the dot syntax to access the returned values. The following example shows how to return a named tuple from a function and access the values from the named tuple that is returned:

```
func getTeam() -> (team:String, wins:Int, percent:Double) {
    let retTuple = ("Red Sox", 99, 0.611)
    return retTuple
}

var t = getTeam()
print("\(t.team) had \(t.wins) wins")
```

In the preceding example, we defined the getTeam() function, which returned a named tuple that contains three values: String, Int, and Double. Within the function, we created the tuple that we were going to return. Notice that we did not need to define the tuple that we were going to return as a named tuple, as the value types within the tuple matched the value types in the function definition. We can now call the function as we would any other function, and use the dot syntax to access the values of the tuple that is returned. In the preceding example, the code would print out the following line:

```
Red Sox had 99 wins
```

In the previous sections, we returned non-nil values from our function; however, that is not always what we need our code to do. What happens if we need to return a nil value from a function? The following code would not be valid and would cause a `Nil is incompatible with return type String` exception:

```
func getName() ->String {
    return nil
}
```

This code throws an exception because we have defined the return type as a string value, but we are attempting to return a `nil` value. If there is a reason to return nil, we need to define the return type as an optional type to let the code calling it know that the value may be nil. To define the return type as an optional type, we use the question mark (?) in the same way as we did when we defined a variable as an optional type. The following example shows how to define an optional return type:

```
func getName() ->String? {
    return nil
}
```

The preceding code would not cause an exception.

We can also set a tuple as an optional type, or any value within a tuple as an optional type. The following example shows how we would return a tuple as an optional type:

```
func getTeam2(id: Int) -> (team:String, wins:Int, percent:Double)? {
    if id == 1 {
        return ("Red Sox", 99, 0.611)
    }
    return nil
}
```

In the following example, we could return a tuple as it was defined within our function definition or `nil`; either option is valid. If we needed an individual value within our tuple to be `nil`, we would need to add an optional type within our tuple. The following example shows how to return a value of nil within the tuple:

```
func getTeam() -> (team:String, wins:Int, percent:Double?) {
    let retTuple: (String, Int, Double?) = ("Red Sox", 99, nil)
    return retTuple
}
```

In the preceding example, we set the `percent` value to either `Double` or `nil`.

Now, let's see how we can add external parameter names for our functions.

Adding external parameter names

In the preceding examples in this section, we defined the parameters' names and value types in the same way we would define parameters in C code. In Swift, we are not limited to this syntax as we can also use external parameter names.

External parameter names are used to indicate the purpose of each parameter when we call a function. An external parameter name for each parameter needs to be defined in conjunction with its local parameter name. The external parameter name is added before the local parameter name in the function definition. The external and local parameter names are separated by a space.

Let's look at how to use external parameter names. But before we do, let's review how we have previously defined functions. In the following two examples, we will define a function without external parameter names, and then redefine it with external parameter names:

```
func winPercentage(team: String, wins: Int, loses: Int) -> Double{
    return Double(wins) / Double(wins + loses)
}
```

In the preceding example, the `winPercentage()` function has three parameters. These parameters are `team`, `wins`, and `loses`. The `team` parameter should be a `String` type, while the `wins` and `loses` parameters should be `Int` types. The following line of code shows how to call the `winPercentage()` function:

```
var per = winPercentage(team: "Red Sox", wins: 99, loses: 63)
```

Now, let's define the same function with external parameter names:

```
func winPercentage(baseballTeam team: String, withWins wins: Int,
andLoses losses: Int) -> Double {
    return Double(wins) / Double(wins + losses)
}
```

In the preceding example, we redefined the `winPercentage()` function with external parameter names. In this redefinition, we have the same three parameters: `team`, `wins`, and `losses`. The difference is how we have defined the parameters. When using external parameters, we define each parameter with both an external parameter name and a local parameter name, separated by a space.

In the preceding example, the first parameter had an external parameter name of baseballTeam and an internal parameter name of team.

When we call a function with external parameter names, we need to include the external parameter names in the function call. The following code shows how to call this function:

```
var per = winPercentage(baseballTeam:"Red Sox", withWins:99,
andLoses:63)
```

While using external parameter names requires more typing, it does make your code easier to read. In the preceding example, it is easy to see that the function is looking for the name of a baseball team, the second parameter is the number of wins, and the last parameter is the number of losses.

Using variadic parameters

A **variadic** parameter is one that accepts zero or more values of a specified type. Within the function's definition, we define a variadic parameter by appending three periods (...) to the parameter's type name. The values of a variadic parameter are made available to the function as an array of the specified type. The following example shows how we would use a variadic parameter with a function:

```
func sayHello(greeting: String, names: String...) {
    for name in names {
        print("\(greeting) \(name)")
    }
}
```

In the preceding example, the sayHello() function takes two parameters. The first parameter is of the String type, which is the greeting to use. The second parameter is a variadic parameter of the String type, which is the names to send the greeting to. Within the function, a variadic parameter is an array that contains the type specified; therefore, in our example, the names parameter is an array of String values. In this example, we used a for-in loop to access the values within the names parameter.

The following line of code shows how to call the sayHello() function with a variadic parameter:

```
sayHello(greeting:"Hello", names: "Jon", "Kara")
```

The preceding line of code prints a greeting to each of the names, as shown here:

```
Hello Jon
Hello Kara
```

Now, let's take a look at what `inout` parameters are.

inout parameters

If we want to change the value of a parameter and we want those changes to persist once the function ends, we need to define the parameter as an `inout` parameter. Any changes made to an `inout` parameter are passed back to the variable that was used in the function call.

Two things to keep in mind when we use `inout` parameters are that these parameters cannot have default values and that they cannot be variadic parameters.

Let's look at how to use inout parameters to swap the values of two variables:

```
func reverse(first: inout String, second: inout String) {
    let tmp = first
    first = second
    second = tmp
}
```

This function will accept two parameters and swap the values of the variables that are used in the function call. When we make the function call, we put an ampersand (&) in front of the variable name, indicating that the function can modify its value. The following example shows how to call the `reverse` function:

```
var one = "One"
var two = "Two"
reverse(first: &one, second: &two)

print("one: \(one) two: \(two)")
```

In the preceding example, we set variable one to a value of One and variable two to a value of Two. We then called the `reverse()` function with the one and two variables. Once the `reverse()` function has returned, the variable named one will contain the value Two, while the variable named two will contain the value One.

Two things to note about `inout` parameters: a variadic parameter cannot be an `inout` parameter and an `inout` parameter cannot have a default value.

Omitting argument labels

All the functions in this chapter have used labels when passing arguments into the functions. If we do not want to use labels, we can omit them by using an underscore. The following example illustrates this:

```
func sayHello(_ name: String, greeting: String) {
    print("\(greeting) \(name)")
}
```

Notice the underscore prior to the `name` label in the parameter list. This indicates that the `name` label should not be used when calling this function. Now, we are able to call this function without using the `name` label:

```
sayHello("Jon", greeting: "Hi")
```

This call would print out `Hi Jon`.

Now, let's put what we have covered together and see a more complex example.

Putting it all together

To reinforce what we have learned in this chapter, let's look at one more example. For this example, we will create a function that will test whether a string value contains a valid IPv4 address. An IPv4 address is the address assigned to a computer that uses the **Internet Protocol** (**IP**) to communicate. An IP address consists of four numeric values that range from 0-255, separated by a dot (period). The following is a code example of a valid IP address; that is, `10.0.1.250`:

```
func isValidIP(ipAddr: String?) ->Bool {

    guard let ipAddr = ipAddr else {
        return false
    }
    let octets = ipAddr.split { $0 == "."}.map{String($0)}
    guard octets.count == 4 else {
        return false
    }
    for octet in octets {
```

```
        guard validOctet(octet: octet) else {
            return false
        }
    }
    return true
}
```

Since the sole parameter in the isValidIp() function is an optional type, the first thing we do is verify that the ipAddR parameter is not nil. To do this, we use a guard statement with optional binding. If the optional binding fails, we return a Boolean false value because nil is not a valid IP address.

If the ipAddr parameter contains a non-nil value, we split the string into an array of strings, using the dots as delimiters. Since an IP address is supposed to contain four numbers separated by a dot, we use the guard statement again to check whether the array contains four elements. If it does not, we return false because we know that the ipAddr parameter did not contain a valid IP address.

We then use the split() function of the String type to split the string into four substrings, where each substring contains one octet of the address. These substrings are stored in the octets array.

Then, we loop through the values in the array that we created by splitting the original ipAddr parameter at the dots and passing the values to the validOctet() function. If all four values are verified by the validOctet() function, we have a valid IP address and we return a Boolean true value; however, if any of the values fail the validOctet() function, we return a Boolean false value. Now, let's look at the code for the validOctet() function:

```
func validOctet(octet: String) ->Bool {
    guard let num = Int(octet),num >= 0 && num <256 else {
        return false
    }
    return true
}
```

The validOctet() function has one String parameter, named octet. This function will verify that the octet parameter contains a numeric value between 0 and 255; if it does, the function will return a Boolean true value. Otherwise, it will return a Boolean false value.

Summary

In this chapter, we covered what functions are and how to use them. You will use functions in every serious application that you write. In the next chapter, we will look at classes and structures. Classes and structures can contain functions, but these functions are known as methods.

8

Classes, Structures, and Protocols

The first programming language that I learned was BASIC. It was a good language to begin programming with, but once I traded in my Commodore Vic-20 for a PCjr (yes, I had a PCjr and I really enjoyed it), I realized that there were other, more advanced languages out there, and I spent a lot of time learning Pascal and C. It wasn't until I started college that I heard the term **object-oriented programming language**. At that time, object-oriented programming languages were so new that there were no real courses on them, but I was able to experiment a little with C++. After I graduated, I left object-oriented programming behind, and it really wasn't until several years later, when I started to experiment with C++ again, that I really discovered the power and flexibility of object-oriented programming. In this chapter, we will cover the following topics:

- What are classes and structures?
- How to add properties and property observers to classes and structures
- How to add methods to classes and structures
- How to add initializers to classes and structures
- How and when to use access controls
- How to create a class hierarchy
- How to extend a class

What are classes and structures?

In Swift, classes and structures are very similar. If we really want to master Swift, it is very important to not only understand what makes classes and structures so similar, but to also understand what sets them apart, because they are the building blocks of our applications. Apple describes them as follows:

> *Classes and structures are general-purpose, flexible constructs that become the building blocks of your program's code. You define properties and methods to add functionality to your classes and structures by using the already familiar syntax of constants, variables, and functions.*

Let's begin by taking a quick look at some of the similarities between classes and structures.

Similarities between classes and structures

In Swift, classes and structures are more similar than they are in other languages, such as Objective-C. The following is a list of some of the features that classes and structures share:

- **Properties**: These are used to store information in our classes and structures
- **Methods**: These provide functionality for our classes and structures
- **Initializers**: These are used when initializing instances of our classes and structures
- **Subscripts**: These provide access to values using the subscript syntax
- **Extensions**: These help extend both classes and structures

Now, let's take a quick look at some of the differences between classes and structures.

Differences between classes and structures

While classes and structures are very similar, there are also several very important differences. The following is a list of some of the differences between classes and structures in Swift:

- **Type**: A structure is a value type, while a class is a reference type
- **Inheritance**: A structure cannot inherit from other types, while a class can
- **Deinitializers**: Structures cannot have custom deinitializers, while a class can

Throughout this chapter, we will be emphasizing the differences between classes and structures to help us understand when to use each. Before we really dive into classes and structures, let's look at the difference between value types (structures) and reference types (classes). To fully understand when to use classes and structures and how to properly use them, it is important to understand the difference between value and reference types.

Value versus reference types

Structures are value types. When we pass instances of a structure within our application, we pass a copy of the structure and not the original structure. Classes are reference types; therefore, when we pass an instance of a class within our application, a reference to the original instance is passed. It is very important to understand this difference. We will give a very high-level view here and will provide additional details in *Chapter 18, Memory Management*. When we pass structures within our application, we are passing copies of the structures and not the original structures. Since the function gets its own copy of the structure, it can change it as needed without affecting the original instance of the structure. When we pass an instance of a class within our application, we are passing a reference to the original instance of the class. Since we're passing the instance of the class to the function, the function is getting a reference to the original instance; therefore, any changes made within the function will remain once the function exits. To illustrate the difference between value and reference types, let's look at a real-world object: a book. If we have a friend who wants to read *Mastering Swift 5.3*, we could either buy them their own copy or share ours. If we bought our friend their own copy of the book, any notes they made within the book would remain in their copy of the book and would not be reflected in our copy. This is how passing by value works with structures and variables. Any changes that are made to the structure or variable within the function are not reflected in the original instance of the structure or variable. If we share our copy of the book, any notes they made within the book would stay in the book when they return it to us. This is how passing by reference works. Any changes that are made to the instance of the class remain when the function exits.

Creating a class or structure

We use the same syntax to define classes and structures. The only difference is that we define a class using the class keyword and a structure using the struct keyword.

Let's look at the syntax that's used to create both classes and structures:

```
class MyClass {
    // MyClass definition
}

struct MyStruct {
    // MyStruct definition
}
```

In the preceding code, we define a new class named `MyClass` and a new structure named `MyStruct`. This effectively creates two new Swift types, named `MyClass` and `MyStruct`. When we name a new type, we want to use the standard naming convention set by Swift, where the name is in camel case, with the first letter being uppercase. This is also known as `PascalCase`. Any method or property defined within the class or structure should also be named using camel case, with the first letter being uppercase. Empty classes and structures are not that useful, so let's look at how we can add properties to our classes and structures.

Properties

Properties associate values with a class or a structure. There are two types of properties:

- **Stored properties**: These will store variable or constant values as part of an instance of a class or structure. Stored properties can also have property observers that can monitor the property for changes and respond with custom actions when the value of the property changes.

- **Computed properties**: These do not store a value themselves but instead retrieve and possibly set other properties. The value returned by a computed property can also be calculated when it is requested.

Stored properties

A stored property is a variable or constant that is stored as part of an instance of a class or structure. These are defined with the var and let keywords, just like normal variables and constants. In the following code, we will create a structure named `MyStruct` and a class named `MyClass`. The structure and the class both contain two stored properties, c and v. The stored property, c, is a constant because it is defined with the let keyword, and v is a variable because it is defined with the var keyword. Let's look at the following code:

```
struct MyStruct
{
    let c = 5
    var v = ""
}

class MyClass
{
    let c = 5
    var v = ""
}
```

As we can see from the preceding example, the syntax to define a stored property is the same for both classes and structures. Let's look at how we would create an instance of both the structure and class. The following code creates an instance of the MyStruct structure, named myStruct, and an instance of the MyClass class, named myClass:

One of the differences between structures and classes is that, by default, a structure creates an initializer that lets us populate the stored properties when we create an instance of the structure. Therefore, we could also create an instance of MyStruct like this:

```
var myStruct = MyStruct(v: "Hello")
```

In the preceding example, the initializer is used to set the v variable, and the c constant will still contain the number 5, which is defined in the structures. If we did not give the constant an initial value, as shown in the following example, the default initializer would be used to set the constant as well:

```
struct MyStruct {
    let c: Int
    var v = ""
}
```

The following example shows how the initializer for this new structure would work:

```
var myStruct = MyStruct(c: 10, v: "Hello")
```

This allows us to define a constant where we set the value when we initialize the class or structure at runtime, rather than hardcoding the value of the constant within the type. The order in which the parameters appear in the initializer is the order in which we defined them. In the previous example, we defined the c constant first, therefore, it is the first parameter in the initializer. We defined the v parameter next, therefore, it is the second parameter in the initializer.

Starting in Swift 5.1 with SE-0242, the initializer for structures has been enhanced so that default values can be added to any parameter, making the parameter optional in the initializer. Let's create a new structure that illustrates this:

```
struct MyStruct {
    var a: Int
    var b = "Hello"
    var c = "Jon"
}
```

In this code, we define three parameters, a, b, and c, where both the b and c parameters have default values. We are now able to initialize the MyStruct structure in any of the following ways:

```
let myStruct1 = MyStruct(a: 2)
let myString2 = MyStruct(a: 3, b: "Bonjour")
let myString3 = MyStruct(a: 4, b: "Bonjour", c: "Kara")
```

We are able to leave the c parameter or the b and c parameters undefined within the initializer because we set default values when we defined the parameters. One thing to note is the following code will throw an error:

```
let myString3 = MyStruct(b: "Hello", c: "Kara")
```

When we defined the parameters within the structure, we defined parameter a first, followed by b, and then c, which means the order within the initializer is also a followed by b, and then c. When we make multiple parameters that are optional, we cannot leave off one of the parameters but still include others that come after it, therefore we cannot leave off parameter a and still include parameters b and c.

To set or read a stored property, we use the standard dot syntax. Let's look at how we would set and read stored properties in Swift:

```
var x = myClass.c
myClass.v = "Howdy"
```

In the first line of code, we read the c property and store it into a variable named x. In the second line of code, we set the v property to the Howdy string. Before we move on to computed properties, let's create both a structure and a class that will represent an employee. We will be using and expanding these throughout this chapter to show how classes and structures are similar, and how they differ:

```
struct EmployeeStruct {
    var firstName = ""
    var lastName = ""
     var salaryYear = 0.0
}

class EmployeeClass {
    var firstName = ""
    var lastName = ""
    var salaryYear = 0.0
}
```

The employee structure is named EmployeeStruct, and the employee class is named EmployeeClass. Both the class and structure have three stored properties: firstName, lastName, and salaryYear. Within the structure and class, we can access these properties by using the name of the property and the self keyword. Every instance of a structure or class has a property named self. This property refers to the instance itself; therefore, we can use it to access the properties within the instance. The following examples show how we can access the properties with the self keyword within the instance of the structure or class:

```
self.firstName = "Jon" self.lastName = "Hoffman"
```

Computed properties

Computed properties are properties that do not have backend variables, which are used to store the values associated with the property but are hidden from the external code. The values of a computed property are usually computed when code requests it. You can think of a computed property as a function disguised as a property. Let's look at how we would define a read-only computed property:

```
var salaryWeek: Double {
    get{
        self.salaryYear/52
    }
}
```

To create a read-only computed property, we begin by defining it as if it were a normal variable with the var keyword, followed by the variable name, a colon, and the variable type. What comes next is different; we add a curly bracket at the end of the declaration and then define a getter method, which is called when the value of our computed property is requested. In this example, the getter method divides the current value of the salaryYear property by 52 to get the employee's weekly salary.

We can simplify the definition of the read-only computed property by removing the get keyword, as shown in the following example:

```
var salaryWeek: Double {
    self.salaryYear/52
}
```

Computed properties are not limited to being read-only; we can also write to them. To enable the salaryWeek property to be writeable, we will add a setter method. The following example shows how we add a setter method that will set the salaryYear property, based on the value being passed into the salaryWeek property:

```
var salaryWeek: Double {
    get {
        self.salaryYear/52
    }
    set(newSalaryWeek){
        self.salaryYear = newSalaryWeek*52
    }
}
```

We can simplify the setter definition by not defining a name for the new value. In this case, the value will be assigned to a default variable named newValue, as shown in the following example:

```
var salaryWeek: Double {
    get {
        self.salaryYear/52
    }
    set{
        self.salaryYear = newValue*52
    }
}
```

The salaryWeek computed property, as written in the preceding examples, could be added to either the EmployeeClass class or the EmployeeStruct structure without any modifications. Let's see how we can do this by adding the salaryWeek property to our EmployeeClass class:

```
class EmployeeClass {
    var firstName = ""
    var lastName = ""
    var salaryYear = 0.0

    var salaryWeek: Double {
        get {
            self.salaryYear/52
        }
        set(newSalaryWeek) {
            self.salaryYear = newSalaryWeek*52
        }
    }
}
```

Now, let's look at how we can add the salaryWeek computed property to the EmployeeStruct structure:

```
struct EmployeeStruct {
    var firstName = ""
    var lastName = ""
     var salaryYear = 0.0
    var salaryWeek: Double {
        get {
            self.salaryYear/52
        }
        set(newSalaryWeek) {
            self.salaryYear = newSalaryWeek*52
        }
    }
}
```

As we can see, the class and structure definitions are the same so far, except for the initial class or struct keywords that are used to define them. We read and write to a computed property exactly as we would to a stored property. Code that is external to the class or structure should not be aware that the property is a computed property. Let's see this in action by creating an instance of the EmployeeStruct structure:

```
var f = EmployeeStruct(firstName: "Jon", lastName: "Hoffman",
salaryYear: 39_000)
print(f.salaryWeek) //prints 750.00 to the console f.salaryWeek = 1000
print(f.salaryWeek) //prints 1000.00 to the console
print(f.salaryYear) //prints 52000.00 to the console
```

The preceding example starts off by creating an instance of the `EmployStruct` structure with the `salaryYear` value being set to 39,000. Next, we print the value of the `salaryWeek` property to the console. This value is currently 750.00. We then set the `salaryWeek` property to 1,000.00 and print out both the `salaryWeek` and `salaryYear` properties to the console. The values of the `salaryWeek` and `salaryYear` properties are now 1,000.00 and 52,000, respectively. As we can see, in this example, setting either the `salaryWeek` or `salaryYear` properties changes the values returned by both. Computed properties can be very useful for offering different views of the same data. For example, if we had a value that represented the length of something, we could store the length in centimeters and then use computed properties that calculate the values for meters, millimeters, and kilometers. Now, let's look at property observers.

Property observers

Property observers are called every time the value of the property is set. We can add property observers to any non-lazy stored property. We can also add property observers to any inherited stored or computed property by overriding the property in the subclass, which we will look at in the *Overriding properties* section. There are two property observers that we can set in Swift: `willSet` and `didSet`. The `willSet` observer is called right before the property is set, and the `didSet` observer is called right after the property is set. One thing to note about property observers is that they are not called when the value is set during initialization. Let's look at how we can add a property observer to the salary property of our `EmployeeClass` class and `EmployeeStruct` structure:

```
var salaryYear: Double = 0.0 {
    willSet(newSalary) {
        print("About to set salaryYear to \(newSalary)")
    }
    didSet {
        if salaryWeek > oldValue {
            print("\(firstName) got a raise.")
        } else {
            print("\(firstName) did not get a raise.")
        }
    }
}
```

When we add a property observer to a stored property, we need to include the type of the value being stored within the definition of the property. In the preceding example, we did not need to define our salaryYear property as a Double type; however, when we add property observers, the definition is required. After the property definition, we define the willSet observer, which simply prints out the new value that the salaryYear property will be set to. We also define a didSet observer, which will check whether the new value is greater than the old value, and if so, it will print out that the employee got a raise; otherwise, it will print out that the employee did not get a raise. As with the getter method with computed properties, we do not need to define the name for the new value of the willSet observer. If we do not define a name, the new value is put in a constant named newValue. The following example shows how we can rewrite the previous willSet observer without defining a name for the new value:

```
willSet {
    print("About to set salaryYear to \(newValue)")
}
```

As we have seen, properties are mainly used to store information associated with a class or structure. Methods are mainly used to add the business logic to a class or structure. Let's look at how we can add methods to a class or structure.

Methods

Methods are functions that are associated with an instance of a class or structure. A method, like a function, will encapsulate the code for a specific task or functionality that is associated with the class or structure. Let's look at how we can define methods for classes and structures. The following code will return the full name of the employee by using the firstName and lastName properties:

```
func fullName() -> String {
    firstName + " " + lastName
}
```

We define this method exactly as we would define any function. A method is simply a function that is associated with a specific class or structure, and everything that we learned about functions in the previous chapters applies to methods. The fullName() function can be added directly to the EmployeeClass class or EmployeeStruct structure without any modification. To access a method, we use the same dot syntax we used to access properties.

The following code shows how we access the `fullName()` method of a class and a structure:

```
var e = EmployeeClass()
var f = EmployeeStruct(firstName: "Jon", lastName: "Hoffman",
salaryYear: 50000)

e.firstName = "Jon"
e.lastName = "Hoffman"
e.salaryYear = 50000.00

print(e.fullName()) //Jon Hoffman is printed to the console
print(f.fullName()) //Jon Hoffman is printed to the console
```

In the preceding example, we initialize an instance of both the `EmployeeClass` class and the `EmployeeStruct` structure. We populate the structure and class with the same information and then use the `fullName()` method to print the full name of the employee to the console. In both cases, `Jon Hoffman` is printed to the console. There is a difference in how we define methods for classes and structures that need to update property values. Let's look at how we define a method that gives an employee a raise within the `EmployeeClass` class:

```
func giveRaise(amount: Double) {
    salaryYear += amount
}
```

If we add the preceding code to our `EmployeeClass`, it works as expected, and when we call the method with an amount, the employee gets a raise. However, if we try to add this method as it is written to the `EmployeeStruct` structure, we receive a mark method and a `mutating to make self mutable` error. By default, we are not allowed to update property values within a method of a structure. If we want to modify a property, we can mutate the behavior for that method by adding the `mutating` keyword before the `func` keyword of the method declaration. Therefore, the following code would be the correct way to define the `giveRaise(amount:)` method for the `EmployeeStruct` structure:

```
mutating func giveRase(amount: Double) {
    self.salaryYear += amount
}
```

In the preceding examples, we use the `self` property to refer to the current instance of the type within the instance itself, so when we write `self.salaryYear`, we ask for the value of the `salaryYear` property for the current instance of the type.

The `self` property should only be used when necessary. We are using it in these examples to illustrate what it is and how to use it.

The `self` property is mainly used to distinguish between local and instance variables that have the same name. Let's look at an example that illustrates this. We can add this function to either the `EmployeeClass` or `EmployeeStruct` type:

```
func isEqualFirstName(firstName: String) -> Bool {
    self.firstName == firstName
}
```

In the preceding example, the method accepts an argument named `firstName`. There is also a property within the type that has the same name. We use the `self` property to specify that we want the instance property with the `firstName` name, and not the local variable with this name. Other than the `mutating` keyword being required for methods that change the value of the structure's properties, methods can be defined and used exactly as functions are defined and used. Therefore, everything we learned about functions in *Chapter 6*, *Functions*, can be applied to methods. There are times when we want to initialize properties or perform some business logic when a class or structure is first initialized. For this, we will use an initializer.

Custom initializers

Initializers are called when we initialize a new instance of a type (class or structure). Initialization is the process of preparing an instance for use. The initialization process can include setting initial values for stored properties, verifying that external resources are available, or setting up the UI properly. Initializers are generally used to ensure that the instance of the class or structure is properly initialized prior to first use. Initializers are special methods that are used to create a new instance of a type. We define an initializer similarly to defining other methods, but we must use the `init` keyword as the name of the initializer to tell the compiler that this method is an initializer. In its simplest form, the initializer does not accept any arguments. Let's look at the syntax that's used to write a simple initializer:

```
init() {
    //Perform initialization here
}
```

This format works for both classes and structures. By default, all classes and structures have an empty default initializer that can be overridden. We used these default initializers when we initialized the `EmployeeClass` class and `EmployeeStruct` structure in the previous section. Structures also have an additional default initializer, which we saw with the `EmployeeStruct` structure, which accepts a value for each stored property and initializes them with those values. Let's look at how we add custom initializers to the `EmployeeClass` class and the `EmployeeStruct` structure. In the following code, we create three custom initializers that will work for both the `EmployeeClass` class and the `EmployeeStruct` structure:

```
init() {
    firstName =""
    lastName = ""
    salaryYear = 0.0
}
init(firstName: String, lastName: String) {
    self.firstName = firstName
    self.lastName = lastName
    salaryYear = 0.0
}
init(firstName: String, lastName: String, salaryYear: Double) {
    self.firstName = firstName
    self.lastName = lastName
    self.salaryYear = salaryYear
}
```

The first initializer, `init()`, will set all of the stored properties to their default values. The second initializer, `init(firstName: String, lastName: String)`, will populate the `firstName` and `lastName` properties with the values of the arguments. The third initializer, `init(firstName: String, lastName: String, salaryYear: Double)`, will populate all the properties with the values of the arguments. In the previous example, we can see that in Swift, an initializer does not have an explicit return value, but it does return an instance of the type. This means that we do not define a return type for the initializer or have a return statement within the initializer. Let's look at how we could use these initializers:

```
var g = EmployeeClass()
var h = EmployeeStruct(firstName: "Me", lastName: "Moe")
var i = EmployeeClass(firstName: "Me", lastName: "Moe", salaryYear:
45_000)
```

The g instance of `EmployeeClass` uses the `init()` initializer to create an instance of the `EmployeeClass` class; therefore, all the properties of this instance contain their default values. The h instance of `EmployeeStruct` uses the `init(firstName: String, lastName: String)` initializer to create an instance of the `EmployeeStruct` structure; therefore, the `firstName` property is set to `Me` and the `lastName` property is set to `Moe`, which are the two arguments passed into the initializer. The `salaryYear` property is still set to the default value of `0.0`. The i instance of `EmployeeClass` uses the `init(firstName: String, lastName: String, salaryYear: Double0)` initializer to create an instance of the `EmployeeClass` class; therefore, the `firstName` property is set to `Me`, the `lastName` property is set to `Moe`, and the `salaryYear` property is set to `45_000`. Since all the initializers are identified with the `init` keyword, the parameters and parameter types are used to identify which initializer to use. A class, unlike a structure, can have a deinitializer. A deinitializer is called just before an instance of the class is destroyed and removed from memory. In *Chapter 18, Memory Management*, we will show examples of the deinitializer and see when it is called. Let's look at internal and external parameter names with initializers.

Internal and external parameter names

Just like functions, the parameters associated with an initializer can have separate internal and external names. If we do not supply external parameter names for our parameters, Swift will automatically generate them for us. In the previous examples, we did not include external parameter names in the definition of the initializers, so Swift created them for us using the internal parameter name as the external parameter name. If we wanted to supply our own parameter names, we would do so by putting the external parameter name before the internal parameter name, exactly as we do with any normal function. Let's look at how we can define our own external parameter names by redefining one of the initializers within our `EmployeeClass` class:

```
init(employeeWithFirstName firstName: String, lastName lastName:
String, andSalary salaryYear: Double) {
    self.firstName = firstName
    self.lastName = lastName
    self.salaryYear = salaryYear
}
```

In the preceding example, we created the `init(employeeWithFirstName firstName: String, lastName lastName: String, andSalary salaryYear: Double)` initializer. This initializer will create an instance of the `EmployeeClass` class and populate the instance properties with the value of the arguments. In this example, each of the parameters has both external and internal property names. Let's look at how we would use this initializer, with the external property names:

```
var i = EmployeeClass(withFirstName: "Me", lastName: "Moe", andSalary:
45000)
```

Notice that we are now using the external parameter names as defined in the initializer. Using external parameter names can help make our code more readable and help differentiate between different initializers. So, what will happen if our initializer fails? For example, what if our class relies on a specific resource, such as a web service that is not currently available? This is where failable initializers come in.

Failable initializers

A failable initializer is an initializer that may fail to initialize the resources needed for a class or a structure, thereby rendering the instance unusable. When using a failable initializer, the result of the initializer is an optional type, containing either a valid instance of the type or nil. An initializer can be made failable by adding a question mark (?) after the init keyword. Let's look at how we can create a failable initializer that will not allow a new employee to be initialized with a salary of less than $20,000 a year:

```
init?(firstName: String, lastName: String, salaryYear: Double) {
    self.firstName = firstName
    self.lastName = lastName
    self.salaryYear = salaryYear
    if self.salaryYear < 20_000 {
        return nil
    }
}
```

In the previous examples, we did not include a return statement within the initializer because Swift does not need to return the initialized instance; however, in a failable initializer, if the initialization fails, it must return nil. If the initializer successfully initializes the instance, we do not need to return anything. Therefore, in our example, if the yearly salary that is passed in is less than $20,000 a year, we return nil, indicating that the initialization failed, otherwise nothing will be returned. Let's look at how we would use a failable initializer to create an instance of a class or structure:

```
if let f = EmployeeClass(firstName: "Jon", lastName: "Hoffman",
salaryYear: 29_000) {
    print(f.fullName())
} else {
    print("Failed to initialize")
}
```

In the previous example, we initialize the instance of the `EmployeeClass` class with a yearly salary of greater than $20,000; therefore, the instance gets initialized correctly and the full name of `Jon Hoffman` is printed to the console. Now, let's try to initialize an instance of the `EmployeeClass` class with a yearly salary of less than $20,000 to see how it fails:

```
if let f = EmployeeClass(firstName: "Jon", lastName: "Hoffman",
salaryYear: 19_000) {
    print(f.fullName())
} else {
    print("Failed to initialize")
}
```

In the preceding example, the yearly salary that we are attempting to initialize for our employee is less than $20,000, therefore the initialization fails and a `Failed to initialize` message is printed to the console.

There are times when we want to restrict access to certain parts of our code. For this, we use access controls.

Access controls

Access controls enable us to hide implementation details and only expose the interfaces we want to expose. This feature is handled with access controls. We can assign specific access levels to both classes and structures. We can also assign specific access levels to properties, methods, and initializers that belong to our classes and structures. In Swift, there are five access levels:

- **Open**: This is the most visible access control level. It allows us to use the property, method, class, and so on anywhere we want to import the module. Basically, anything can use an item that has an access-control level of open. Anything that is marked open can be subclassed or overridden by any item within the module they are defined in and any module that imports the module it is defined in. This level is primarily used by frameworks to expose the framework's public API. The open-access control is only available to classes and members of a class.

- **Public**: This access level allows us to use the property, method, class, and so on anywhere we want to import the module. Basically, anything can use an item that has an access-control level of public. Anything that is marked public can be subclassed or overridden only by any item within the module they are defined in. This level is primarily used by frameworks to expose the framework's public API.

- **Internal**: This is the default access level. This access level allows us to use the property, method, class, and so on in the module the item is defined in. If this level is used in a framework, it lets other parts of the framework use the item but code outside the framework will be unable to access it.

- **Fileprivate**: This access control allows access to the properties and methods from any code within the same source file that the item is defined in.

- **Private**: This is the least visible access-control level. It only allows us to use the property, method, class, and so on, within extensions of the declaration defined in the source file that defines it.

When we are developing frameworks, the access controls really become useful. We will need to mark the public-facing interfaces as public or open so that other modules, such as applications that import the framework, can use them. We will then use the internal and private access-control levels to mark the interfaces that we want to use internally to the framework and the source file, respectively. To define access levels, we place the name of the level before the definition of the entity. The following code shows examples of how we can add access levels to several entities:

```
private struct EmployeeStruct {}
public class EmployeeClass {}
internal class EmployeeClass2 {}
public var firstName = "Jon"
internal var lastName = "Hoffman"
private var salaryYear = 0.0
public func fullName() -> String {}
private func giveRaise(amount: Double) {}
```

There are some limitations with access controls, but these limitations are there to ensure that access levels in Swift follow a simple guiding principle: no entity can be defined in terms of another entity that has a lower (more restrictive) access level. This means that we cannot assign a higher (less restrictive) access level to an entity when it relies on another entity that has a lower (more restrictive) access level. The following examples demonstrate this principle:

- We cannot mark a method as being public when one of the arguments or the return type has an access level of private, because external code would not have access to the private type

- We cannot set the access level of a method or property to public when the class or structure has an access level of private, because external code would not be able to access the constructor when the class is private

Now let's look at a new feature in Swift 5.2, key-path expressions as functions.

Key-path expressions as functions

SE-0249 in Swift 5.2 introduced a great shortcut which enables us to easily access the properties of objects in a particular collection. What this means is if we iterate over a collection using the map algorithm, we are able to use key-path expressions (\Root. value) to access the properties of the items in the collection. Let's look at an example using the employee structure we created earlier. We will start by creating three employees and adding them to an array:

```
let employee1 = EmployeeStruct(firstName: "Jon", lastName: "Hoffman",
salaryYear: 90000)
let employee2 = EmployeeStruct(firstName: "Kailey", lastName:
"Hoffman", salaryYear: 32000)
let employee3 = EmployeeStruct(firstName: "Kara", lastName: "Hoffman",
salaryYear: 28000)

let employeeCollection = [employee1, employee2, employee3]
```

Now that we have an array of employees, let's retrieve all of the first names of our employees. We could loop through our array and pull out the names one by one, but if we combine the map algorithm that we saw in *Chapter 5, Using Swift Collections*, with this new feature, we could retrieve all first names like this:

```
let firstNames = employeeCollection.map(\.firstName)
```

With this code, the firstName array will contain the first name for each employee in our employeeCollection array.

Let's look at another new feature with Swift 5.2, calling a type as a function.

Calling a type as a function

With SE-0253 in Swift 5.2, we are able to call a type as a function. To explain it a little better, instances of types that have a method whose name is callAsFunction can be called as if they were a function. Let's look at an example of this. We will start off by creating a Dice type that can be used to create an instance of any size dice:

```
struct Dice {
    var highValue: Int
    var lowValue: Int

    func callAsFunction() -> Int {
        Int.random(in: lowValue...highValue)
```

```
        }
    }
```

Notice the method within the function called callAsFunction(). This function generates a random number using the `lowValue` and `highValue` properties. Since we named this method `callAsFunction`, we are able to call it using the instance's name as if it were a function. Let's see how this works by creating a six-sided dice and generating a random value:

```
let d6 = Dice(highValue: 6, lowValue: 1)
let roll = d6()
```

The `roll` variable will contain a random value generated from the `callAsFunction()` method. This enables us to simplify how we call certain functions. In the previous example, we are able to generate the roll of the dice by simply calling `d6()` rather than calling the instance with a function name like `d6.generateRoll()`.

Now let's look at what inheritance is.

Inheritance

The concept of inheritance is a basic object-oriented development concept. Inheritance allows a class to be defined as having a certain set of characteristics, and then other classes can be derived from that class. The derived class inherits all of the features of the class it is inheriting from (unless the derived class overrides those characteristics) and then usually adds additional characteristics of its own.

 Inheritance is one of the fundamental differences that separates classes from structures. Classes can be derived from a parent or superclass, but a structure cannot.

With inheritance, we can create what is known as a class hierarchy. In a class hierarchy, the class at the top of the hierarchy is known as the base class, and the derived classes are known as subclasses. We are not limited to only creating subclasses from a base class, we can also create subclasses from other subclasses. The class that a subclass is derived from is known as the parent or superclass. In Swift, a class can have only one parent class. This is known as single inheritance.

Subclasses can call and access the properties, methods, and subscripts of their superclass. They can also override the properties, methods, and subscripts of their superclass.

Subclasses can add property observers to properties that they inherit from a superclass so that they can be notified when the values of the properties change. Let's look at an example that illustrates how inheritance works in Swift. We will start off by defining a base class named `Plant`. The `Plant` class will have two properties: height and age. It will also have one method: `growHeight()`. The height property will represent the height of the plant, the age property will represent the age of the plant, and the `growHeight()` method will be used to increase the height of the plant. Here is how we would define the `Plant` class:

```
class Plant {
    var height = 0.0
    var age = 0
    func growHeight(inches: Double) {
        height += inches;
    }
}
```

Now that we have our `Plant` base class, let's see how we would define a subclass of it. We will name this subclass `Tree`. The `Tree` class will inherit the age and height properties of the `Plant` class and add one more property, named `limbs`. It will also inherit the `growHeight()` method of the `Plant` class and add two more methods: `limbGrow()`, where new limbs are grown, and `limbFall()`, where limbs fall off the tree. Let's have a look at the following code:

```
class Tree: Plant {
    var limbs = 0
    func limbGrow() {
        self.limbs += 1
    }
    func limbFall() {
        self.limbs -= 1
    }
}
```

We indicate that a class has a superclass by adding a colon and the name of the superclass to the end of the class definition. In this example, we indicated that the `Tree` class has a superclass named `Plant`. Now, let's look at how we could use the `Tree` class that inherited the age and height properties from the `Plant` class:

```
var tree = Tree()
tree.age = 5
tree.height = 4
tree.limbGrow()
tree.limbGrow()
```

The preceding example begins by creating an instance of the `Tree` class. We then set the `Age` and `height` properties to 5 and 4, respectively, and added two limbs to the tree by calling the `limbGrow()` method twice. We now have a base class named `Plant` that has a subclass named `Tree`. This means that the super (or parent) class of `Tree` is the `Plant` class. This also means that one of the subclasses (or child classes) of `Plant` is named `Tree`. There are, however, lots of different kinds of trees in the world. Let's create two subclasses from the `Tree` class. These subclasses will be the `PineTree` class and the `OakTree` class:

```
class PineTree: Tree {
    var needles = 0
}

class OakTree: Tree{
    var leaves = 0
}
```

The class hierarchy now looks like this:

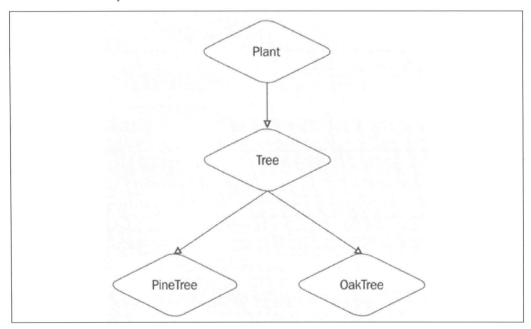

Figure 8.1: Inheritance class hierarchy

It is important to keep in mind that, in Swift, a class can have multiple subclasses; however, a class can have only one superclass. There are times when a subclass needs to provide its own implementation of a method or property that it inherited from its superclass. This is known as **overriding**.

Overriding methods and properties

To override a method, property, or subscript, we need to prefix the definition with the override keyword. This tells the compiler that we intend to override something in the superclass, and that we did not make a duplicate definition by mistake. The override keyword prompts the Swift compiler to verify that the superclass (or one of its parents) has a matching declaration that can be overridden. If it cannot find a matching declaration in one of the superclasses, an error will be thrown.

Overriding methods

Let's look at how we can override a method. We will start by adding a getDetails() method to the Plant class that we will then override in the child classes. The following code shows the code for the new Plant class:

```
class Plant {
    var height = 0.0
    var age = 0
    func growHeight(inches: Double) {
        self.height += inches;
    }

    func getDetails() -> String {
        return "Plant Details"
    }
}
```

Now, let's see how we can override the getDetails() method in the Tree class:

```
class Tree: Plant {
    private var limbs = 0
    func limbGrow() {
        self.limbs += 1
    }
    func limbFall() {
        self.limbs -= 1
    }
    override func getDetails() -> String {
        return "Tree Details"
    }
}
```

The thing to note here is that we do not use the override keyword in the Plant class because it is the first class to implement this method; however, we do include it in the Tree class since we are overriding the getDetails() method from the Plant class. Now, let's see what happens if we call the getDetails() method from an instance of the Plant and Tree classes:

```
var plant = Plant()
var tree = Tree()
print("Plant: \(plant.getDetails())")
print("Tree: \(tree.getDetails())")
```

The previous example will print the following two lines to the console:

```
Plant: Plant Details
Tree: Tree Details
```

As we can see, the getDetails() method in the Tree subclass overrides the getDetails() of its parent Plant class. Inside the Tree class, we can still call the getDetails() method (or any overridden method, property, or subscript) of its superclass by using the super prefix. We will begin by replacing the getDetails() method in the Plant class with the following method, which will generate a string that contains the values of the height and age properties:

```
func getDetails() -> String {
    return "Height:\(height) age:\(age)"
}
```

Now, we will replace the getDetails() method for the Tree class with the following method, which will call the getDetails() method of the superclass:

```
override func getDetails() -> String {
    let details = super.getDetails()
    return "\(details) limbs:\(limbs)"
}
```

In the preceding example, we begin by calling the getDetails() method of the superclass (the Plant class in this case) to get a string that contains the tree's height and age. We then build a new string object that combines the results of the getDetails() method and a new string that contains the number of limbs from the Tree class. This new string is then returned. Let's look at what happens if we call this new method:

```
var tree = Tree()
tree.age = 5
```

```
tree.height = 4
tree.limbGrow()
tree.limbGrow()
print(tree.getDetails())
```

If we run the preceding code, the following line will be printed to the console:

```
Height: 4.0
age: 5
limbs: 2
```

As we can see, the string that is returned contains the `height` and `age` information from the `Plant` class and the `limbs` information from the `Tree` class.

Overriding properties

We can provide custom getters and setters to override any inherited property. When we override a property, we must provide the name and the type of property we are overriding so that the compiler can verify that one of the classes in the class hierarchy has a matching property to override. Let's see how we can override a property by adding the following property to our `Plant` class:

```
var description: String {
    return "Base class is Plant."
}
```

The `description` property is a basic read-only property. This property returns the `Base class is Plant` string. Now, let's override this property by adding the following property to the `Tree` class:

```
override var description: String {
    return "\(super.description) I am a Tree class."
}
```

The same `override` keyword is used when overriding both properties and methods. This keyword tells the compiler that we want to override a property so that the compiler can verify that another class in the class hierarchy contains a matching property to override. We then implement the property as we would any other property. Calling the `description` property for an instance of the `Tree` class will result in the `Base class is Plant. I am a Tree class` string being returned. There are times when we want to prevent a subclass from overriding the properties and methods. There are also times when we want to prevent an entire class from being subclassed. Let's see how we can do this.

Preventing overrides

To prevent overrides or subclassing, we can use the `final` keyword. To use the `final` keyword, we add it before the item's definition. Examples are `final func`, `final var`, and `final class`. Any attempt to override an item marked with this keyword will result in a compile-time error.

Protocols

There are times when we would like to describe the implementations (methods, properties, and other requirements) of a type without actually providing any implementation. For this, we can use protocols. Protocols define a blueprint of methods, properties, and other requirements for a class or a structure. A class or a structure can then provide an implementation that conforms to those requirements. The class or structure that provides the implementation is said to conform to the protocol. Protocols are very important to the Swift language. The entire Swift standard library is based on them, and we will be looking at protocols and how to use them in *Chapter 9, Protocols and Protocol Extensions*, and *Chapter 10, Protocol Oriented Design*.

Protocol syntax

The syntax to define a protocol is very similar to how we define a class or a structure. The following example shows the syntax that's used to define a protocol:

```
protocol MyProtocol {
    //protocol definition here
}
```

We state that a class or structure conforms to a protocol by placing the name of the protocol after the type's name, separated by a colon. Here is an example of how we would state that a structure conforms to the `MyProtocol` protocol:

```
struct MyStruct: MyProtocol {
    // Structure implementation here
}
```

A type can conform to multiple protocols. We list the protocols that the type conforms to by separating them with commas. The following example shows how we would state that our structure conforms to multiple protocols:

```
struct MyStruct: MyProtocol, AnotherProtocol, ThirdProtocol {
    // Structure implementation here
}
```

If we need a class to both inherit from a superclass and implement a protocol, we would list the superclass first, followed by the protocols. The following example illustrates this:

```
class MyClass: MySuperClass, MyProtocol, MyProtocol2 {
    // Class implementation here
}
```

Property requirements

A protocol can require that the conforming type provides certain properties with a specified name and type. The protocol does not say whether the property should be a stored or computed property because the implementation details are left up to the conforming type. When defining a property within a protocol, we must specify whether the property is a read-only or read-write property by using the get and set keywords. Let's look at how we would define properties within a protocol by creating a protocol named FullName:

```
protocol FullName {
    var firstName: String { get set }
    var lastName: String { get set }
}
```

The FullName protocol defines two properties, which any type that conforms to the protocol must implement. These are the firstName and lastName properties, and both are read-write properties. If we wanted to specify that the property is read-only, we would define it with only the get keyword, like this:

```
var readOnly: String { get }
```

Let's see how we can create a Scientist class that conforms to this protocol:

```
class Scientist: FullName {
    var firstName = ""
    var lastName = ""
}
```

If we had forgotten to include either of the required properties, we would have received an error message letting us know the property we forgot. We also need to make sure that the type of the property is the same. For example, if we change the definition of the lastName property in the Scientist class to var lastName = 42, we will also receive an error message because the protocol specifies that we must have a lastName property of the string type.

Method requirements

A protocol can require that the conforming class or structure provides certain methods. We define a method within a protocol exactly as we do within a class or structure, except without the method body. Let's add a `fullName()` method to our `FullName` protocol and `Scientist` class:

```
protocol FullName {
    var firstName: String { get set }
    var lastName: String { get set }
    func fullName() -> String
}
```

Now, we need to add a `fullName()` method to our `Scientist` class so that it will conform to the protocol:

```
class Scientist: FullName {
    var firstName = ""
    var lastName = ""
    var field = ""

    func fullName() -> String {
        return "\(firstName) \(lastName) studies \(field)"
    }
}
```

Structures can conform to Swift protocols exactly as classes do. In fact, the majority of the Swift standard library are structures that implement the various protocols that make up the standard library. The following example shows how we can create a `FootballPlayer` structure that also conforms to the `FullName` protocol:

```
struct FootballPlayer: FullName {
    var firstName = ""
    var lastName = ""
    var number = 0

    func fullName() -> String {
        return "\(firstName) \(lastName) has the number \(number)"
    }
}
```

When a class or structure conforms to a Swift protocol, we can be sure that it has implemented the required properties and methods. This can be very useful when we want to ensure that certain properties or methods are implemented over various classes, as our preceding examples show. Protocols are also very useful when we want to decouple our code from requiring specific types. The following code shows how we would decouple our code using the FullName protocol, the Scientist class, and the FootballPlayer structure that we have already built:

```
var scientist = Scientist()
scientist.firstName = "Kara"
scientist.lastName = "Hoffman"
scientist.field = "Physics"

var player = FootballPlayer()
player.firstName = "Dan"
player.lastName = "Marino"
player.number = 13

var person: FullName
person = scientist
print(person.fullName())
person = player
print(person.fullName())
```

In the preceding code, we begin by creating an instance of the Scientist class and the FootballPlayer structure. We then create a person variable that is of the FullName (protocol) type and set it to the scientist instance that we just created. We then call the fullName() method to retrieve our description. This will print out the Kara Hoffman studies Physics message to the console. We then set the person variable equal to the player instance and call the fullName() method again. This will print out the Dan Marino has the number 13 message to the console. As we can see, the person variable does not care what the actual implementation type is. Since we defined the person variable to be of the FullName type, we can set the variable to an instance of any type that conforms to the FullName protocol. This is called polymorphism. We will cover polymorphism and protocols more in *Chapter 9, Protocols and Protocol Extensions*, and *Chapter 10, Protocol Oriented Design*.

Extensions

With extensions, we can add new properties, methods, initializers, and subscripts, or make an existing type conform to a protocol without modifying the source code for the type. One thing to note is that extensions cannot override the existing functionality. To define an extension, we use the `extension` keyword, followed by the type that we are extending.

The following example shows how we would create an extension that extends the `string` class:

```
extension String {
    //add new functionality here
}
```

Let's see how extensions work by adding a `reverse()` method and a `firstLetter` property to Swift's standard `string` class:

```
extension String {
    var firstLetter: Character? {
        get {
            return self.first
        }
    }

    func reverse() -> String {
        var reverse = ""
        for letter in self {
            reverse = "\(letter)" + reverse
        }
        return reverse
    }
}
```

When we extend an existing type, we define properties, methods, initializers, subscripts, and protocols in exactly the same way as we would normally define them in a standard class or structure. In the string extension example, we can see that we define the `reverse()` method and the `firstLetter` property exactly as we would define them in a normal type. We can then use these methods exactly as we would use any other method, as the following example shows:

```
var myString = "Learning Swift is fun"
print(myString.reverse())
print(myString.firstLetter!)
```

Swift 4 did add the reversed() method to the string type, which should be preferred over the one we created here. This example just illustrates how to use extensions. Extensions are very useful for adding extra functionality to an existing type from external frameworks, even for Apple's frameworks, as demonstrated in this example. It is preferred to use extensions to add extra functionality to types from external frameworks rather than subclassing, because it allows us to continue to use the type throughout our code rather than changing the type to the subclass. Before we finish this chapter, let's take another look at optional chaining now that we have an understanding of classes and structures.

Property wrappers

Property wrappers were introduced in Swift 5.1 with SE-0258 and they enable property values to be wrapped using a custom type. In order to perform this wrapping, we must create a custom attribute and a type that will handle the attribute. To see an example of this, let's say that we want to trim all of the whitespace characters from the beginning and the ending of our string values. We could do this by using the getter and setter methods of our properties to trim the whitespace characters; however, we would have to put this logic in for each property that we wanted to trim. With property wrappers, we would do this much more easily. We will start off by creating our custom type that will be used as a wrapper; we will name it Trimmed:

```swift
@propertyWrapper
struct Trimmed {
    private var str: String = ""

    var wrappedValue: String {
        get { str }
        set { str = newValue.trimmingCharacters(in:
.whitespacesAndNewlines) }
    }

    init(wrappedValue: String) {
        self.wrappedValue = wrappedValue
    }
}
```

The previous code starts off by using the @propertyWrapper attribute to define that this type can be used as a property wrapper. Any type that is defined as a property wrapper must have a non-static property named wrappedValue, which we define as a `String` type within our Trimmed type. Finally, we create an initializer that is used to set the wrappedValue property.

If we look back at the `EmployeeStruct` structure that we created earlier in the chapter, we defined two `String` properties like this:

```
var firstName = ""
var lastName = ""
```

If we wanted to trim all of the whitespaces from the beginning and ending of these properties, all we would need to do now is to add an @Trimmed attribute to them like this:

```
@Trimmed var firstName = ""
@Trimmed var lastName = ""
```

Now if we created new instances of the `EmployeeStruct` structure like this (notice the spaces in the initializer):

```
let employee1 = EmployeeStruct(firstName: " Jon ", lastName: " Hoffman
")
```

The `firstName` and `lastName` properties will contain the values with the whitespace characters automatically removed.

Optional chaining

Optional binding allows us to unwrap one optional at a time, but what would happen if we had optional types embedded within other optional types? This would force us to have optional binding statements embedded within other optional binding statements. There is a better way to handle this: by using optional chaining. Before we look at optional chaining, let's see how this would work with optional binding. We will start off by defining three types that we will be using for our examples in this section:

```
class Collar {
    var color: String
    init(color: String) {
        self.color = color
    }
}

class Pet {
    var name: String
    var collar: Collar?
    init(name: String) {
```

```
            self.name = name
    }
}

class Person {
    var name: String
    var pet: Pet?
    init(name: String) {
        self.name = name
    }
}
```

In this example, we begin by defining a `Collar` class, which has one property defined. This property is named `color`, which is of the string type. We can see that the `color` property is not an optional; therefore, we can safely assume that it will always have a valid value. Next, we define a `Pet` class that has two properties defined. These properties are named `name` and `collar`. The `name` property is of the string type and the `collar` property is an optional that may contain an instance of the `Collar` type or may contain no value. Finally, we define a `Person` class, which also has two properties. These properties are named `name` and `pet`. The `name` property is of the string type and the `pet` property is an optional that may contain an instance of the `Pet` type or may contain no value. For the examples that follow, let's use the following code to initialize the classes:

```
var jon = Person(name: "Jon")
var buddy = Pet(name: "Buddy")
jon.pet = buddy
var collar = Collar(color: "red")
buddy.collar = collar
```

Now, let's say that we want to get the color of the collar for a person's pet; however, the person may not have a pet (the `pet` property may be `nil`) or the pet may not have a collar (the `collar` property may be `nil`). We could use optional binding to drill down through each layer, as shown in the following example:

```
if let tmpPet = jon.pet, let tmpCollar = tmpPet.collar {
    print("The color of the collar is \(tmpCollar.color)")
} else {
    print("Cannot retrieve color")
}
```

While this example is perfectly valid and would print out a The color of the collar is red message, the code is rather messy and hard to follow because we have multiple optional binding statements on the same line, where the second optional binding statement is dependent on the first one. Optional chaining allows us to drill down through multiple optional type layers of properties, methods, and subscripts in one line of code. These layers can be chained together and if any layer returns nil, the entire chain gracefully fails and returns nil. If none of the values returns nil, the last value of the chain is returned. Since the results of optional chaining may be a nil value, the results are always returned as an optional type, even if the final value we are retrieving is a non-optional type. To specify optional chaining, we place a question mark (?) after each of the optional values within the chain. The following example shows how to use optional chaining to make the preceding example much cleaner and easier to read:

```
if let color = jon.pet?.collar?.color {
    print("The color of the collar is \(color)")
} else {
    print("Cannot retrieve color")
}
```

In this example, we put a question mark after the pet and collar properties to signify that they are of the optional type and that, if either value is nil, the whole chain will return nil. This code would also print out the The color of the collar is red message; however, it is much easier to read than the preceding example because it clearly shows us what optionals we are dependent on.

Summary

In this chapter, we took an in-depth look at classes and structures. We saw what makes them so similar and also what makes them so different. In the upcoming chapters, it will be important to remember that classes are reference types while structures are value types. We also looked at protocols and extensions. As this chapter ends, we end the introduction to the Swift programming language. At this point, we have enough knowledge of the Swift language to begin writing our own applications; however, there is still much to learn. In the following chapters, we will look in more depth at some of the concepts that we've already discussed, such as protocols and subscripts. We will also see how we can use protocol-oriented programming techniques to write easy-to-manage code. Finally, we will have chapters that will help us write better code, such as a sample Swift style guide, and a chapter on design patterns.

9
Protocols and Protocol Extensions

While watching the presentations from WWDC 2015 about protocol extensions and **protocol-oriented programming (POP)**, I will admit that I was very skeptical. I have worked with **object-oriented programming (OOP)** for so long that I was unsure whether this new programming paradigm would solve all of the problems that Apple was claiming it would. Since I am not one who lets my skepticism get in the way of trying something new, I set up a new project that mirrored the one I was currently working on, but wrote the code using Apple's recommendations for POP. I also used protocol extensions extensively in the code. I can honestly say that I was amazed by how much cleaner the new project was compared to the original one. I believe that protocol extensions are going to be one of those defining features that set one programming language apart from the rest.

In this chapter, you will learn about the following topics:

- How are protocols used as a type?
- How do we implement polymorphism in Swift using protocols?
- How do we use protocol extensions?
- Why we would want to use protocol extensions?

While protocol extensions are basically syntactic sugar, they are, in my opinion, one of the most important additions to the Swift programming language. With protocol extensions, we are able to provide method and property implementations to any type that conforms to a protocol. To really understand how useful protocols and protocol extensions are, let's get a better understanding of protocols.

While classes, structures, and enumerations can all conform to protocols in Swift, for this chapter, we will be focusing on classes and structures. Enumerations are used when we need to represent a finite number of cases, and while there are valid use cases where we would have an enumeration conform to a protocol, they are rare in my experience. Just remember that anywhere we refer to a class or structure, we can also use an enumeration.

Let's begin exploring protocols by seeing how they are full-fledged types in Swift.

Protocols as types

Even though no functionality is implemented in a protocol, they are still considered a full-fledged type in the Swift programming language and can be used like any other type. This means that we can use protocols as a parameter type or as a return type in a function.

We can also use them as the type for variables, constants, and collections. Let's take a look at some examples. For these few examples, we will use the following `PersonProtocol` protocol:

```
protocol PersonProtocol {
    var firstName: String { get set }
    var lastName: String { get set }
    var birthDate: Date { get set }
    var profession: String { get }

init(firstName: String,lastName: String, birthDate: Date)
}
```

In this first example, a protocol is used as a parameter type and a return type for a function:

```
func updatePerson(person: PersonProtocol) -> PersonProtocol {
    // Code to update person goes here
return person
}
```

In this example, the `updatePerson()` function accepts one parameter of the `PersonProtocol` protocol type and returns a value of the `PersonProtocol` protocol type. This next example shows how to use a protocol as a type for constants, variables, or properties:

```
var myPerson: PersonProtocol
```

In this example, we create a variable of the PersonProtocol protocol type that is named myPerson. Protocols can also be used as the item type for storing a collection, such as arrays, dictionaries, or sets:

```
var people: [PersonProtocol] = []
```

In this final example, we created an array of the PersonProtocol protocol type. Even though the PersonProtocol protocol does not implement any functionality, we can still use protocols when we need to specify a type. However, a protocol cannot be instantiated in the same way as a class or a structure. This is because no functionality is implemented in a protocol. As an example, when trying to create an instance of the PersonProtocol protocol, as shown in the following example, we would receive a compile-time error:

```
var test = PersonProtocol(firstName: "Jon", lastName: "Hoffman",
birthDate:bDateProgrammer)
```

We can use the instance of any type that conforms to our protocol wherever the protocol type is required. As an example, if we've defined a variable to be of the PersonProtocol protocol type, we can then populate that variable with any class or structure that conforms to this protocol. For this example, let's assume that we have two types, named SwiftProgrammer and FootballPlayer, that conform to the PersonProtocol protocol:

```
var myPerson: PersonProtocol

myPerson = SwiftProgrammer(firstName: "Jon", lastName: "Hoffman",
birthDate: bDateProgrammer)

print("\(myPerson.firstName) \(myPerson.lastName)")

myPerson = FootballPlayer(firstName: "Dan", lastName: "Marino",
birthDate:bDatePlayer)

print("\(myPerson.firstName) \(myPerson.lastName)")
```

In this example, we start off by creating the myPerson variable of the PersonProtocol protocol type. We then set the variable with an instance of the SwiftProgrammer type and print out the first and last names. Next, we set the myPerson variable to an instance of the FootballPlayer type and print out the first and last names again. One thing to note is that Swift does not care whether the instance is a class or structure. The only thing that matters is that the type conforms to the PersonProtocol protocol type.

We can use the `PersonProtocol` protocol as the type for an array, which means that we can populate the array with instances of any type that conforms to the protocol. Once again, it does not matter whether the type is a class or a structure, as long as it conforms to the `PersonProtocol` protocol.

Polymorphism with protocols

What we saw in the previous examples is a form of polymorphism. The word **polymorphism** comes from the Greek roots **poly**, meaning many, and **morphe**, meaning form. In programming languages, polymorphism is a single interface to multiple types (many forms). In the previous example, the single interface was the `PersonProtocol` protocol and the multiple types were any type that conforms to that protocol.

Polymorphism gives us the ability to interact with multiple types in a uniform manner. To illustrate this, we can extend the previous example where we created an array of the `PersonProtocol` types and looped through the array. We can then access each item in the array using the properties and methods defined in the `PersonProtocol` protocol, regardless of the actual type. Let's see an example of this:

```
for person in people {
    print("\(person.firstName)\(person.lastName):\(person.profession)")
}
```

When we define the type of a variable, constant, collection type, and so on to be a protocol type, we can use the instance of any type that conforms to that protocol. This is a very important concept to understand and is one of the many things that make protocols and protocol extensions so powerful.

When we use a protocol to access instances, as shown in the previous example, we are limited to using only properties and methods that are defined in the protocol itself. If we want to use properties or methods that are specific to the individual types, we need to cast the instance to that type.

Typecasting with protocols

Typecasting is a way to check the type of the instance and/or to treat the instance as a specified type. In Swift, we use the `is` keyword to check whether an instance is a specific type, and the `as` keyword to treat the instance as a specific type.

To start, let's see how we would check the instance type using the `is` keyword. The following example shows how this is done:

```
for person in people {
    if let p = person as? SwiftProgrammer {
        print("\(person.firstName) is a Swift Programmer")
    }
}
```

In this example, we use the `if` conditional statement to check whether each element in the `people` array is an instance of the `SwiftProgrammer` type and, if so, we print that the person is a Swift programmer to the console. While this is a good method to check whether we have an instance of a specific class or structure, it is not very efficient if we want to check for multiple types. It would be more efficient to use a `switch` statement, as shown in the next example:

```
for person in people {
    switch person {
        case is SwiftProgrammer:
            print("\(person.firstName) is a Swift Programmer")
        case is FootballPlayer:
            print("\(person.firstName) is a Football Player")
        default:
            print("\(person.firstName) is an unknown type")
    }
}
```

In the previous example, we showed how to use the `switch` statement to check the instance type for each element of the array. To do this check, we use the `is` keyword in each of the `case` statements in an attempt to match the instance type.

In *Chapter 6, Control Flow*, we saw how to filter conditional statements with the `where` statement. We can also use the `where` statement with the `is` keyword to filter the array, as shown in the following example:

```
for person in people where person is SwiftProgrammer {
    print("\(person.firstName) is a Swift Programmer")
}
```

Now let's look at how we can cast an instance of a class or structure to a specific type. To do this, we would use the `as` keyword. Since the cast can fail if the instance is not of the specified type, the `as` keyword comes in two forms: `as?` and `as!`. With the `as?` form, if the casting fails, it returns `nil`, and with the `as!` form, if the casting fails, we get a runtime error. Therefore, it is recommended to use the `as?` form unless we are absolutely sure of the instance type or we perform a check of the instance type prior to doing the cast.

While we do show examples of typecasting with `as!` in this book, so you are aware that it is there, we highly recommend that you do not use it in your projects because it can cause a runtime error.

Let's look at how we would use the `as?` keyword to cast an instance of a class or structure to a specified type:

```
for person in people {
    if let p = person as? SwiftProgrammer {
        print("\(person.firstName) is a Swift Programmer")
    }
}
```

Since the `as?` keyword returns an optional, we use optional binding to perform the cast, as shown in this example.

Now that we have covered the basics of protocols, let's dive into one of the most exciting features of Swift: protocol extensions.

Protocol extensions

Protocol extensions allow us to extend a protocol to provide method and property implementations to conforming types. They also allow us to provide common implementations to all the conforming types, eliminating the need to provide an implementation in each individual type or the need to create a class hierarchy. While protocol extensions may not seem too exciting, once you see how powerful they really are, they will transform the way you think about and write code.

Let's begin by looking at how we would use protocol extensions within a very simplistic example. We will start by defining a protocol named Dog, as follows:

```
protocol Dog {
    var name: String { get set }
    var color: String { get set }
}
```

With this protocol, we state that any type that conforms to the Dog protocol must have the two properties of the String type, named name and color. Next, let's define the three types that conform to this Dog protocol. We will name these types JackRussel, WhiteLab, and Mutt. The following code shows how we would define these types:

```
struct JackRussel: Dog{
    var name: String
    var color: String
}
class WhiteLab: Dog{
    var name: String
    var color: String
    init(name: String, color: String) {
        self.name = name
        self.color = color
    }
}

struct Mutt: Dog{
    var name: String
    var color: String
}
```

We purposely created the JackRussel and Mutt types as structures and the WhiteLab type as a class to show the differences between how the two types are set up, and to illustrate how they are treated the same when it comes to protocols and protocol extensions.

The biggest difference we can see in this example is that structure types provide a default initiator, but in the class we must provide the initiator to populate the properties.

Now let's say that we want to provide a method named speak to each type that conforms to the protocol. Prior to protocol extensions, we would have started off by adding the method definition to the protocol, as shown in the following code:

```
protocol Dog{
    var name: String { get set }
    var color: String { get set }
    func speak() -> String
}
```

Once the method is defined in the protocol, we would then need to provide an implementation of the method in every type that conforms to the protocol. Depending on the number of types that conformed to this protocol, this could take a bit of time to implement and it could affect a lot of code. The following code sample shows how we might implement this method:

```
struct JackRussel: Dog{
    var name: String
    var color: String
    func speak() -> String {
        return "Woof"
    }
}

class WhiteLab: Dog{
    var name: String
    var color: String

    init(name: String, color: String) {
        self.name = nameself.color = color}

    func speak() -> String {
        return "Woof"
    }
}

struct Mutt: Dog{
    var name: String
    var color: String
    func speak() -> String {
        return "Woof Woof"
    }
}
```

While this method works, it is not very efficient because any time we update the protocol, we need to update all the types that conform to it, and therefore duplicate a lot of code, as shown in this example. If we need to change the default behavior of the speak() method, we would have to go into each implementation and change the method. This is where protocol extensions come in.

With protocol extensions, we could take the speak() method definition out of the protocol itself and define it with the default behavior in the protocol extension.

 If we are implementing a method in a protocol extension, we are not required to define it in the protocol.

The following code shows how we would define the protocol and the protocol extension:

```
protocol Dog{
    var name: String { get set }
    var color: String { get set }
}

extension Dog{
    func speak() -> String {
      return "Woof Woof"
    }
  }
```

We begin by defining the Dog protocol with the original two properties. We then create a protocol extension that extends it and contains the default implementation of the speak() method. With this code, there is no need to provide an implementation of the speak() method in all of the types that conform to the Dog protocol because they automatically receive the implementation as part of the protocol.

Let's see how this works by setting the three types that conform to the Dog protocol back to their original implementations; then they should receive the speak() method from the protocol extension:

```
struct JackRussel: Dog{
    var name: String
    var color: String
}
class WhiteLab: Dog{
    var name: String
    var color: String
    init(name: String, color: String) {
        self.name = name
        self.color = color
    }
}

struct Mutt: Dog{
    var name: String
    var color: String
}
```

We can now use each of the types, as shown in the following code:

```
let dash = JackRussel(name: "Dash", color: "Brown and White")
let lily = WhiteLab(name: "Lily", color: "White")
let maple = Mutt(name: "Buddy", color: "Brown")
let dSpeak = dash.speak() // returns "woof woof"
let lSpeak = lily.speak() // returns "woof woof"
let bSpeak = maple.speak() // returns "woof woof"
```

As we can see in this example, by adding the speak() method to the Dog protocol extension, we are automatically adding that method to all the types that conform to the protocol. The speak() method in the protocol extension can be considered a default implementation of the method because we are able to override it in the type implementations. As an example, we could override the speak() method in the Mutt structure, as shown in the following code:

```
struct Mutt: Dog{
    var name: String
    var color: String
    func speak() -> String {
        return "I am hungry"
    }
}
```

When we call the speak() method for an instance of the Mutt type, it will return the I am hungry string.

 In this chapter, we named our protocols with the protocol suffix. This was done to make it very clear that this was a protocol. This is not how we would normally name our types. The following example gives a better example of how we would properly name protocols. You can read additional information about Swift's naming conventions in the Swift API design guidelines: https://swift.org/documentation/api-design-guidelines/#general-conventions.

Now that we have seen how to use protocols and protocol extensions, let's look at a more real-world example.

A real-world example

In numerous apps across multiple platforms (iOS, Android, and Windows), I have needed to validate user input as it is entered. This validation can be done very easily with regular expressions; however, we do not want various regular expressions littered throughout our code. It is very easy to solve this problem by creating different classes or structures that contain the validation code. However, we would have to organize these types to make them easy to use and maintain. Prior to protocol extensions in Swift, I would use a protocol to define the validation requirements and then create structures that would conform to the protocol for each validation that I needed. Let's look at this pre-protocol extension method.

A regular expression is a sequence of characters that defines a particular pattern. This pattern can then be used to search a string to see whether the string matches the pattern or contains a match of the pattern. Most major programming languages contain a regular expression parser, and if you are not familiar with regular expressions, it may be worthwhile to learn more about them.

The following code shows the `TextValidating` protocol that defines the requirements for any type that we want to use for text validation:

```
protocol TextValidating {
    var regExMatchingString: String { get }
    var regExFindMatchString: String { get }
    var validationMessage: String { get }
    func validateString(str: String) -> Bool

    func getMatchingString(str: String) -> String?
}
```

The Swift API design guidelines (`https://swift.org/documentation/api-design-guidelines/`) state that protocols that describe what something is should be named as a noun, while protocols that describe a capability should be named with a suffix of -able, - ible, or -ing. With this in mind, we named the text validation protocol `TextValidating`.

In this protocol, we define three properties and two methods that any type that conforms to a protocol must implement. The three properties are as follows:

- `regExMatchingString`: This is a regular expression string used to verify that the input string contains only valid characters.

- `regExFindMatchString`: This is a regular expression string used to retrieve a new string from the input string that contains only valid characters. This regular expression is generally used when we need to validate the input in real time as the user enters information, because it will find the longest matching prefix of the input string.

- `validationMessage`: This is the error message that's displayed if the input string contains non-valid characters.

The two methods for this protocol are as follows:

- `validateString`: This method will return `true` if the input string contains only valid characters. The `regExMatchingString` property will be used in this method to perform the match.

- `getMatchingString`: This method will return a new string that contains only valid characters. This method is generally used when we need to validate the input in real time as the user enters information because it will find the longest matching prefix of the input string. We will use the `regExFindMatchString` property in this method to retrieve the new string.

Now let's see how we can create a structure that conforms to this protocol. The following structure would be used to verify that the input string contains only alpha characters:

```
struct AlphaValidation1: TextValidating {
    static let sharedInstance = AlphaValidation1()
    private init(){}
    let regExFindMatchString = "^[a-zA-Z]{0,10}"
    let validationMessage = "Can only contain Alpha characters"
    var regExMatchingString: String {
        get {
            return regExFindMatchString + "$"
        }
    }
    func validateString(str: String) -> Bool {
        if let _ = str.range(of: regExMatchingString, options:
                    .regularExpression) {
        return true
    } else {
        return false
        }
    }
    func getMatchingString(str: String) -> String? {
        if let newMatch = str.range(of: regExFindMatchString,
```

```
                          options:.regularExpression) {
        return String(str[newMatch])
    } else {
        return nil
        }
    }
}
```

In this implementation, the `regExFindMatchString` and `validationMessage` properties are stored properties, and the `regExMatchingString` property is a computed property.

We also implement the `validateString()` and `getMatchingString()` methods within the structure.

Normally, we would have several different types that conform to the protocol, where each one would validate a different type of input. As we can see from the `AlphaValidation1` structure, there is a bit of code involved with each validation type. A lot of the code would also be duplicated in each type. The code for both methods and the `regExMatchingString` property would probably be duplicated in every validation class. This is not ideal, but if we want to avoid creating a class hierarchy with a superclass that contains the duplicate code (it is recommended that we prefer value types over reference types), prior to protocol extensions, we had no other choice. Now let's see how we would implement this using protocol extensions.

With protocol extensions, we need to think about the code a little differently. The big difference is that we neither need nor want to define everything in the protocol. With standard protocols, all the methods and properties that you would want to access using a protocol interface would have to be defined within the protocol.

With protocol extensions, it is preferable for us not to define a property or method in the protocol if we are going to be defining it within the protocol extension. Therefore, when we rewrite our text validation types with protocol extensions, `TextValidating` would be greatly simplified to look like this:

```
protocol TextValidating {
    var regExFindMatchString: String { get }
    var validationMessage: String { get }
}
```

In the original `TextValidating` protocol, we defined three properties and two methods. As we can see in this new protocol, we are only defining two properties. Now that we have our `TextValidating` protocol defined, let's create the protocol extension for it:

```
extension TextValidating {
    var regExMatchingString: String {
        get {
            return regExFindMatchString + "$"
        }
    }
    func validateString(str: String) -> Bool {
        if let _ = str.range(of:regExMatchingString,
                    options:.regularExpression){
        return true
    } else {
        return false
        }
    }
    func getMatchingString(str: String) -> String? {
        if let newMatch = str.range(of:regExFindMatchString,
                            options:.regularExpression) {
        return str.substring(with: newMatch)
    } else {
        return nil
        }
    }
}
```

In the TextValidating protocol extension, we define the two methods and the property that were defined in the original TextValidating protocol but were not defined in the new one. Now that we have created the protocol and protocol extension, we are able to define our new text validation types. In the following code, we define three structures that we will use to validate text as a user types it in:

```
struct AlphaValidation: TextValidating {
    static let sharedInstance = AlphaValidation()
    private init(){}
    let regExFindMatchString = "^[a-zA-Z]{0,10}"
    let validationMessage = "Can only contain Alpha characters"
}

struct AlphaNumericValidation: TextValidating {
    static let sharedInstance = AlphaNumericValidation()
    private init(){}
    let regExFindMatchString = "^[a-zA-Z0-9]{0,15}"
    let validationMessage = "Can only contain Alpha Numeric characters"
}
```

```
struct DisplayNameValidation: TextValidating {
    static let sharedInstance = DisplayNameValidation()
    private init(){}
    let regExFindMatchString = "^[\\s?[a-zA-Z0-9\\-_\\s]]{0,15}"
    let validationMessage = "Can only contain Alphanumeric Characters"
}
```

In each of the text-validation structures, we create a static constant and a private initializer so that we can use the structure as a singleton. For more information on the singleton pattern, please see *The singleton design pattern* section of *Chapter 20, Adopting Design Patterns in Swift*.

After we define the singleton pattern, all we do in each type is set the values for the `regExFindMatchString` and `validationMessage` properties. Now we have virtually no duplicate code. The only code that is duplicated is the code for the singleton pattern, and that is not something we would want to put in the protocol extension because we would not want to force the singleton pattern on all the conforming types.

We can now use the text validation types, as shown in the following code:

```
var testString = "abc123"

var alpha = AlphaValidation.sharedInstance alpha.getMatchingString(str:
testString)
alpha.validateString(str: testString)
```

In the previous code snippet, a new string is created to validate and get the shared instance of the `AlphaValidation` type. Then `getMatchingString()` is used to retrieve the longest matching prefix of the test string, which will be abc. Then, the `validateString()` method is used to validate the test string, but since the test string contains numbers, the method will return `false`.

Now the question is, do we really need to use protocols?

Do I need to use protocols?

Do you need to use protocols and protocol extensions when you already know OOP? The short answer is no; however, it is highly recommended. In *Chapter 10, Protocol-Oriented Design*, we look at what makes protocol-oriented design so powerful to show you why you should prefer protocols with POP over OOP. By understanding protocols and protocol-oriented design, you will understand the Swift standard library better.

Adopting protocols using a synthesized implementation

Swift can automatically provide protocol conformance for the Equatable, Hashable, and Comparable protocols in specific cases. What this means is we do not need to write the boilerplate code to implement these protocols, and instead we can use the synthesized implementations. This only works if the structures or enumerations (not classes) contain only stored properties (for structures) or associated values (for enumerations) that conform to the Equatable, Hashable, and Comparable protocols.

The Equatable, Hashable, and Comparable protocols are provided by the Swift standard library. Any type that conforms to the Equatable protocols can use the equals operator (==) to compare two instances of the type. Any type that uses the Comparable protocol can use comparative operators to compare two instances of the type. Finally, any type that conforms to the Hashable protocol can be hashed into a Hasher instance to produce an integer hash.

Let's look at one example of this. We will start off by creating a simple structure that will store names:

```swift
struct Name {
    var firstName = ""
    var lastName = ""
}
```

We can now create three instances of the Name structure, as shown in the following code:

```swift
let name1 = Name(firstName: "Jon", lastName: "Hoffman")
let name2 = Name(firstName: "John", lastName: "Hoffman")
let name3 = Name(firstName: "Jon", lastName: "Hoffman")
```

If we tried to compare the instances of the Name structure, as shown in the following code, we could receive a compile-time error because the Name structure does not conform to the Equatable protocol:

```swift
name1 == name2
name1 == name3
```

In order to have the ability to compare instances of the Name structure, all that is needed is to state that the structure conforms to the Equatable protocol, and the boilerplate code to do the comparison will be automatically added at compile time. The following code shows us how this is done:

```
struct Name: Equatable {
    var firstName = ""
    var lastName = ""
}
```

Notice that the only thing we changed was to add the Equatable protocol to the structure definition. We are now able to successfully compare instances of the Name structure.

Swift's standard library

The Swift standard library defines a base layer of functionality for writing Swift applications. Everything we have used so far in this book is from the Swift standard library. The library defines the fundamental data types, such as the String, Int, and Double types. It also defines collections, optionals, global functions, and all the protocols that these types conform to.

One of the best sites to see everything that makes up the standard library is http:// swiftdoc.org. This site lists all the types, protocols, operators, and globals that make up the standard library and contains documentation for all of it.

Let's look at how protocols are used in the standard library by looking at the documentation. When you first visit the home page, you will be greeted with a searchable list of everything that makes up the standard library. There is also a complete list of all Swift types that you can select from. Let's look at the Swift Array type by clicking on the **Array** link. This will take you to the documentation page for the Array type.

These documentation pages are extremely useful and contain a lot of information about the various types that make up the standard library, including samples of how to use them. For our discussion, we are interested in the section labeled **Inheritance**:

Figure 9.1: Documentation on Inheritance

From the inheritance section, we can see that the Array conforms to 7 protocols. If you click on some of the protocols, such as the MutableCollection protocol, you will notice that they conform to other protocols. This may not make a lot of sense at this point but in the next chapter, *Chapter 10, Protocol-Oriented Design*, we will look at how to design our applications and frameworks using a protocol-oriented approach, and then we will have a better understanding of how the Swift standard library is written.

Summary

In this chapter, we saw that protocols are treated as full-fledged types by Swift. We also saw how polymorphism can be implemented in Swift with protocols. We concluded this chapter with an in-depth look at protocol extensions and saw how we would use them in Swift. Protocols and protocol extensions are the backbone of Apple's new POP paradigm. This new model for programming has the potential to change the way we write and think about code. While we did not specifically cover POP in this chapter, getting to grips with the topics in this chapter gives us the solid understanding of protocols and protocol extensions needed to learn about this new programming model. In the next chapter, we will look at how to use protocols and protocol extensions when we are designing our application.

10
Protocol-Oriented Design

When Apple announced Swift 2 at the **World Wide Developers Conference (WWDC)** in 2016, they also declared that Swift was the world's first **protocol-oriented programming (POP)** language. From its name, we might assume that POP is all about protocol; however, that would be a wrong assumption. POP is about so much more than just protocol; it is actually a new way of not only writing applications but also thinking about programming.

In this chapter, we will cover the following topics:

- What is the difference between OOP and POP design?
- What is protocol-oriented design?
- What is protocol composition?
- What is protocol inheritance?

Days after Dave Abrahams did his presentation on POP at WWDC 2016, there were numerous tutorials on the internet about POP that took a very object-oriented approach to it. With this statement, I mean the approach taken by these tutorials focused on replacing the superclass with protocols and protocol extensions. While protocols and protocol extensions are arguably two of the more important concepts of POP, these tutorials seem to be missing some very important concepts.

In this chapter, we will be comparing a protocol-oriented design with an object-oriented design to highlight some of the conceptual differences between the two. We will look at how we can use protocols and protocol extensions to replace superclasses, and how a protocol-oriented design will give us a cleaner and easier-to-maintain code base. To do this, we will look at how to define animal types for a video game in both an object-oriented and a protocol-oriented way. Let's start off by defining the requirements for our animals.

Requirements

When we develop applications, we usually have a set of requirements that we need to develop against. With that in mind, let's define the requirements for the animal types that we will be creating in this chapter:

- We will have three categories of animals: land, sea, and air.

- Animals may be members of multiple categories. For example, an alligator can be a member of both the land and sea categories.

- Animals may attack and/or move when they are on a tile that matches the categories they are in.

- Animals will start off with a certain number of hit points, and if those hit points reach 0 or less, then they will be considered dead.

For our example here, we will define two animals, `Lion` and `Alligator`, but we know that the number of animal types will grow as we develop the game.

We will start off by looking at how we would design the animal types using an object-oriented approach.

Object-oriented design

Before we start writing code, let's create a very basic diagram that shows how we would design the **Animal** class hierarchy. In this diagram, we will simply show the classes without much detail. This diagram will help us picture the class hierarchy in our minds. *Figure 10.1* shows the class hierarchy for the object-oriented design:

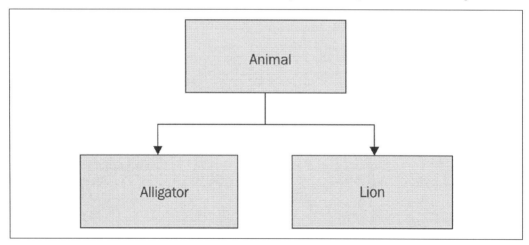

Figure 10.1: Animal class hierarchy

Figure 10.1 shows that we have one superclass named **Animal**, and two subclasses named Alligator and Lion. We may think with the three categories (land, air, and sea) that we would want to create a larger class hierarchy where the middle layer would contain the classes for the land, air, and sea animals. This would allow us to separate the code for each animal category; however, that is not possible with our requirements. The reason this is not possible is that any of the animal types can be members of multiple categories, and with a class hierarchy, each class can have one and only one superclass. This means that the Animal superclass will need to contain the code required for each of the three categories.

Let's begin by looking at the code for the Animal superclass.

We will start the Animal superclass by defining 10 properties. These properties will define what type of animal it is and what type of attacks/movements it can do. We also define a property that will keep track of the remaining hit points for the animal.

We define these properties as internal variables. We will need to set these properties in the subclasses; however, we do not want external entities, outside of our module that defines the animals, to change them. The preference is for these to be constants, but with an object-oriented approach; a subclass cannot set/change the value of a constant defined in a superclass. For this to work, the subclass will need to be defined in the same module as the Animal superclass:

```
class Animal {
    internal var landAnimal = false
    internal var landAttack = false
    internal var landMovement = false

    internal var seaAnimal = false
    internal var seaAttack = false
    internal var seaMovement = false

    internal var airAnimal = false
    internal var airAttack = false
    internal var airMovement = false

    internal var hitPoints = 0
}
```

Next, we define an initializer that will set the properties. We will set all the properties to false by default, and the hit points to zero. It will be up to the subclasses to set the appropriate properties that apply:

```
init() {
    landAnimal = false
    landAttack = false
    landMovement = false
    airAnimal = false
    airAttack = false
    airMovement = false
    seaAnimal = false
    seaAttack = false
    seaMovement = false
    hitPoints = 0
}
```

Since our properties are internal, we need to create some getter methods so that we can retrieve their values. We will also create a couple of additional methods that check if the animal is alive. We will need another method that deducts hit points when the animal takes a hit:

```
func isLandAnimal() -> Bool {
    return landAnimal
}
func canLandAttack() -> Bool {
    return landAttack
}
func canLandMove() -> Bool {
    return landMovement
}
func isSeaAnimal() -> Bool {
    return seaAnimal
}
func canSeaAttack() -> Bool {
    return seaAttack
}
func canSeaMove() -> Bool {
    return seaMovement
}
func isAirAnimal() -> Bool {
    return airAnimal
}
func canAirAttack() -> Bool {
    return airAttack
}
```

```swift
func canAirMove() -> Bool {
    return airMovement
}
func doLandAttack() {}
func doLandMovement() {}
func doSeaAttack() {}
func doSeaMovement() {}
func doAirAttack() {}
func doAirMovement() {}
func takeHit(amount: Int) {
    hitPoints -= amount
}
func hitPointsRemaining() -> Int {
    return hitPoints
}
func isAlive() -> Bool {
    return hitPoints > 0 ? true : false
}
```

Now that we have our `Animal` superclass, we can create the `Alligator` and `Lion` classes, which will be subclasses of the `Animal` class:

```swift
class Lion: Animal {
    override init() {
        super.init() landAnimal = true
        landAttack = true
        landMovement = true
        hitPoints = 20
    }
    override func doLandAttack() {
        print("Lion Attack")
    }
    override func doLandMovement() {
        print("Lion Move")
    }
}

class Alligator: Animal {
    override init() {
        super.init()
        landAnimal = true
        landAttack = true
        landMovement = true
```

```
            seaAnimal = true
            seaAttack = true
            seaMovement = true
            hitPoints = 35
    }
    override func doLandAttack() {
        print("Alligator Land Attack")
    }
    override func doLandMovement() {
        print("Alligator Land Move")
    }
    override func doSeaAttack() {
        print("Alligator Sea Attack")
    }
    override func doSeaMovement() {
        print("Alligator Sea Move")
    }
}
```

As we can see, these classes set the functionality needed for each animal. The `Lion` class contains the functionality for a land animal and the `Alligator` class contains the functionality for both land and sea animals.

Another disadvantage of this object-oriented design is that we do not have a single point that defines what type of animal (air, land, or sea) this is. It is very easy to set the wrong flag or add the wrong function when we cut and paste or type in the code. This may lead us to have an animal like this:

```
class landAnimal: Animal {
    override init() {
        super.init()
        landAnimal = true
        airAttack = true
        landMovement = true
        hitPoints = 20
    }
    override func doLandAttack() {
        print("Lion Attack")
    }
    override func doLandMovement() {
        print("Lion Move")
    }
}
```

In the previous code, we set the `landAnimal` property to true; however, we accidentally set `airAttack` to true as well. This will give us an animal that can move on land but cannot attack, since the `landAttack` property is not set. Hopefully, we would catch these types of errors in testing; however, as we will see later in this chapter, a protocol-oriented approach would help prevent coding errors like this.

Since both classes have the same `Animal` superclass, we can use polymorphism to access them through the interface provided by the `Animal` superclass:

```
var animals = [Animal]()
animals.append(Alligator())
animals.append(Alligator())
animals.append(Lion())

for (index, animal) in animals.enumerated() {
    if animal.isAirAnimal() {
        print("Animal at \(index) is Air")
    }
    if animal.isLandAnimal() {
        print("Animal at \(index) is Land")
    }
    if animal.isSeaAnimal() {
        print("Animal at \(index) is Sea")
    }
}
```

The way we designed the animal types here would work; however, there are several drawbacks to this design. The first drawback is the large monolithic `Animal` superclass. Those who are familiar with designing characters for video games probably realize how much functionality is missing from this superclass and its subclasses. This is on purpose so that we can focus on the design and not the functionality. For those who are not familiar with designing characters for video games, trust me when I say that this class may get very large.

Another drawback is not being able to define constants in the superclass that the subclasses can set. We could define various initializers for the superclass that would correctly set the constants for the different animal categories; however, these initializers will become pretty complex and hard to maintain as we add more animals. The builder pattern could help us with the initialization, but as we are about to see, a protocol-oriented design would be even better.

One final drawback that I am going to point out is the use of flags (the `landAnimal`, `seaAnimal`, and `airAnimal` properties) to define the type of animal, and the type of attack and movements an animal can perform. If we do not correctly set these flags, then the animal will not behave correctly. As an example, if we set the `seaAnimal` flag rather than the `landAnimal` flag in the `Lion` class, then the lion will not be able to move or attack on land. Trust me, it is very easy, even for the most experienced developers, to set flags wrongly.

Now let's look at how we would define this same functionality in a protocol-oriented way.

Protocol-oriented design

Just like our object-oriented design, we will start off with a diagram that shows the types needed and the relationships between them. *Figure 10.2* shows our protocol-oriented design:

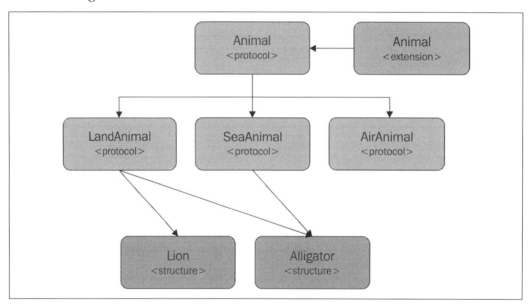

Figure 10.2: Protocol-oriented design

As we can see, the POP design is quite different from the OOP design. In this design, we use three techniques that make POP significantly different from OOP. These techniques are protocol inheritance, protocol composition, and protocol extensions. We looked at protocol extensions in the previous chapter, but we have not covered protocol inheritance or composition yet. It is important to understand these concepts, so before we go into the design, let's look at what protocol inheritance and protocol composition are.

Protocol inheritance

Protocol inheritance is where one protocol can inherit the requirements from one or more additional protocols. This is similar to class inheritance in OOP, but instead of inheriting functionality, we are inheriting requirements. We can also inherit requirements from multiple protocols, whereas a class in Swift can have only one superclass. Let's start off by defining four protocols, named `Name`, `Age`, `Fur`, and `Hair`:

```
protocol Name {
    var firstName: String { get set }
    var lastName: String { get set }
}

protocol Age {
    var age: Double { get set }
}

protocol Fur {
    var furColor: String { get set }
}

protocol Hair {
    var hairColor: String { get set }
}
```

Each of the four protocols has different requirements.

 There is one thing that I would like to point out. If you find yourself creating protocols with single requirements (as shown in this example), you probably want to reconsider your overall design. Protocols should not be this granular because we end up with too many protocols and they become hard to manage. We are using smaller protocols here as examples.

Now let's look at how we can use these protocols and protocol inheritance to create additional protocols. We will define two more protocols, named `Person` and `Dog`:

```
protocol Person: Name, Age, Hair {
    var height: Double { get set }
}

protocol Dog: Name, Age, Fur {
    var breed: String { get set }
}
```

In this example, any type that conforms to the `Person` protocol will need to fulfill the requirements of the `Name`, `Age`, and `Hair` protocols, as well as the requirements defined within the `Person` protocol itself. Any type that conforms to the `Dog` protocol will need to fulfill the requirements of the `Name`, `Age`, and `Fur` protocols as well as the requirements defined within the `Dog` protocol itself. This is the basis of protocol inheritance, where we can have one protocol inherit the requirements of one or more protocols.

Protocol inheritance is extremely powerful because we can define several smaller protocols and mix/match them to create larger protocols. You will want to be careful not to create protocols that are too granular because they will become hard to maintain and manage.

Protocol composition

Protocol composition allows types to conform to more than one protocol. This is one of the many advantages that protocol-oriented design has over object-oriented design. With object-oriented design, a class can have only one superclass. This can lead to very large, monolithic superclasses, as we saw in the *Object-oriented design* section of this chapter. With protocol-oriented design, we are encouraged to create multiple smaller protocols with very specific requirements. Let's look at how protocol composition works.

Let's add another protocol, named `Occupation`, to our example from the *Protocol inheritance* section:

```
protocol Occupation {
    var occupationName: String { get set }
    var yearlySalary:Double { get set }
    var experienceYears: Double { get set }
}
```

Next let's create a new type named `Programmer` that will conform to both the `Person` and `Occupation` protocols:

```
struct Programmer: Person, Occupation {
    var firstName: String
    var lastName: String
    var age: Double
    var hairColor: String
    var height: Double
    var occupationName: String
    var yearlySalary: Double
```

```
        var experienceYears: Double
}
```

In this example, the `Programmer` structure conforms to all the requirements from both the `Person` and `Occupation` protocols. Keep in mind that the `Person` protocol is a composite of the requirements from the `Name`, `Age`, `Hair`, and `Person` protocols; therefore, the `Programmer` type will need to conform to all those protocols plus the `Occupation` protocol.

Once again, I want to warn you not to make your protocols too granular. Protocol inheritance and composition are really powerful features but can also cause problems if used wrongly.

Protocol composition and inheritance may not seem that powerful on their own; however, when we combine them with protocol extensions, we have a very powerful programming paradigm. Let's look at how powerful this paradigm is.

Protocol-oriented design – putting it all together

We will begin by rewriting the `Animal` superclass as a protocol:

```
protocol Animal {
    var hitPoints: Int { get set }
}
```

In the `Animal` protocol, the only item that we are defining is the `hitPoints` property. If we were putting in all the requirements for an animal in a video game, this protocol would contain all the requirements that would be common to every animal. To be consistent with our object-oriented design, we only need to add the `hitPoints` property to this protocol.

Next, we need to add an `Animal` protocol extension, which will contain the functionality that is common for all types that conform to the protocol. Our `Animal` protocol extension would contain the following code:

```
extension Animal {
    mutating func takeHit(amount: Int) {
        hitPoints -= amount
    }
    func hitPointsRemaining() -> Int {
        return hitPoints
    }
}
```

```
    func isAlive() -> Bool {
        return hitPoints > 0 ? true : false
    }
}
```

The `Animal` protocol extension contains the same `takeHit()`, `hitPointsRemaining()`, and `isAlive()` methods that we saw in the `Animal` superclass from the object-oriented example. Any type that conforms to the `Animal` protocol will automatically inherit these three methods.

Now let's define our `LandAnimal`, `SeaAnimal`, and `AirAnimal` protocols. These protocols will define the requirements for the `land`, `sea`, and `air` animals respectively:

```
protocol LandAnimal: Animal {
    var landAttack: Bool { get }
    var landMovement: Bool { get }

    func doLandAttack()
    func doLandMovement()
}

protocol SeaAnimal: Animal {
    var seaAttack: Bool { get }
    var seaMovement: Bool { get }

    func doSeaAttack()
    func doSeaMovement()
}

protocol AirAnimal: Animal {
    var airAttack: Bool { get }
    var airMovement: Bool { get }

    func doAirAttack()
    func doAirMovement()
}
```

Unlike the `Animal` superclass in the object-oriented design, these three protocols only contain the functionality needed for their particular type of animal. Each of these protocols only contains four lines of code, while the `Animal` superclass from the object-oriented example contains significantly more. This makes our protocol design much easier to read and manage. The protocol design is also much safer because the functionalities for the various animal types are isolated in their own protocols rather than being embedded in a giant superclass. We are also able to avoid the use of flags to define the animal category and, instead, define the category of the animal by the protocols it conforms to.

In a full design, we would probably need to add some protocol extensions for each of the animal types, but once again, to be consistent with our object-oriented design, we do not need them for our example here.

Now, let's look at how we would create our `Lion` and `Alligator` types using protocol-oriented design:

```swift
struct Lion: LandAnimal {
    var hitPoints = 20
    let landAttack = true
    let landMovement = true

    func doLandAttack() {
        print("Lion Attack")
    }
    func doLandMovement() {
        print("Lion Move")
    }
}

struct Alligator: LandAnimal, SeaAnimal {
    var hitPoints = 35
    let landAttack = true
    let landMovement = true
    let seaAttack = true
    let seaMovement = true
```

```
    func doLandAttack() {
        print("Alligator Land Attack")
    }
    func doLandMovement() {
        print("Alligator Land Move")
    }
    func doSeaAttack() {
        print("Alligator Sea Attack")
    }
    func doSeaMovement() {
        print("Alligator Sea Move")
    }
}
```

Notice that we specify that the `Lion` type conforms to the `LandAnimal` protocol, while the `Alligator` type conforms to both the `LandAnimal` and `SeaAnimal` protocols. As we saw previously, having a single type that conforms to multiple protocols is called **protocol composition** and is what allows us to use smaller protocols, rather than one giant monolithic superclass, as we did in the object-oriented example.

Both the `Lion` and `Alligator` types originate from the `Animal` protocol; therefore, they will inherit the functionality added with the `Animal` protocol extension. If our animal type protocols also had extensions, then they would also inherit the function added by those extensions. With protocol inheritance, composition, and extensions, our concrete types contain only the functionality needed by the particular animal types that they conform to, unlike in the object-oriented design, where each animal would contain all of the functionality from the huge, single superclass.

Since the `Lion` and `Alligator` types originate from the `Animal` protocol, we can still use polymorphism as we did in the object-oriented example. Let's look at how this works:

```
var animals = [Animal]()

animals.append(Alligator())
animals.append(Alligator())
animals.append(Lion())

for (index, animal) in animals.enumerated() {
    if let _ = animal as? AirAnimal {
        print("Animal at \(index) is Air")
    }
```

```swift
    if let _ = animal as? LandAnimal {
        print("Animal at \(index) is Land")
    }
    if let _ = animal as? SeaAnimal {
        print("Animal at \(index) is Sea")
    }
}
```

In this example, we create an array that will contain `Animal` types named `animals`. We then create two instances of the `Alligator` type and one instance of the `Lion` type that are added to the `animals` array. Finally, we use a `for-in` loop to loop through the array and print out the animal type based on the protocol that the instance conforms to.

Using the where statement with protocols

With protocols, we are able to use the `where` statement to filter the instances of our types. For example, if we only want to get the instances that conform to the `SeaAnimal` protocol, we can create a `for` loop as follows:

```swift
for (index, animal) in animals.enumerated() where animal is SeaAnimal {
    print("Only Sea Animal: \(index)")
}
```

This will retrieve only the animals that conform to the `SeaAnimal` protocol. This is a lot safer than using flags as we did in the object-oriented design example.

Structures versus classes

You may have noticed that in the object-oriented design we used classes, while in the protocol-oriented design example we used structures. Classes, which are reference types, are one of the pillars of object-oriented programming and every major object-oriented programming language uses them. For Swift, Apple has said that we should prefer value types (structures) to reference types (classes). While this may seem odd for anyone who has extensive experience with object-oriented programming, there are several good reasons for this recommendation.

The biggest reason, in my opinion, for using structures (value types) over classes is the performance gain we get. Value types do not incur the additional overhead for reference counting that reference types incur. Value types are also stored on the stack, which provides better performance as compared to reference types, which are stored on the heap. It is also worth noting that copying values is relatively cheap in Swift.

Keep in mind that, as our value types get large, the performance cost of copying can negate the other performance gains of value types. In the Swift standard library, Apple has implemented copy-on-write behavior to reduce the overhead of copying large value types.

With copy-on-write behavior, we do not create a new copy of our value type when we assign it to a new variable. The copy is postponed until one of the instances changes the value. This means that, if we have an array of 1 million numbers, when we pass this array to another array, we will not make a copy of the 1 million numbers until one of the arrays changes. This can greatly reduce the overhead incurred from copying instances of our value types.

Value types are also a lot safer than reference types, because we do not have multiple references pointing to the same instance, as we do with reference types. This really becomes apparent when we are dealing with a multithreaded environment. Value types are also safer because we do not have memory leaks caused by common programming errors, such as the strong reference cycles that we will discuss in *Chapter 18, Memory Management*.

Don't worry if you do not understand some of the items discussed in this section. The thing to understand is that value types, like structures, are safer, and for the most part provide better performance in Swift, as compared to reference types, such as classes.

Summary

As we have read through this chapter and looked at some of the advantages that protocol-oriented design has over object-oriented design, we may think that protocol-oriented design is clearly superior to object-oriented design. However, this assumption would not be entirely correct.

Object-oriented design has been around since the 1970s and is a tried and true programming paradigm. Protocol-oriented design is the new kid on the block and was designed to correct some of the issues with object-oriented design.

Object-oriented and protocol-oriented design have similar philosophies, such as creating custom types that model real-world objects, and polymorphism to use a single interface to interact with multiple types. The difference is how these philosophies are implemented.

To me, the code base in a project that uses protocol-oriented design is much safer, easier to read, and easier to maintain as compared to a project that uses object-oriented design. This does not mean that I am going to stop using object-oriented design altogether. I can still see a need for a class hierarchy in certain instances.

Remember that when we are designing our application, we should always use the right tool for the job. We would not want to use a chainsaw to cut a piece of 2 x 4 lumber, but we also would not want to use a skill saw to cut down a tree. Therefore, the winner is the programmer who has the choice of using different programming paradigms rather than being limited to only one. In the next chapter, we will look at generics.

11
Generics

My first experience with generics was back in 2004, when they were first introduced in the Java programming language. I can still remember picking up my copy of *The Java Programming Language, Fourth Edition*, which covered Java 5, and reading about Java's implementation of generics. Since then, I have used generics in several projects, not only in Java but also in other languages. If you are familiar with generics in other languages, such as Java, the syntax that Swift uses will be very familiar. Generics allow us to write very flexible and reusable code; however, just like with subscripts, we need to make sure that we use them properly and do not overuse them.

In this chapter, we will cover the following topics:

- What are generics?
- How to create and use generic functions
- How to create and use generic types
- How to use associated types with protocols

Introducing generics

The concept of generics has been around for a while, so it should not be a new concept to developers coming from languages such as Java or C#. The Swift implementation of generics is very similar to these languages. For those developers coming from languages that do not have generics, such as **Objective-C**, they might seem a bit foreign at first, but once you start using them, you will realize how powerful they are.

Generics allow us to write very flexible and reusable code that avoids duplication. With a type-safe language, such as Swift, we often need to write functions, classes, and structures that are valid for multiple types. Without generics, we need to write separate functions for each type we wish to support; however, with generics, we can write one generic function to provide the functionality for multiple types. Generics allow us to tell a function or type, "*I know Swift is a type-safe language, but I do not know the type that will be needed yet. I will give you a placeholder for now and will let you know what type to enforce later.*"

In Swift, we have the ability to define both generic functions and generic types. Let's look at generic functions first.

Generic functions

Let's begin by examining the problem that generics try to solve, and then we will see how generics solve this problem. Let's say that we wanted to create functions that swapped the values of two variables, as described in the first part of this chapter; however, for our application, we need to swap two integer types, two Double types, and two String types. The following code shows what these functions could look like:

```swift
func swapInts(a: inout Int,b: inout Int) {
    let tmp = a
    a = b
    b = tmp
}
func swapDoubles(a: inout Double,b: inout Double) {
    let tmp = a
    a = b
    b = tmp
}
func swapStrings(a: inout String, b: inout String) {
    let tmp = a
    a = b
    b = tmp
}
```

With these three functions, we can swap the original values of two `Integer` types, two `Double` types, and two `String` types. Now, let's say, as we develop our application further, we find out that we also need to swap the values of two unsigned `Integer` types, two `Float` types, and even a couple of custom types. We might easily end up with eight or more swap functions. The worst part is that each of these functions contains duplicate code. The only difference between these functions is that the parameter types change. While this solution does work, generics offer a much simpler and more elegant solution that eliminates all the duplicate code. Let's see how we would condense all three of the preceding functions into a single generic function:

```
func swapGeneric<T>(a: inout T, b: inout T) {
    let tmp = a
    a = b
    b = tmp
}
```

Let's look at how we defined the `swapGeneric` function. The function itself looks pretty similar to a normal function, except for the capital `T`. The capital `T`, as used in the `swapGeneric` function, is a placeholder type, and tells Swift that we will be defining the type later. When a type is defined, it will be used in place of all the placeholders.

To define a generic function, we include the placeholder type between two angular brackets (`<T>`) after the function's name. We can then use that placeholder type in place of any type definition within the parameter definitions, the return type, or the function itself. The big thing to keep in mind is that, once the placeholder is defined as a type, all the other placeholders assume that type. Therefore, any variable or constant defined with that placeholder must conform to that type.

There is nothing special about the capital `T`; we could use any valid identifier in place of `T`. We can also use descriptive names, such as key and value, as the Swift language does with dictionaries. The following definitions are perfectly valid:

```
func swapGeneric<G>(a: inout G, b: inout G) {
    //Statements
}
func swapGeneric<xyz>(a: inout xyz, b: inout xyz) {
    //Statements
}
```

In most documentation, generic placeholders are defined with either T (for type) or E (for element). We will, for the purposes of this chapter, use the capital T to define generic placeholders. It is also good practice to use the capital T to define a generic placeholder within our code so that the placeholder is easily recognized when we are looking at the code at a later time.

> If you do not like using the capital T or capital E to define generics, try to be consistent. I would recommend that you avoid the use of different identifiers to define generics throughout your code.

If we need to use multiple generic types, we can create multiple placeholders by separating them with commas. The following example shows how to define multiple placeholders for a single function:

```
func testGeneric<T,E>(a: T, b: E) {
    //Statements
}
```

In this example, we are defining two generic placeholders, T and E. In this case, we can set the T placeholder to one type and the E placeholder to a different type.

Let's look at how to call a generic function. The following code will swap two integers using the swapGeneric<T>(inout a: T, inout b: T) function:

```
var a = 5
var b = 10
swapGeneric(a: &a, b: &b)
print("a:\(a) b:\(b)")
```

If we run this code, the output will be a: 10 b: 5. We can see that we do not have to do anything special to call a generic function. The function infers the type from the first parameter and then sets all the remaining placeholders to that type. Now, if we need to swap the values of two strings, we will call the same function, as follows:

```
var c = "My String 1"
var d = "My String 2"
swapGeneric(a: &c, b: &d)
print("c:\(c) d:\(d)")
```

We can see that the function is called in exactly the same way as we called it when we wanted to swap two integers. One thing that we cannot do is pass two different types into the swap function, because we defined only one generic placeholder. If we attempt to run the following code, we will receive an error:

```
var a = 5
var c = "My String 1"
swapGeneric(a: &a, b: &c)
```

The error that we will receive is that it cannot convert the value of type String to expected argument type Int, which tells us that we are attempting to use a String value when an Int value is expected. The reason the function is looking for an Int value is because the first parameter that we pass into the function is an Int value, and, therefore, all the generic types in the function become Int types.

Now, let's say we have the following function, which has multiple generic types defined:

```
func testGeneric<T,E>(a: T, b: E) {
    print("\(a)\(b)")
}
```

This function would accept parameters of different types; however, since they are of different types, we would be unable to swap the values because they are different. There are also other limitations to generics. For example, we may think that the following generic function would be valid; however, we would receive an error if we tried to implement it:

```
func genericEqual<T>(a: T, b: T) -> Bool{
    return a == b
}
```

We receive an error because the binary operator == cannot be applied to two T operands. Since the type of the arguments is unknown at the time the code is compiled, Swift does not know whether it can use the equal operator on the types, and, therefore, an error is thrown. We might think that this is a limit that will make generics hard to use. However, we have a way to tell Swift that we expect the type, represented by a placeholder, to have a certain functionality. This is done with type constraints.

A type constraint specifies that a generic type must inherit from a specific class or conform to a particular protocol. This allows us to use the methods or properties defined by the parent class or protocol within the generic function. Let's look at how to use type constraints by rewriting the genericEqual function to use the Comparable protocol:

```
func testGenericComparable<T: Comparable>(a: T, b: T) -> Bool{
    a == b
}
```

To specify the type constraint, we put the class or protocol constraint after the generic placeholder, where the generic placeholder and the constraint are separated by a colon. This new function works as we might expect, and it will compare the values of the two parameters and return `true` if they are equal or `false` if they are not.

We can declare multiple constraints just like we declare multiple generic types. The following example shows how to declare two generic types with different constraints:

```
func testFunction<T: MyClass, E: MyProtocol>(a: T, b: E) {
    //Statements
}
```

In this function, the type defined by the `T` placeholder must inherit from the `MyClass` class, and the type defined by the `E` placeholder must conform to the `MyProtocol` protocol. Now that we have looked at generic functions, let's look at generic types.

Generic types

We already had a general introduction to how generic types work when we looked at Swift arrays and dictionaries. A generic type is a class, structure, or enumeration that can work with any type, just like the way Swift arrays and dictionaries work. As we recall, Swift arrays and dictionaries are written so that they can contain any type. The catch is that we cannot mix and match different types within an array or dictionary. When we create an instance of our generic type, we define the type that the instance will work with. After we define that type, we cannot change the type for that instance.

To demonstrate how to create a generic type, let's create a simple `List` class. This class will use a Swift array as the backend storage for the list, and will let us add items to the list or retrieve values from the list.

Let's begin by seeing how to define our generic `List` type:

```
class List<T> {
}
```

The preceding code defines the generic `List` type. We can see that we use the `<T>` tag to define a generic placeholder, just like we did when we defined a generic function. This `T` placeholder can then be used anywhere within the type instead of a concrete type definition.

To create an instance of this type, we would need to define the type of items that our list will hold. The following example shows how to create instances of the generic List type for various types:

```
var stringList = List<String>()
var intList = List<Int>()
var customList = List<MyObject>()
```

The preceding example creates three instances of the List class. The stringList instance can be used with instances of the String type, the intList instance can be used with instances of the integer type, and the customList instance can be used with instances of the MyObject type.

We are not limited to using generics only with classes. We can also define structures and enumerations as generics. The following example shows how to define a generic structure and a generic enumeration:

```
struct GenericStruct<T> {
}
    enum GenericEnum<T> {
}
```

Now let's add the backend storage array to our List class. The items that are stored in this array need to be of the same type that we define when we initiate the class; therefore, we will use the T placeholder for the array's definition. The following code shows the List class with an array named items. The items array will be defined using the T placeholder, so it will hold the same types that we defined for the class:

```
class List<T> {
    var items = [T]()
}
```

This code defines our generic List type and uses T as the type placeholder. We can then use this T placeholder anywhere in the class to define the type of an item. That item will then be of the same type that we defined when we created the instance of the List class. Therefore, if we create an instance of the List type, such as var stringList = List<String>(), the items array will be an array of string instances. If we created an instance of the List type, such as var intList = List<Int>(), the items array will be an array of integer instances.

Now, we need to create the add() method, which will be used to add an item to the list. We will use the T placeholder within the method declaration to define that the item parameter will be of the same type that we declared when we initiated the class. Therefore, if we create an instance of the List type to use the String type, we will be required to use an instance of the String type as the parameter for the add() method. However, if we create an instance of the List type to use the Int type, we will be required to use an instance of the Int type as the parameter for the add() method.

Here is the code for the add() function:

```
func add(item: T) {
    items.append(item)
}
```

To create a standalone generic function, we add the <T> declaration after the function name to declare that it is a generic function; however, when we use a generic method within a generic type, we do not need the <T> declaration. Instead, we just need to use the type that we defined in the class declaration. If we wanted to introduce another generic type, we could define it with the method declaration.

Now, let's add the getItemAtIndex() method, which will return the item from the backend array, at the specified index:

```
func getItemAtIndex(index: Int) -> T? {
    if items.count>index {
        return items[index]
    } else {
        return nil
    }
}
```

The getItemAtIndex() method accepts one argument, which is the index of the item we want to retrieve. We then use the T placeholder to specify that our return type is an optional that might be of the T type or that might be nil. If the backend storage array contains an item at the specified index, we will return that item; otherwise, we return nil.

Now, let's look at our entire generic List class:

```
class List<T> {
    var items = [T]()

    func add(item: T) {
        items.append(item)
```

```
        }

    func getItemAtIndex(index: Int) -> T? {
        guard items.count < index else {
            return items[index]
        }
        return nil
    }
}
```

As we can see, we initially defined the generic T placeholder type in the class declaration. We then used this placeholder type within our class. In our List class, we used this placeholder in three places. We used it as the type for our items array, as the parameter type for our add() method, and as the optional return type in the getItemAtIndex() method.

Now, let's look at how to use the List class. When we use a generic type, we define the type to be used within the class between angled brackets, such as <type>. The following code shows how to use the List class to store instances of the String type:

```
var list = List<String>()
list.add(item: "Hello")
list.add(item: "World")
print(list.getItemAtIndex(index: 1))
```

In the preceding code, we start off by creating an instance of the List type, called list, and specify that it will store instances of the String type. We then use the add() method twice to store two items in the list instance. Finally, we use the getItemAtIndex() method to retrieve the item at index number 1, which will display Optional(World) to the console.

We can also define our generic types with multiple placeholder types, similarly to how we use multiple placeholders in our generic methods. To use multiple placeholder types, we separate them with commas. The following example shows how to define multiple placeholder types:

```
class MyClass<T,E>{
//Code
}
```

We then create an instance of the MyClass type that uses instances of the String and Int types, like this:

```
var mc = MyClass<String, Int>()
```

We can also use type constraints with generic types. Once again, using a type constraint for a generic type is exactly the same as using one with a generic function. The following code shows how to use a type constraint to ensure that the generic type conforms to the Comparable protocol:

```
class MyClass<T: Comparable>{}
```

So far in this chapter, we have seen how to use placeholder types with functions and types. Now let's see how we can conditionally add extensions to a generic type.

Conditionally adding extensions with generics

We can add extensions to a generic type conditionally if the type conforms to a protocol. For example, if we wanted to add a sum() method to our generic List type only if the type for T conforms to the numeric protocol, we could do the following:

```
extension List where T: Numeric {
    func sum () -> T {
        items.reduce (0, +)
    }
}
```

This extension adds the sum() method to any list instance where the T type conforms to the numeric protocol. This means that the list instance in the previous example, where the list was created to hold String instances, would not receive this method.

In the following code, where we create an instance of the List type that contains integers, the instance will receive sum() and can be used as shown:

```
var list2 = List<Int>()
list2.add(item: 2)
list2.add(item: 4)
list2.add(item: 6)
print(list2.sum())
```

The output of this would be 12. We are also able to conditionally add functions inside a generic type or extension.

Conditionally adding functions

Conditionally adding extensions, as we saw in the last section, works great; however, if we had separate functionality that we wished to add for different conditions, we would have to create separate extensions for each condition. Starting in Swift 5.3 with SE-0267, we are able to conditionally add functions to a generic type or extension. Let's take a look at this by rewriting the extension in the previous section:

```
extension List {
    func sum () -> T where T: Numeric {
        items.reduce (0, +)
    }
}
```

With this code, we moved the where T: Numeric clause out of the extensions declaration and into the function declaration. This will conditionally add the function if the type conforms to the Numeric protocol. Now we can add additional functions to the extension with different conditions as shown in the following code:

```
extension List {
    func sum () -> T where T: Numeric {
        items.reduce (0, +)
    }
    func sorted() -> [T] where T: Comparable {
        items.sorted()
    }
}
```

In the previous code, we added an additional function named sorted() that will only be applied to instances where the type conforms to the Comparable protocol. This enables us to put functions with different conditions in the same extension or generic type rather than creating multiple extensions. I would definitely recommend conditionally adding functions, as shown in this section, over conditionally adding extensions, as shown in the previous section.

Now let's look at conditional conformance.

Conditional conformance

Conditional conformance allows a generic type to conform to a protocol only if the type meets certain conditions. For example, if we wanted our List type to conform to the Equatable protocol only if the type stored in the list also conformed to the Equatable protocol, we could use the following code:

```
extension List: Equatable where T: Equatable {
    static func ==(l1:List, l2:List) -> Bool {
        if l1.items.count != l2.items.count {
            return false
        }
        for (e1, e2) in zip(l1.items, l2.items) {
            if e1 != e2 {
                return false
            }
        }
        return true
    }
}
```

This code will add conformance to the `Equatable` protocol to any instance of the `List` type where the type that is stored in the list also conforms to the `Equatable` protocol.

> There is a new function shown here that we have not talked about: the `zip()` function. This function will loop through two sequences, in our case arrays, simultaneously and create pairs (e1 and e2) that we can compare.

The comparison function will first check to see that each array contains the same number of elements and if not, it will return `false`. It then loops through each array, simultaneously comparing the elements of the arrays; if any of the pairs do not match, it will return `false`. If the previous tests pass, `true` is returned, which indicates that the `list` instances are equal because the elements in the list are the same.

Now let's see how we can add generic subscripts to a non-generic type.

Generic subscripts

Prior to Swift 4, if we wanted to use generics with a subscript, we had to define the subscript at the class or structure level. This forced us to make generic methods when it felt like we should be using subscripts. Starting with Swift 4, we can create generic subscripts, where either the subscript's return type or its parameters may be generic. Let's look at how we can create a generic subscript. In this first example, we will create a subscript that will accept one generic parameter:

```
subscript<T: Hashable>(item: T) -> Int {
    return item.hashValue
}
```

When we create a generic subscript, we define the placeholder type after the `subscript` keyword. In the previous example, we define the `T` placeholder type and use a type constraint to ensure that the type conforms to the `Hashable` protocol. This will allow us to pass in an instance of any type that conforms to the `Hashable` protocol.

As we mentioned at the start of this section, we can also use generics for the return type of a subscript. We define the generic placeholder for the return type exactly as we did for the generic parameter. The following example illustrates this:

```
subscript<T>(key: String) -> T? {
    return dictionary[key] as? T
}
```

In this example, we define the `T` placeholder type after the `subscript` keyword, as we did in the previous example. We then use this type as our return type for the subscript.

Associated types

An associated type declares a placeholder name that can be used instead of a type within a protocol. The actual type to be used is not specified until the protocol is adopted. When creating generic functions and types, we used a very similar syntax, as we have seen throughout this chapter. Defining associated types for a protocol, however, is very different. We specify an associated type using the `associatedtype` keyword.

Let's see how to use associated types when we define a protocol. In this example, we will define the `QueueProtocol` protocol, which defines the capabilities that need to be implemented by the queue that implements it:

```
protocol QueueProtocol {
    associatedtype QueueType
    mutating func add(item: QueueType)
    mutating func getItem() -> QueueType?
    func count() -> Int
}
```

In this protocol, we defined one associated type, named `QueueType`. We then used this associated type twice within the protocol: once as the parameter type for the `add()` method and once when we defined the return type of the `getItem()` method as an optional type that might return an associated type of `QueueType` or `nil`.

Any type that implements the QueueProtocol protocol must be able to specify the type to use for the QueueType placeholder, and must also ensure that only items of that type are used where the protocol uses the QueueType placeholder.

Let's look at how to implement QueueProtocol in a non-generic class called IntQueue. This class will implement the QueueProtocol protocol using the Integer type:

```
class IntQueue: QueueProtocol {
    var items = [Int]()
    func add(item: Int) {
        items.append(item)
    }
    func getItem() -> Int? {
        return items.count > 0 ? items.remove(at: 0) : nil
    }
    func count() -> Int {
        return items.count
    }
}
```

In the IntQueue class, we begin by defining our backend storage mechanism as an array of integer types. We then implement each of the methods defined in the QueueProtocol protocol, replacing the QueueType placeholder defined in the protocol with the Int type. In the add() method, the parameter type is defined as an instance of Int type, and in the getItem() method, the return type is defined as an optional that might return an instance of Int type or nil.

We use the IntQueue class as we would use any other class. The following code shows this:

```
var intQ = IntQueue()
intQ.add(item: 2)
intQ.add(item: 4)
print(intQ.getItem()!)
intQ.add(item: 6)
```

We begin by creating an instance of the IntQueue class, named intQ. We then call the add() method twice to add two values of the integer type to the intQ instance. We then retrieve the first item in the intQ instance by calling the getItem() method. This line will print the number 2 to the console. The final line of code adds another instance of the integer type to the intQ instance.

In the preceding example, we implemented the QueueProtocol protocol in a non-generic way. This means that we replaced the placeholder types with an actual type. QueueType was replaced by the Int type. We can also implement QueueProtocol with a generic type. Let's see how we would do this:

```
class GenericQueue<T>: QueueProtocol {
    var items = [T]()
    func add(item: T) {
        items.append(item)
    }
    func getItem() -> T? {
        return items.count > 0 ? items.remove(at:0) : nil
    }
    func count() -> Int {
        return items.count
    }
}
```

As we can see, the GenericQueue implementation is very similar to the IntQueue implementation, except that we define the type to use as the generic placeholder T. We can then use the GenericQueue class as we would use any generic class. Let's look at how to use the GenericQueue class:

```
var intQ2 = GenericQueue<Int>()
intQ2.add(item: 2)
intQ2.add(item: 4)
print(intQ2.getItem()!)
intQ2.add(item: 6)
```

We begin by creating an instance of the GenericQueue class that will use the Int type and name it intQ2. Next, we call the add() method twice to add two instances of the integer type to the intQ2 instance. We then retrieve the first item in the queue that was added using the getItem() method and print the value to the console. This line will print the number 2 to the console.

We can also use type constraints with associated types. When the protocol is adopted, the type defined for the associated type must inherit from the class or conform to the protocol defined by the type constraint. The following line defines an associated type with a type constraint:

```
associatedtype QueueType: Hashable
```

In this example, we specify that when the protocol is implemented, the type defined for the associated type must conform to the Hashable protocol.

Summary

Generic types can be incredibly useful, and they are also the basis of the Swift standard collection types (arrays and dictionaries); however, as mentioned in the introduction to this chapter, we have to be careful to use them correctly.

We saw a couple of examples in this chapter that show how generics can make our lives easier. The swapGeneric() function that was shown at the beginning of the chapter is a good use of a generic function because it allows us to swap two values of any type we choose, while only implementing the swap code once.

The generic List type is also a good example of how to make custom collection types that can be used to hold any type. The way that we implemented the generic List type in this chapter is similar to how Swift implements an array and dictionary with generics.

In the next chapter, we will look at error handling with Swift and how we can make a feature available only if the device that the user is using has a certain version of the OS.

12

Error Handling and Availability

When I first started writing applications with Objective-C, one of the most noticeable deficiencies was the lack of exception handling. Most modern programming languages, such as Java and C#, use `try...catch` blocks, or something similar, for exception handling. While Objective-C did have the `try...catch` block, it wasn't used within the Cocoa framework itself, and it never really felt like a true part of the language. I have significant experience in C, so I was able to understand how Apple's frameworks received and responded to errors. To be honest, I sometimes preferred this method, even though I had grown accustomed to exception handling with Java and C#. When Swift was first introduced, I was hoping that Apple would put true error handling into the language so that we would have the option of using it; however, it was not in the initial release of Swift. It wasn't until Swift 2 was released that Apple added error handling to Swift. While this kind of error handling may look similar to exception handling in Java and C#, there are some very significant differences.

We will cover the following topics in this chapter:

- How to represent errors
- How to use the `do-catch` block in Swift
- How to use the `defer` statement
- How to use the availability attribute

Let's get started!

Native error handling

Languages such as Java and C# generally refer to the error handling process as exception handling. Within the Swift documentation, Apple refers to this process as error handling. While on the outside, Java and C# exception handling may look somewhat similar to Swift's error handling, there are some significant differences that those familiar with exception handling in other languages will notice throughout this chapter.

Representing errors

Before we can really understand how error handling works in Swift, we must see how we can represent an error. In Swift, errors are represented by values of types that conform to the Error protocol. Swift's enumerations are very well suited to modeling error conditions because we generally have a finite number of error conditions to represent.

Let's look at how we would use an enumeration to represent an error. For this, we will define a fictitious error named MyError with three error conditions, Minor, Bad, and Terrible:

```
enum MyError: Error {
    case Minor
    case Bad
    case Terrible
}
```

In this example, we defined that the MyError enumeration conforms to the Error protocol and also defined three error conditions: Minor, Bad, and Terrible. That is all there is to defining basic error conditions.

We can also use the associated values with our error conditions to add more details about the error condition. Let's say that we want to add a description to the Terrible error condition. We would do so like this:

```
enum MyError: Error {
    case Minor
    case Bad
    case Terrible(description:String)
}
```

Those who are familiar with exception handling in Java and C# can see that representing errors in Swift is a lot cleaner and easier, because we do not need to create a lot of boilerplate code or a full class. With Swift, it can be as simple as defining an enumeration with our error conditions. Another advantage is that it is very easy to define multiple error conditions and group them together so that all the related error conditions are of one type.

Now, let's learn how to model errors in Swift. For this example, we'll look at how we would assign numbers to players on a baseball team. For a baseball team, every new player who is called up is assigned a unique number. This number must also be within a certain range, because only two numbers fit on a baseball jersey.

Therefore, we would have three error conditions: the number is too large, the number is too small, and the number is not unique. The following example shows how we might represent these error conditions:

```
enum PlayerNumberError: Error {
    case NumberTooHigh(description: String)
    case NumberTooLow(description: String)
    case NumberAlreadyAssigned
}
```

With the `PlayerNumberError` type, we define three very specific error conditions that tell us exactly what went wrong. These error conditions are also grouped together in one type since they are all related to assigning the players' numbers.

This method of defining errors allows us to define very specific errors that let our code know exactly what went wrong if an error condition occurs. It also lets us group the errors so that all related errors can be defined in the same type.

Now that we know how to represent errors, let's look at how to throw errors.

Throwing errors

When an error occurs in a function, the code that called the function must be made aware of it; this is called **throwing an error**. When a function throws an error, it assumes that the code that called the function, or some code further up the chain, will catch and recover appropriately from the error.

To throw an error from a function, we use the `throws` keyword. This keyword lets the code that called it know that an error may be thrown from the function. Unlike exception handling in other languages, we do not list the specific error types that may be thrown.

Since we do not list the specific error types that may be thrown from a function within the function's definition, it would be good practice to list them in the documentation and comments for the function. This allows other developers who use the function to know what error types to catch.

Soon, we will look at how to throw errors. But first, let's add a fourth error to the `PlayerNumberError` type that we defined earlier. This demonstrates how easy it is to add error conditions to our error types. This error condition is thrown if we are trying to retrieve a player by their number, but no player has been assigned that number.

The new `PlayerNumberError` type will now look similar to this:

```
enum PlayerNumberError: Error {
    case NumberTooHigh(description: String)
    case NumberTooLow(description: String)
    case NumberAlreadyAssigned
    case NumberDoesNotExist
}
```

To demonstrate how to throw errors, let's create a `BaseballTeam` structure that will contain a list of players for a given team. These players will be stored in a dictionary object named `players`. We will use the player's number as the key because we know that each player must have a unique number. The `BaseballPlayer` type, which will be used to represent a single player, will be a `typealias` for a tuple type, and is defined like this:

```
typealias BaseballPlayer = (firstName: String, lastName: String,
number: Int)
```

In this `BaseballTeam` structure, we will have two methods. The first one will be named `addPlayer()`. This method will accept one parameter of the `BaseballPlayer` type and attempt to add the player to the team. This method can also throw one of three error conditions: `NumberTooHigh`, `NumberTooLow`, or `NumberAlreadyExists`. Here is how we would write this method:

```
mutating func addPlayer(player: BaseballPlayer) throws {
    guard player.number < maxNumber else {
        throw PlayerNumberError.NumberTooHigh(description: "Max
        number is \(maxNumber)")
    }
```

```
        guard player.number > minNumber else {
            throw PlayerNumberError.NumberTooLow(description: "Min number
            is \(minNumber)")
        }
        guard players[player.number] == nil else {
            throw PlayerNumberError.NumberAlreadyAssigned
        }
        players[player.number] = player
    }
```

We can see that the `throws` keyword is added to the method's definition. The `throws` keyword lets any code that calls this method know that it may throw an error and that the error must be handled. We then use the three `guard` statements to verify that the number is not too large, not too small, and is unique in the `players` dictionary. If any of these conditions are not met, we throw the appropriate error using the `throw` keyword. If we make it through all three checks, the player is then added to the `players` dictionary.

The second method that we will be adding to the `BaseballTeam` structure is the `getPlayerByNumber()` method. This method will attempt to retrieve the baseball player that has been assigned a given number. If no player is assigned that number, this method will throw a `NumberDoesNotExist` error. The `getPlayerByNumber()` method will look similar to this:

```
func getPlayerByNumber(number: Int) throws -> BaseballPlayer {
    if let player = players[number] {
        return player
    } else {
        throw PlayerNumberError.NumberDoesNotExist
    }
}
```

We have added the `throws` keyword to this method definition as well; however, this method also has a return type. When we use the `throws` keyword with a return type, it must be placed before the return type in the method's definition.

Within the method, we attempt to retrieve the baseball player with the number that is passed into the method. If we can retrieve the player, we return it; otherwise, we throw the `NumberDoesNotExist` error. Note that if we throw an error from a method that has a return type, a return value is not required.

Now, let's learn how to catch an error with Swift.

Catching errors

When an error is thrown from a function, we need to catch it in the code that called it; this is done using the do-catch block. We use the try keyword, within the do-catch block, to identify the places in the code that may throw an error. The do-catch block with a try statement has the following syntax:

```
do {
    try [Some function that throws]
    [Code if no error was thrown]
} catch [pattern] {
    [Code if function threw error]
}
```

If an error is thrown, it is propagated out until it is handled by a catch clause. The catch clause consists of the catch keyword, followed by a pattern to match the error against. If the error matches the pattern, the code within the catch block is executed.

Let's look at how to use the do-catch block by calling both the getPlayerByNumber() and addPlayer() methods of the BaseballTeam structure. Let's look at the getPlayerByNumber() method first, since it only throws one error condition:

```
do {
    let player = try myTeam.getPlayerByNumber(number: 34)
    print("Player is \(player.firstName) \(player.lastName)")
} catch PlayerNumberError.NumberDoesNotExist {
    print("No player has that number")
}
```

Within this example, the do-catch block calls the getPlayerByNumber() method of the BaseballTeam structure. This method will throw the NumberDoesNotExist error condition if no player on the team has been assigned this number; therefore, we attempt to match this error in the catch statement.

Any time an error is thrown within a do-catch block, the remainder of the code within the block is skipped and the code within the catch block that matches the error is executed. Therefore, in our example, if the NumberDoesNotExist error is thrown by the getPlayerByNumber() method, the first print statement is never reached.

We do not have to include a pattern after the catch statement. If a pattern is not included after the catch statement, or if we put in an underscore, the catch statement will match all the error conditions. For example, either one of the following two catch statements will catch all errors:

```
do {
    // our statements
} catch {
    // our error conditions
}
do {
    // our statements
} catch _ {
    // our error conditions
}
```

If we want to capture the error, we can use the `let` keyword, as shown in the following example:

```
do {
    // our statements
} catch let error {
    print("Error:\(error)")
}
```

Now, let's look at how to use the `catch` statement, similar to a `switch` statement, to catch different error conditions. To do this, we will call the `addPlayer()` method of the `BaseballTeam` structure:

```
do {
    try myTeam.addPlayer(player:("David", "Ortiz", 34))
} catch PlayerNumberError.NumberTooHigh(let description) {
    print("Error: \(description)")
} catch PlayerNumberError.NumberTooLow(let description) {
    print("Error: \(description)")
} catch PlayerNumberError.NumberAlreadyAssigned {
    print("Error: Number already assigned")
}
```

In this example, we have three `catch` statements. Each `catch` statement has a different pattern to match; therefore, they will each match a different error condition. As you may recall, the `NumberTooHigh` and `NumberToLow` error conditions have associated values. To retrieve the associated values, we use the `let` statement within parentheses, as shown in the preceding example.

It is always good practice to make your last `catch` statement an empty `catch` statement so that it will catch any errors that did not match any of the patterns in the previous `catch` statements. Therefore, the previous example should be rewritten like this:

```
do {
    try myTeam.addPlayer(player:("David", "Ortiz", 34))
} catch PlayerNumberError.NumberTooHigh(let description) {
    print("Error: \(description)")
} catch PlayerNumberError.NumberTooLow(let description) {
    print("Error: \(description)")
} catch PlayerNumberError.NumberAlreadyAssigned {
    print("Error: Number already assigned")
} catch {
    print("Error: Unknown Error")
}
```

We can also let the errors propagate out rather than immediately catching them. To do this, we just need to add the throws keyword to the function definition. For instance, in the following example, rather than catching the error, we could let it propagate out to the code that called the function, like this:

```
func myFunc() throws {
    try myTeam.addPlayer(player:("David", "Ortiz", 34))
}
```

If we are certain that an error will not be thrown, we can call the function using a forced-try expression, which is written as try!. The forced-try expression disables error propagation and wraps the function call in a runtime assertion so no error will be thrown from this call. If an error is thrown, you will get a runtime error, so be very careful when using this expression.

 It is highly recommended that you avoid using the forced-try expression in production code since it can cause a runtime error and cause your application to crash.

When I work with exceptions in languages such as Java and C#, I see a lot of empty catch blocks. This is where we need to catch the exception, because one might be thrown; however, we do not want to do anything with it. In Swift, the code would look something like this:

```
do {
    let player = try myTeam.getPlayerByNumber(number: 34)
    print("Player is \(player.firstName) \(player.lastName)")
} catch {}
```

Code like this is one of the things that I dislike about exception handling. Well, the Swift developers have an answer for this: try?. This attempts to perform an operation that may throw an error and converts it into an optional value; therefore, the result of the operation will be either nil if an error is thrown, or the result of the operation if no error is thrown.

Since the results of try? are returned in the form of an optional, we would normally use this with optional binding. We could rewrite the previous example like this:

```
if let player = try? myTeam.getPlayerByNumber(number: 34) {
    print("Player is \(player.firstName) \(player.lastName)")
}
```

As we can see, this makes our code much cleaner and easier to read.

If we need to perform a cleanup action, regardless of whether we had any errors, we can use a defer statement. We use defer statements to execute a block of code just before the code execution leaves the current scope. The following example shows how we can use the defer statement:

```
func deferFunction(){
    print("Function started")
    var str: String?

    defer {
        print("In defer block")
        if let s = str {
            print("str is \(s)")
        }
    }
    str = "Jon"
    print("Function finished")
}
```

If we called this function, the first line to be printed to the console would be Function started. The code's execution would skip over the defer block, and Function finished would then be printed to the console. Finally, the defer block of code would be executed just before we leave the function's scope, and we would see the In defer block message. The following is the output of this function:

```
Function started
Function finished
In defer block
str is Jon
```

The defer block will always be called before the execution leaves the current scope, even if an error is thrown. The defer statement is very useful when we want to make sure we perform all the necessary cleanup, even if an error is thrown. For example, if we successfully open a file to write to, we will always want to make sure we close that file, even if we encounter an error during the write operation.

In this case, we could put the file-closed functionality in a defer block to make sure that the file is always closed prior to leaving the current scope.

Multi-pattern catch clauses

In the previous section, we had code that looked like this:

```
do {
    try myTeam.addPlayer(player:("David", "Ortiz", 34))
} catch PlayerNumberError.NumberTooHigh(let description) {
    print("Error: \(description)")
} catch PlayerNumberError.NumberTooLow(let description) {
    print("Error: \(description)")
} catch PlayerNumberError.NumberAlreadyAssigned {
    print("Error: Number already assigned")
} catch {
    print("Error: Unknown Error")
}
```

You will notice that the catch clause for the PlayerNmberError.NumberTooHigh and PlayerNumberError.NumberTooLow errors contains duplicate code. When you are developing, it is always good to find a way to eliminate duplicate code like this. However, prior to Swift 5.3, we did not have a choice. Swift introduced multi-pattern catch clauses with SE-0276 in Swift 5.3 to help reduce duplicate code like this. Let's take a look at this by rewriting the previous code to use a multi-pattern catch clause:

```
do {
    try myTeam.addPlayer(player:("David", "Ortiz", 34))
} catch PlayerNumberError.NumberTooHigh(let description),
PlayerNumberError.NumberTooLow(let description) {
    print("Error: \(description)")
} catch PlayerNumberError.NumberAlreadyAssigned {
    print("Error: Number already assigned")
} catch {
    print("Error: Unknown Error")
}
```

Notice that in the first `catch` clause, we are now catching both the `PlayerNmberError.NumberTooHigh` and `PlayerNumberError.NumberTooLow` errors and that the errors are separated by a comma.

Next, we'll look at how to use the new availability attribute with Swift.

The availability attribute

Developing our applications for the latest **Operating System (OS)** version gives us access to all the latest features for the platform that we are developing for. However, there are times when we want to also target older platforms. Swift allows us to use the availability attribute to safely wrap code to run only when the correct version of the operating system is available. This was first introduced in Swift 2.

 The availability attribute is only available when we use Swift on Apple platforms.

The availability block essentially lets us, if we are running the specified version of the operating system or higher, run this code or otherwise run some other code. There are two ways in which we can use the availability attribute. The first way allows us to execute a specific block of code that can be used with an `if` or a `guard` statement. The second way allows us to mark a method or type as available only on certain platforms.

The availability attribute accepts up to six comma-separated arguments, which allow us to define the minimum version of the operating system or application extension needed to execute our code. These arguments are as follows:

- `iOS`: This is the minimum iOS version that is compatible with our code.
- `OSX`: This is the minimum OS X version that is compatible with our code.
- `watchOS`: This is the minimum watchOS version that is compatible with our code.
- `tvOS`: This is the minimum tvOS version that is compatible with our code.
- `iOSApplicationExtension`: This is the minimum iOS application extension that is compatible with our code.
- `OSXApplicationExtension`: This is the minimum OS X application extension that is compatible with our code.

After the argument, we specify the minimum version that is required. We only need to include the arguments that are compatible with our code. As an example, if we are writing an iOS application, we only need to include the iOS argument in the availability attribute. We end the argument list with an * (asterisk) as it is a placeholder for future versions. Let's look at how we would execute a specific block of code only if we met the minimum requirements:

```
if #available(iOS 9.0, OSX 10.10, watchOS 2, *) {
    //Available for iOS 9, OSX 10.10, watchOS 2 or above
    print("Minimum requirements met")
} else {
    //Block on anything below the above minimum requirements
    print("Minimum requirements not met")
}
```

In this example, the `if #available(iOS 9.0, OSX 10.10, watchOS 2, *)` line of code prevents the block of code from executing when the application is run on a system that does not meet the specified minimum operating system version. In this example, we also use the `else` statement to execute a separate block of code if the operating system does not meet the minimum requirements.

We can also restrict access to a function or a type. In the previous code, the `available` attribute was prefixed with the # (pound, also known as **octothorpe** and **hash**) character. To restrict access to a function or type, we prefix the `available` attribute with an @ (at) character. The following example shows how we could restrict access to a type and function:

```
@available(iOS 9.0, *)
    func testAvailability() {
        // Function only available for iOS 9 or above
}
@available(iOS 9.0, *)
    struct TestStruct {
        // Type only available for iOS 9 or above
}
```

In the previous example, we specified that the `testAvailability()` function and the `testStruct()` type could only be accessed if the code was run on a device that has iOS version 9 or newer. In order to use the `@available` attribute to block access to a function or type, we must wrap the code that calls that function or type with the `#available` attribute.

The following example shows how we could call the `testAvailability()` function:

```
if #available(iOS 9.0, *) {
    testAvailability()
} else {
    // Fallback on earlier versions
}
```

In this example, the `testAvailability()` function is only called if the application is running on a device that has iOS version 9 or later.

Summary

In this chapter, we looked at Swift's error handling features. While we are not required to use these features in our custom types, they do give us a uniform way to handle and respond to errors. Apple has also started to use this form of error handling in their frameworks. It is recommended that we use error handling in our code.

We also looked at the availability attribute, which allows us to develop applications that take advantage of the latest features of our target operating systems, while still allowing our applications to run on older versions. In the next chapter, we'll take a look at how to write custom subscripts.

13
Custom Subscripting

Custom subscripts were added to Objective-C in 2012. At that time, Chris Lattner was already two years into developing Swift and, like other good features, subscripts were added to the Swift language. I have not used custom subscripts in many other languages; however, I do find myself using subscripts extensively when I am developing in Swift. The syntax for using subscripts seems like a natural part of the language, possibly because they were part of the language when it was released and not added in later. Once you start using them, you may find them indispensable.

In this chapter, we will cover the following topics:

- What are custom subscripts?
- Adding custom subscripts to classes, structures, or enumerations
- Creating read/write and read-only subscripts
- Using external names without custom subscripts
- Using multidimensional subscripts

Introducing subscripts

Subscripts, in the Swift language, are used as shortcuts for accessing elements of a collection, list, or sequence. We can use them in our custom types to set or retrieve the values by index rather than by using getter and setter methods. Subscripts, if used correctly, can significantly enhance the usability and readability of our custom types.

We can define multiple subscripts for a single type. When types have multiple subscripts, the appropriate subscript will be chosen based on the type of index passed in with the subscript. We can also set external parameter names for our subscripts that can help distinguish between subscripts that have the same types.

We use custom subscripts just like we use subscripts for arrays and dictionaries. For example, to access an element in an array, we use the `Array[index]` syntax. When we define a custom subscript for our custom types, we also access them with the same `ourType[key]` syntax.

When creating custom subscripts, we should try to make them feel like a natural part of the class, structure, or enumeration. As mentioned previously, subscripts can significantly enhance the usability and readability of our code, but if we try to overuse them, they will not feel natural and will be hard to use and understand.

In this chapter, we will look at several examples of how we can create and use custom subscripts. However, before we see how to use custom subscripts, let's review how subscripts are used with Swift arrays to understand how subscripts are used within the Swift language itself. We should use subscripts in a similar manner to how Apple uses them within the language to make our custom subscripts easy to understand and use.

Subscripts with Swift arrays

The following example shows how to use subscripts to access and change the values of an array:

```
var arrayOne = [1, 2, 3, 4, 5, 6]
print(arrayOne[3])  //Displays '4'
arrayOne[3] = 10
print(arrayOne[3])  //Displays '10'
```

In the preceding example, we create an array of integers and then use the subscript syntax to display and change the element at index three. Subscripts are mainly used to set or retrieve information from a collection. We generally do not use subscripts when specific logic needs to be applied to determine which item to select. As an example, we would not want to use subscripts to append an item to the end of the array or to retrieve the number of items in the array. To append an item to the end of an array, or to get the number of items in an array, we use functions or properties, such as the following:

```
arrayOne.append(7)  //append 7 to the end of the array
arrayOne.count  //returns the number of items in an array
```

Subscripts in our custom types should follow the same standard set by the Swift language itself, so other developers that use our types are not confused by the implementation. The key to knowing when to use subscripts, and when not to, is to understand how they will be used.

Creating and using custom subscripts

Let's look at how to define a subscript that is used to read and write to a backend array. Reading and writing to a backend storage class is one of the most common uses of custom subscripts. However, as we will see in this chapter, we do not need to have a backend storage class. The following code shows how to use a subscript to read and write to an array:

```swift
class MyNames {
    private var names = ["Jon", "Kailey", "Kara"]
    subscript(index: Int) -> String {
        get {
            return names[index]
        }
        set {
            names[index] = newValue
        }
    }
}
```

As we can see, the syntax for subscripts is similar to how we define properties within a class using the get and set keywords. The difference is that we declare the subscript using the subscript keyword. We then specify one or more inputs and the return type.

We can now use the custom subscript just like we used subscripts with arrays and dictionaries. The following code shows how to use the subscript in the preceding example:

```swift
var nam = MyNames()
print(nam[0])  //Displays 'Jon'
nam[0] = "Buddy"
print(nam[0])  //Displays 'Buddy'
```

In the preceding code, we create an instance of the MyNames class and display the original name at index 0. We then change the name at index 0 and redisplay it. In this example, we use the subscript that is defined in the MyNames class to retrieve and set elements of the names array within the class.

While we could make the names array available for external code to access directly, this would lock our code into using an array to store the data. In the future, if we wanted to change the backend storage mechanism to a dictionary object, or even an SQLite database, we would have a difficult time doing so because all of the external code would also have to be changed. Subscripts are very good at hiding how we store information within our custom types; therefore, external code that uses these custom types does not rely on specific storage implementations.

If we gave direct access to the names array, we would also be unable to verify that the external code was inserting valid information into the array. With subscripts, we can add validation to our setters to verify that the data being passed in is correct before adding it to the array. As an example, in the previous example, we could have added in a validation to verify that the names only contain alpha characters and certain special characters that are valid in names. This can be very useful when we are creating a framework or a library.

Read-only custom subscripts

We can also make the subscript read-only by either not declaring a setter method within the subscript or by not implicitly declaring the getter and setter methods. The following code shows how to declare a read-only property by not declaring a getter or setter method:

```
//No getter/setters implicitly declared
subscript(index: Int) -> String {
    return names[index]
}
```

The following example shows how to declare a read-only property by only declaring a getter method:

```
//Declaring only a getter
subscript(index: Int) -> String {
    get {
        return names[index]
    }
}
```

In the first example, we do not define either a getter or setter method; therefore, Swift sets the subscript as read-only, and the code acts as if it were in a getter definition. In the second example, we specifically set the code in a getter definition. Both examples are valid read-only subscripts. One thing to note is that write-only subscripts are not valid in Swift.

Calculated subscripts

While the preceding example is very similar to using stored properties in a class or structure, we can also use subscripts in a similar manner to computed properties. Let's look at how to do this:

```
struct MathTable {
    var num: Int
    subscript(index: Int) -> Int {
        return num * index
    }
}
```

In the preceding example, we used an array as the backend storage mechanism for the subscript. In this example, we use the value of the subscript to calculate the return value. We would use this subscript as follows:

```
var table = MathTable(num: 5)
print(table[4])
```

This example displays the calculated value of 5 (the number defined in the initialization) multiplied by 4 (the subscript value), which is equal to 20.

Subscript values

In the preceding subscript examples, all of the subscripts accepted integers as the value for the subscript; however, we are not limited to integers. In the following example, we will use a `String` type as the value for the subscript. The `subscript` keyword will also return a `String` type:

```
struct Hello {
    subscript (name: String) -> String {
        return "Hello \(name)"
    }
}
```

In this example, the subscript takes a string as the value within the subscript and returns a message saying `Hello`. Let's look at how to use this subscript:

```
let greeting = Hello["Jon"]
```

In the previous code, the greeting constant would contain the string `Hello Jon`.

Static subscripts

Static subscripts were introduced in Swift 5.1 with SE-0254. This functionality enables us to use the subscript without having to create an instance of the type. Let's see how this works:

```swift
struct Hello {
    static subscript (name: String) -> String {
        return "Hello \(name)"
    }
}
```

In the previous code, we create a structure named `Hello` and within this structure we define a `subscript`. The thing to note is the `static` keyword prior to the subscript declaration. We are now able to use this subscript as shown in the next line of code:

```swift
let greeting = Hello["Jon"]
```

In the previous code, the `greeting` constant would contain the string `Hello Jon`. Note that we did not have to create an instance of the `Hello` structure to use the subscript.

External names for subscripts

As mentioned earlier in this chapter, we can have multiple subscript signatures for our custom types. The appropriate subscript will be chosen based on the type of index passed into the subscript. However, there are times when we may wish to define multiple subscripts that have the same type. For this, we could use external names in a similar way to how we define external names for the parameters of a function.

Let's rewrite the original `MathTable` structure to include two subscripts that each accept an integer as the subscript type. However, one will perform a multiplication operation, and the other will perform an addition operation:

```swift
struct MathTable {
    var num: Int
    subscript(multiply index: Int) -> Int {
        return num * index
    }
    subscript(add index: Int) -> Int {
        return num + index
    }
}
```

As we can see, in this example we define two subscripts, and each subscript accepts an integer type. The difference between the two subscripts is the external name within the definition. In the first subscript, we define an external name, `multiply`, because we multiply the value of the subscript by the `num` property within this subscript. In the second `subscript`, we define an external name, `add`, because we add the value of the subscript to the `num` property within the subscript.

Let's look at how to use these two subscripts:

```
var table = MathTable(num: 5)
print(table[multiply: 4])  //Displays 20 because 5*4=20
print(table[add: 4])  //Displays 9 because 5+4=9
```

If we run this example, we will see that the correct subscript is used, based on the external name within the subscript.

Using external names within our subscript is very useful if we need multiple subscripts of the same type. I would not recommend using external names unless they are needed to distinguish between multiple subscripts.

Multidimensional subscripts

While the most common subscripts are those that take a single parameter, subscripts are not limited to single parameters. They can take any number of input parameters, and these parameters can be of any type.

Let's look at how we could use a multidimensional subscript to implement a Tic-Tac-Toe board. A Tic-Tac-Toe board looks similar to the following diagram:

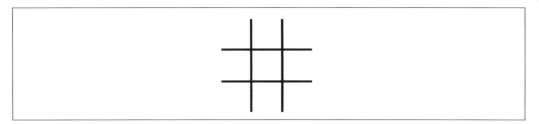

Figure 13.1: Empty Tic-Tac-Toe board

The board can be represented by a two-dimensional array, where each dimension has three elements. The upper-left box of the board would be represented by the coordinates 0,0, while the lower-right box of the board would be represented by the coordinates 2,2. The middle box would have the coordinates 1,1. Each player will take turns placing their pieces (typically x or o) onto the board until one player has three pieces in a line or the board is full.

Let's look at how we could implement a Tic-Tac-Toe board using a multidimensional array and multidimensional subscripts:

```
struct TicTacToe {
    var board = [["","",""],["","",""],["","",""]]
    subscript(x: Int, y: Int) -> String {
        get {
            return board[x][y]
        }
        set {
            board[x][y] = newValue
        }
    }
}
```

We start the TicTacToe structure by defining a 3×3 array, also known as a matrix, which will represent the game board. We then define a subscript that can be used to set and retrieve player pieces on the board. The subscript will accept two integer values. We define multiple parameters for our subscripts by putting the parameters between parentheses. In this example, we are defining the subscript with the parameters (x: Int, y: Int). We can then use the x and y variable names within our subscripts to access the values that are passed in.

Let's look at how to use this subscript to set the user's pieces on the board:

```
var board = TicTacToe()
board[1,1] = "x"
board[0,0] = "o"
```

If we run this code, we will see that we added the x piece to the center square and the o piece to the upper-left square, so our game board will look similar to the following:

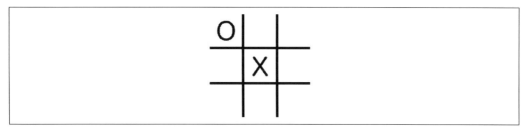

Figure 13.2: Tic-Tac-Toe board with two player pieces

We are not limited to using only one type for our multidimensional subscripts. For example, we could have a subscript of (x: Int, y: Double, z: String).

We can also add external names for our multidimensional subscript types to help identify what values are used for and to distinguish between subscripts that have the same types. Let's take a look at how to use multiple types and external names with subscripts by creating a subscript that will return an array of string instances based on the values of the subscript:

```
struct SayHello {
    subscript(messageText message: String, messageName name: String,
number: Int) -> [String]{
        var retArray: [String] = []
        for _ in 0..<number {
            retArray.append("\(message) \(name)")
        }
        return retArray
    }
}
```

In the `SayHello` structure, we define our subscript as follows:

```
subscript(messageText message: String, messageName name: String,
number: Int) -> [String]
```

This defines a subscript with three elements. Each element has an external name (`messageText`, `messageName`, and `number`) and an internal name (`message`, `name`, and `number`). The first two elements are of the `String` type and the last one is an `Integer` type. We use the first two elements to create a message for the user that will repeat the number of times defined by the last (`number`) element. We will use this subscript as follows:

```
var message = SayHello()
var ret = message[messageText:"Bonjour", messageName:"Jon", number:5]
```

If we run this code, we will see that the `ret` variable contains an array of five strings, where each string equals `Bonjour Jon`. Now let's look at one of the most controversial new additions to the Swift language – dynamic member lookup.

Dynamic member lookup

Dynamic member lookup enables a call to a property that will be dynamically resolved at runtime. This may not make a lot of sense without seeing an example, so let's look at one. Let's say that we had a structure that represented a baseball team. This structure has a property that represents the city the team was from and another property that represents the nickname of the team. The following code shows this structure:

```
struct BaseballTeam {
    let city: String
    let nickName: String
}
```

In this structure, if we wanted to retrieve the full name of the baseball team, including the city and nickname, we could easily create a method as shown in the following example:

```
func fullname() -> String {
    return "\(city) \(nickName)"
}
```

This is how you would do it in most object-oriented programming languages. However, in our code, which uses the BaseballTeam structure, we would retrieve the city and nickname as properties with the dot notation and the full name as a method. The following code shows how we would use both the city property and the fullname method:

```
var redsox = BaseballTeam(city: "Boston", nickName: "Red Sox")
let city = redsox.city
let fullname = redsox.fullname()
```

We can create a much cleaner interface using dynamic member lookups. To use dynamic member lookups, the first thing we need to do is to add the @dynamicMemberLookup attribute when we define the BaseballTeam structure, as shown in the following code:

```
@dynamicMemberLookup
struct BaseballTeam {
    let city: String
    let nickName: String
    let wins: Double
    let losses: Double
    let year: Int
}
```

Now we will need to add the lookup to the BaseballTeam structure. This is done by implementing the subscript(dynamicMember:) subscript. The following code shows how we would create a lookup to retrieve both the full name and the winning percentage for the BaseballTeam structure:

```
subscript(dynamicMember key: String) -> String {
    switch key {
```

```
    case "fullname":
        return "\(city) \(nickName)"
    case "percent":
        let per = wins/(wins+losses) return String(per)
    default:
        return "Unknown request"
    }
}
```

This code will retrieve the key passed in and uses a switch statement, using that key, to determine what information to return from the subscript. With this code added to the BaseballTeam structure, we can use the lookup as shown in the following example:

```
var redsox = BaseballTeam(city: "Boston", nickName: "Red Sox", wins:
108, losses: 54, year: 2018)

print("The \(redsox.fullname) won \(redsox.percent) of their games in \
(redsox.year)")
```

Notice how we are able to access both fullname and percent from the instance of the BaseballTeam structure as if they were normal properties. This makes our code much cleaner and easier to read. However, there is one thing to keep in mind when using lookups like this: there is no way to control what keys are passed into the lookup.

In the previous example, we called fullname and percent; however, we could just as easily have called flower or dog with no warning from the compiler. This is why there is a lot of controversy attached to dynamic member lookup, because there is no compile-time warning if you do something wrong.

If you use dynamic member lookup, make sure you verify the key and handle any instances when something unexpected is sent, as we did with the previous example using the default case of the switch statement.

Now that we have seen how to use subscripts, let's take a quick look at when not to use custom subscripts.

When not to use a custom subscript

As we have seen in this chapter, creating custom subscripts can really enhance our code. However, we should avoid overusing them or using them in a way that is not consistent with standard subscript usage. The way to avoid overusing subscripts is to examine how subscripts are used in Swift's standard libraries.

Let's look at the following example:

```swift
class MyNames {
    private var names:[String] = ["Jon", "Kailey", "Kara"]
    var number: Int {
        get {
            return names.count
        }
    }

    subscript(add name: String) -> String {
        names.append(name)
            return name
    }
    subscript(index: Int) -> String {
        get {
            return names[index]
        }
        set {
            names[index] = newValue
        }
    }
}
```

In the preceding example, within the `MyNames` class, we define an array of names that are used within our application. As an example, let's say that within our application we display this list of names and allow users to add names to it. Within the `MyNames` class, we then define the following subscript, which allows us to append a new name to the array:

```swift
subscript(add name: String) -> String {
    names.append(name)
    return name
}
```

This would be a poor use of subscripts because its usage is not consistent with how subscripts are used within the Swift language itself—we are using it to accept a parameter and add that value. This might cause confusion when the class is used. It would be more appropriate to rewrite this subscript as a function, such as the following:

```swift
func append(name: String) {
    names.append(name)
}
```

Remember, when you are using custom subscripts, make sure that you are using them appropriately.

Summary

As we saw in this chapter, adding support for subscripts to our custom types can greatly enhance their readability and usability. We saw that subscripts can be used to add an abstraction layer between our backend storage class and external code. Subscripts can also be used in a similar manner to computed properties, where the subscript is used to calculate a value. As we noted, the key with subscripts is to use them appropriately and in a manner that is consistent with subscripts in the Swift language.

In the next chapter, we will look at what closures are and how to use them.

14
Working with Closures

Today, most major programming languages have functionalities similar to those of closures in Swift. Some of these implementations are really hard to use (Objective-C blocks), while others are easy (Java lambdas and C# delegates). I have found that the functionality that closures provide is especially useful when developing frameworks. I have also used them extensively when communicating with remote services over a network connection. While blocks in Objective-C are incredibly useful, the syntax used to declare a block is absolutely horrible. Luckily, when Apple was developing the Swift language, they made the syntax of closures much easier to use and understand.

In this chapter, we will cover the following topics:

- What are closures?
- How to create a closure
- How to use a closure
- What are some examples of useful closures?
- How to avoid strong reference cycles within closures

An introduction to closures

Closures are self-contained blocks of code that can be passed around and used throughout our application. We can think of the Int type as a type that contains an integer, and the String type as a type that contains a string. In this context, a closure can be thought of as a type that contains a block of code. This means that we can assign closures to a variable, pass them as arguments to functions, and return them from a function.

Closures can capture and store references to any variable or constant from the context in which they were defined. This is known as closing over the variables or constants and, for the most part, Swift will handle the memory management for us. The only exception is in creating a strong reference cycle, and we will look at how to resolve this in the *Creating strong reference cycles with closures* section of *Chapter 18, Memory Management*.

Closures in Swift are similar to blocks in Objective-C; however, closures in Swift are a lot easier to use and understand. Let's look at the syntax used to define a closure in Swift:

```
{
(<#parameters#>) -> <#return-type#> in <#statements#>
}
```

The syntax used to create a closure looks very similar to the syntax we use to create functions, and in Swift, global and nested functions are closures. The biggest difference in the format between closures and functions is the in keyword. The in keyword is used in place of curly brackets to separate the definition of the closure's parameter and return types from the body of the closure.

There are many uses for closures, and we will go over a number of them later in this chapter, but first, we need to understand the basics of closures. Let's start by looking at some very basic closures so that we can get a better understanding of what they are, how to define them, and how to use them.

Simple closures

We will begin by creating a very simple closure that does not accept any arguments and does not return any value. All it does is print Hello World to the console. Let's look at the following code:

```
let clos1 = { () -> Void in
    print("Hello World")
}
```

In this example, we create a closure and assign it to the clos1 constant. Since there are no parameters defined between the parentheses, this closure will not accept any parameters. Also, the return type is defined as Void; therefore, this closure will not return any value. The body of the closure contains one line, which prints Hello World to the console.

There are many ways to use closures; in this example, all we want to do is execute it. We can execute the closure as follows:

```
clos1()
```

After executing the closure, we will see that Hello World is printed to the console. At this point, closures may not seem that useful, but as we get further along in this chapter, we will see how useful and powerful they can be.

Let's look at another simple example. This closure will accept one String parameter named name but will not return a value. Within the body of the closure, we will print out a greeting to the name passed into the closure through the name parameter. Here is the code for this second closure:

```
let clos2 = {
    (name: String) -> Void in
    print("Hello \(name)")
}
```

The big difference between the clos2 closure and the clos1 closure is that we define a single String parameter between the parentheses. As we can see, we define parameters for closures just like we define parameters for functions. We can execute this closure in the same way in which we executed the clos1 closure. The following code shows how this is done:

```
clos2("Jon")
```

This example, when executed, will print the Hello Jon message to the console. Let's look at another way we can use the clos2 closure. One thing to note in this example is that the named parameters in a closure do not require the parameter name to be used.

Our original definition of closures stated that Closures are self-contained blocks of code that can be passed around and used throughout our application. This tells us that we can pass our closures from the context that they were created into other parts of our code. Let's look at how to pass our clos2 closure into a function. We will define a function that accepts our clos2 closure, as follows:

```
func testClosure(handler: (String) -> Void) {
    handler("Dasher")
}
```

We define the function just like we would any other function; however, in the parameter list, we define a parameter named `handler`, and the type defined for the `handler` parameter is `(String) -> Void`. If we look closely, we can see that the `(String) -> Void` definition of the `handler` parameter matches the parameter and return types that we defined for the `clos2` closure. This means that we can pass the `clos2` closure into the function. Let's look at how to do this:

```
testClosure(handler: clos2)
```

We call the `testClosure()` function just like any other function, and the closure that is being passed in looks like any other variable. Since the `clos2` closure is executed in the `testClosure()` function, we will see the message `Hello Dasher` printed to the console when this code is executed. As we will see a little later in this chapter, the ability to pass closures to functions is what makes closures so exciting and powerful. As the final piece to the closure puzzle, let's look at how to return a value from a closure. The following example shows this:

```
let clos3 = {
    (name: String) -> String in
    return "Hello \(name)"
}
```

The definition of the `clos3` closure looks very similar to how we defined the `clos2` closure. The difference is that we changed the `Void` return type to a `String` type. Then, in the body of the closure, instead of printing the message to the console, we used the return statement to return the message. We can now execute the `clos3` closure just like the previous two closures or pass the closure to a function like we did with the `clos2` closure. The following example shows how to execute the `clos3` closure:

```
var message = clos3("Buddy")
```

After this line of code is executed, the message variable will contain the `Hello Buddy` string. The previous three examples of closures demonstrate the format and how to define a typical closure. Those who are familiar with Objective-C can see that the format of closures in Swift is a lot cleaner and easier to use. The syntax for creating closures that we have shown so far in this chapter is pretty short; however, we can shorten it even more. In this next section, we will look at how to do this.

Shorthand syntax for closures

In this section, we will look at a couple of ways to shorten the syntax.

 Using the shorthand syntax for closures is really a matter of personal preference. A lot of developers like to make their code as small and compact as possible, and they take great pride in doing so. However, at times this can make the code hard to read and understand for other developers.

The first shorthand syntax for closures that we are going to look at is one of the most popular, which is the syntax we saw when we were using algorithms with arrays in *Chapter 5*, Using Swift Collections. This format is mainly used when we want to send a really small (usually one line) closure to a function, like we did with the algorithms for arrays. Before we look at this shorthand syntax, we need to write a function that will accept a closure as a parameter:

```
func testFunction(num: Int, handler:() -> Void) {
    for _ in 0..<num {
        handler()
    }
}
```

This function accepts two parameters; the first parameter is an integer named num, and the second parameter is a closure named handler, which does not have any parameters and does not return any value. Within the function, we create a for loop that will use the num integer to define how many times it loops. Within the for loop, we call the handler closure that was passed into the function. Now let's create a closure and pass it to testFunction() as follows:

```
let clos = { () -> Void in
    print("Hello from standard syntax")
}
testFunction(num: 5, handler: clos)
```

This code is very easy to read and understand; however, it does take five lines of code. Now let's look at how to shorten it by writing the closure inline within the function call:

```
testFunction(num: 5,handler: {print("Hello from Shorthand closure")})
```

In this example, we created the closure inline within the function call, using the same syntax that we used with the algorithms for arrays. The closure is placed in between two curly brackets ({}), which means the code to create the closure is {print("Hello from Shorthand closure")}. When this code is executed, it will print out the Hello from Shorthand closure message five times on the screen. The ideal way to call the testFunction() with a closure, for both compactness and readability, would be as follows:

```
testFunction(num: 5) {
    print("Hello from Shorthand closure")
}
```

Having the closure as the final parameter allows us to leave off the label when calling the function. This example gives us both compact and readable code. Let's look at how to use parameters with this shorthand syntax. We will begin by creating a new function that will accept a closure with a single parameter. We will name this function testFunction2. The following example shows what the new testFunction2 function does:

```
func testFunction2(num: Int, handler: (_ : String)->Void) {
    for _ in 0..<num {
        handler("Me")
    }
}
```

In testFunction2, we define the closure like this: (_ : String)->Void. This definition means that the closure accepts one parameter and does not return any value. Now let's look at how to use the same shorthand syntax to call this function:

```
testFunction2(num: 5){
    print("Hello from \($0)")
}
```

The difference between this closure definition and the previous one is $0. The $0 parameter is shorthand for the first parameter passed into the function. If we execute this code, it prints out the Hello from Me message five times. Using the dollar sign ($) followed by a number with inline closures allows us to define the closure without having to create a parameter list in the definition. The number after the dollar sign defines the position of the parameter in the parameter list. Let's examine this format a bit more, because we are not limited to only using the dollar sign ($) and number shorthand format with inline closures. This shorthand syntax can also be used to shorten the closure definition by allowing us to leave the parameter names off. The following example demonstrates this:

```
let clos5: (String, String) -> Void = {
    print("\($0) \($1)")
}
```

In this example, the closure has two string parameters defined; however, we do not give them names. The parameters are defined like this: (String, String). We can then access the parameters within the body of the closure using $0 and $1. Also, note that the closure definition is after the colon (:), using the same syntax that we use to define a variable type rather than inside the curly brackets. When we use anonymous arguments, this is how we would define the closure. It will not be valid to define the closure as follows:

```
let clos5b = { (String, String) in
    print("\($0) \($1)")
}
```

In this example, we will receive an error letting us know that this format is not valid. Next, let's look at how we would use the clos5 closure:

```
clos5("Hello", "Kara")
```

Since Hello is the first string in the parameter list, it is accessed with $0, and as Kara is the second string in the parameter list, it is accessed with $1. When we execute this code, we will see the Hello Kara message printed to the console. This next example is used when the closure doesn't return any value. Rather than defining the return type as Void, we can use parentheses, as the following example shows:

```
let clos6: () -> () = {
    print("Howdy")
}
```

In this example, we define the closure as () -> (). This tells Swift that the closure does not accept any parameters and also does not return a value. We will execute this closure as follows:

```
clos6()
```

As a personal preference, I am not very fond of this shorthand syntax. I think the code is much easier to read when the Void keyword is used rather than the parentheses.

We have one more shorthand closure example to demonstrate before we begin showing some really useful examples of closures. In this last example, we will demonstrate how we can return a value from the closure without the need to include the return keyword. If the entire closure body consists of only a single statement, we can omit the return keyword, and the results of the statement will be returned. Let's look at an example of this:

```
let clos7 = {(first: Int, second: Int) -> Int in first + second }
```

In this example, the closure accepts two parameters of the Int type and will return an instance of the Int type. The only statement within the body of the closure adds the first parameter to the second parameter. However, if you notice, we do not include the return keyword before the additional statement. Swift will see that this is a single-statement closure and will automatically return the results, just as if we put the return keyword before the additional statement. We do need to make sure the result type of our statement matches the return type of the closure.

All of the examples shown in the previous two sections were designed to show how to define and use closures. On their own, these examples do not really show off the power of closures and they do not show how incredibly useful closures are. The remainder of this chapter will demonstrate the power and usefulness of closures in Swift.

Using closures with Swift arrays

In *Chapter 5, Using Swift Collections*, we looked at several built-in algorithms that we can use with Swift's arrays. In that chapter, we briefly looked at how to add simple rules to each of these algorithms with very basic closures. Now that we have a better understanding of closures, let's look at how we can expand on these algorithms using more advanced closures.

Using closures with Swift's array algorithms

In this section, we will primarily be using the map algorithm for consistency purposes; however, we can use the basic ideas demonstrated with any of the algorithms. We will start by defining an array to use:

```
let guests = ["Jon", "Kailey", "Kara"]
```

This array contains a list of names and the array is named guests. This array will be used for the majority of the examples in this section. Now that we have our guests array, let's add a closure that will print a greeting to each of the names in the array:

```
guests.map { name in
    print("Hello \(name)")
}
```

Since the map algorithm applies the closure to each item of the array, this example will print out a greeting for each name within the array. After the first section in this chapter, we should have a pretty good understanding of how this closure works. Using the shorthand syntax that we saw in the previous section, we could reduce the preceding example down to the following single line of code:

```
guests.map {
    print("Hello \($0)")}
```

This is one of the few times, in my opinion, where the shorthand syntax may be easier to read than the standard syntax. Now, let's say that rather than printing the greeting to the console, we wanted to return a new array that contained the greetings. For this, we would return a String type from our closure, as shown in the following example:

```
var messages = guests.map {
    (name:String) -> String in
    return "Welcome \(name)"
}
```

When this code is executed, the messages array will contain a greeting to each of the names in the guests array, while the array will remain unchanged. We could access the greetings as follows:

```
for message in messages {
    print("\(message)")
}
```

The preceding examples in this section showed how to add a closure to the map algorithm inline. This is good if we only had one closure that we wanted to use with the map algorithm, but what if we had more than one closure that we wanted to use, or if we wanted to use the closure multiple times or reuse it with different arrays? For this, we could assign the closure to a constant or variable and then pass in the closure, using its constant or variable name, as needed. Let's look at how to do this. We will begin by defining two closures.

One of the closures will print a greeting for each element in the array, and the other closure will print a goodbye message for each element in the array:

```
let greetGuest = { (name:String) -> Void in
    print("Hello guest named \(name)")
}

let sayGoodbye = { (name:String) -> Void in
    print("Goodbye \(name)")
}
```

Now that we have two closures, we can use them with the map algorithm as needed. The following code shows how to use these closures interchangeably with the guests array:

```
guests.map(greetGuest)
guests.map(sayGoodbye)
```

When we use the greetGuest closure with the guests array, the greeting message is printed to the console, and when we use the sayGoodbye closure with the guests array, the goodbye message is printed to the console. If we had another array named guests2, we could use the same closures for that array, as shown in the following example:

```
guests.map(greetGuest)
guests2.map(greetGuest)
guests.map(sayGoodbye)
guests2.map(sayGoodbye)
```

All of the examples in this section so far have either printed a message to the console or returned a new array from the closure. We are not limited to such basic functionality in our closures. For example, we can filter the array within the closure, as shown in the following example:

```
let greetGuest2 = {
    (name:String) -> Void in
    if (name.hasPrefix("K")) {
        print("\(name) is on the guest list")
    } else {
        print("\(name) was not invited")
    }
}
```

In this example, we print out a different message depending on whether the name starts with the letter K.

As mentioned earlier in the chapter, closures have the ability to capture and store references to any variable or constant from the context in which they were defined. Let's look at an example of this. Let's say that we have a function that contains the highest temperature for the last seven days at a given location and this function accepts a closure as a parameter. This function will execute the closure on the array of temperatures. The function can be written as follows:

```
func temperatures(calculate:(Int)->Void) {
    var tempArray = [72,74,76,68,70,72,66]
    tempArray.map(calculate)
}
```

This function accepts a closure, defined as (Int)-> Void. We then use the map algorithm to execute this closure for each item of the tempArray array. The key to using a closure correctly in this situation is to understand that the temperatures function does not know, or care, about what goes on inside the calculate closure. Also, be aware that the closure is also unable to update or change the items within the function's context, which means that the closure cannot change any other variable within the temperature's function; however, it can update variables in the context that it was created in.

Let's look at the function that we will create the closure in. We will name this function testFunction:

```
func testFunction() {
    var total = 0
    var count = 0
    let addTemps = {
        (num: Int) -> Void in
        total += num
        count += 1
    }
    temperatures(calculate: addTemps)
    print("Total: \(total)")
    print("Count: \(count)")
    print("Average: \(total/count)")
}
```

In this function, we begin by defining two variables, named `total` and `count`, where both variables are of the `Int` type. We then create a closure named `addTemps` that will be used to add all the temperatures from the `temperatures` function together. The `addTemps` closure will also count how many temperatures there are in the array. To do this, the `addTemps` closure calculates the sum of each item in the array and keeps the total in the `total` variable that was defined at the beginning of the function. The `addTemps` closure also keeps track of the number of items in the array by incrementing the `count` variable for each item. Notice that neither the `total` nor `count` variables are defined within the closure; however, we are able to use them within the closure because they were defined in the same context as the closure.

We then call the `temperatures` function and pass it the `addTemps` closure. Finally, we print the `Total`, `Count`, and `Average` temperature to the console. When `testFunction` is executed, we will see the following output to the console:

```
Total: 498
Count: 7
Average: 71
```

As we can see from the output, the `addTemps` closure is able to update and use items that are defined within the context that it was created in, even when the closure is used in a different context.

Now that we have looked at using closures with the array map algorithm, let's look at using closures by themselves. We will also look at the ways we can clean up our code to make it easier to read and use.

Non-contiguous elements from an array

In *Chapter 5, Using Swift Collections*, we showed how to retrieve non-contiguous sub-elements from an array using the `subrange` method with a closure. Now that we know a little more about closures, let's take a look at this again.

The code we used in *Chapter 5, Using Swift Collections*, retrieved the even numbers from an array of integers. Let's look at this code again:

```
var numbers = [1,2,3,4,5,6,7,8,9,10]
let evenNum = numbers.subranges(where: { $0.isMultiple(of: 2) })
//numbers[evenNum] contains 2,4,6,8,10
```

In this example, we used `isMultiple(of: )` from the `Int` type to retrieve all elements that are even numbers. Since the `subranges(where: )` method takes a closure, we can use other logic as well. For example, if we wanted to retrieve all elements that were equal to or less than 6, we could use the following line of code:

```
let newNumbers = numbers.subrange(where: { $0 <= 6 })
```

Now that we are familiar with closures, we can see some of the possibilities of the
subrange(where:) method.

Uninitialized arrays

Swift 5.2 with SE-0245 introduced a new initializer for arrays that does not pre-fill
the values with a default value. This initializer enables us to provide a closure to fill
in the values however we like. Let's take a look at how to do this by creating an array
that will contain the value of 20 dice rolls:

```
let capacity = 20
let diceRolls = Array<Int>(unsafeUninitializedCapacity: capacity) {
buffer, initializedCount in
    for x in 0..<capacity {
        buffer[x] = Int.random(in: 1...6)
    }
    initializedCount = capacity
}
```

We begin by setting a constant that contains the capacity for the array. We do this
because we need to provide that value in several spots within the initializer and by
using the constant, if we need to change this capacity at a later time, then it only
needs to be changed in one spot.

The rest of the code initializes the array. The closure provides an unsafe mutable
buffer pointer, which we named buffer in the previous code, that can be used to
write the values for the array too. We use a for loop to populate the array with
random integer values from 1 to 6.

There are some general rules when you are using this initializer:

- You do not need to use the full capacity that you ask for; however, you
  cannot use more. In our example, we ask for a capacity of 20 elements, which
  means we can use less than 20, but we cannot use more than 20.

- If you do not initialize an element, then it will probably be filled with
  random data (very bad idea). In our example, where we request a capacity
  of 20 elements, if we only populated the first 10 elements then the second 10
  elements would contain random garbage.

- If initializedCount is not set then it will default to 0 and all of the data will
  be lost.

- This is a very handy initializer to use but it is also very easy to make a mistake with it. We could also rewrite the diceRolls initializer using the map array algorithm, as the following code shows:

```
let diceRolls = (0...20).map { _ in Int.random(in: 1...6) }
```

However, this would be less efficient because initializing the array as shown in the first example is internally optimized for better performance. If you are not worried about the best performance, then the map algorithm is much easier to read and understand.

Now let's look at how we can use closures to change functionality at runtime.

Changing functionality

Closures also give us the ability to change the functionality of types on the fly. In *Chapter 11, Generics*, we saw that generics give us the ability to write functions that are valid for multiple types. With closures, we are able to write functions and types whose functionality can change, based on the closure that is passed in. In this section, we will show you how to write a function whose functionality can be changed with a closure.

Let's begin by defining a type that will be used to demonstrate how to swap out a functionality. We will name this type TestType:

```
struct TestType {
    typealias GetNumClosure = ((Int, Int) -> Int)

    var numOne = 5
    var numTwo = 8
    var results = 0;

    mutating func getNum(handler: GetNumClosure) -> Int {
        results = handler(numOne,numTwo)
        print("Results: \(results)")
        return results
    }
}
```

We begin this type by defining a typealias for our closure, which is named GetNumClosure. Any closure that is defined as a GetNumClosure closure will take two integers and return a single integer. Within this closure, we assume that it does something with the integers that we pass in to get the value to return, but it really doesn't have to do anything with the integers. To be honest, this class doesn't really care what the closure does as long as it conforms to the GetNumClosure type. Next, we define three integers, named numOne, numTwo, and results.

We also define a method named getNum(). This method accepts a closure that conforms to the GetNumClosure type as its only parameter. Within the getNum() method, we execute the closure by passing in the numOne and numTwo variables, and the integer that is returned is put into the results class variable. Now let's look at several closures that conform to the GetNumClosure type that we can use with the getNum() method:

```
var max: TestType.GetNumClosure = {
    if $0 > $1 {
        return $0
    } else {
        return $1
    }
}

var min: TestType.GetNumClosure = {
    if $0 < $1 {
        return $0
    } else {
        return $1
    }
}

var multiply: TestType.GetNumClosure = {
    return $0 * $1
}

var second: TestType.GetNumClosure = {
    return $1
}

var answer: TestType.GetNumClosure = {
    var _ = $0 + $1
    return 42
}
```

In this code, we define five closures that conform to the `GetNumClosure` type:

- `max`: This returns the maximum value of the two integers that are passed
- `in min`: This returns the minimum value of the two integers that are passed
- `in multiply`: This multiplies both the values that are passed in and returns the product
- `second`: This returns the second parameter that was passed in
- `answer`: This returns the answer to life, the universe, and everything

In the `answer` closure, we have an extra line that looks like it does not have a purpose:

```
var _ = $0 + $1
```

We do this deliberately because the following code is not valid:

```
var answer: TestType.GetNumClosure = {
    return 42
}
```

This type gives us the error Contextual type for closure argument list expects two arguments, which cannot be implicitly ignored. As we can see by the error, Swift will not let us ignore the expected parameters within the body of the closure. In the second closure, Swift assumes that there are two parameters because $1 specifies the second parameter. We can now pass each one of these closures to the `getNum()` method to change the functionality of the function to suit our needs. The following code illustrates this:

```
var myType = TestType()

myType.getNum(handler: max)
myType.getNum(handler: min)
myType.getNum(handler: multiply)
myType.getNum(handler: second)
myType.getNum(handler: answer)
```

When this code is run, we will receive the following results for each of the closures:

```
For Max:
Results: 8
For Min:
Results: 5
For Multiply:
Results: 40
```

```
For Second:
Results: 8
For Answer:
Results: 42
```

The last example we are going to show you is one that is used a lot in frameworks, especially ones that have a functionality that is designed to be run asynchronously.

Selecting a closure based on results

In the final example, we will pass two closures to a method, and then, depending on some logic, one or possibly both of the closures will be executed. Generally, one of the closures is called if the method was successfully executed and the other closure is called if the method failed.

Let's start by creating a type that will contain a method that will accept two closures and then execute one of the closures based on the defined logic. We will name this type TestType. Here is the code for the TestType type:

```swift
class TestType {
    typealias ResultsClosure = ((String) -> Void)

    func isGreater(numOne: Int, numTwo: Int, successHandler:
ResultsClosure,failureHandler: ResultsClosure) {
        if numOne > numTwo {
            successHandler("\(numOne) is greater than \(numTwo)")
        }
        else {
            failureHandler("\(numOne) is not greater than \(numTwo)")
        }

    }
}
```

We begin this type by creating a typealias that defines the closure that we will use for both the successful and failure closures. We will name this typealiasResultsClosure. This example also illustrates why you should use a typealias rather than retyping the closure definition. It saves us a lot of typing and prevents us from making mistakes. In this example, if we do not use a typealias, we would need to retype the closure definition four times, and if we need to change the closure definition, we would need to change it in four spots. With the type alias, we only need to type the closure definition once and then use the alias throughout the remaining code.

We then create a method named `isGreater`, which takes two integers as the first two parameters, and two closures as the next two parameters. The first closure is named `successHandler`, and the second closure is named `failureHandler`. Within this method, we check whether the first integer parameter is greater than the second. If the first integer is greater, the `successHandler` closure is executed; otherwise, the `failureHandler` closure is executed. Now, let's create two closures outside of the `TestType` structure. The code for these two closures is as follows:

```
var success: TestType.ResultsClosure = {
    print("Success: \($0)")
}
var failure: TestType.ResultsClosure = {
    print("Failure: \($0)")
}
```

Note that both closures are defined as the `TestClass.ResultsClosure` type. In each closure, we simply print a message to the console to let us know which closure was executed. Normally, we would put some functionality in the closure. We will then call the method with both the closures, as follows:

```
var test = TestType()
test.isGreater(numOne: 8, numTwo: 6, successHandler: success,
failureHandler: failure)
```

Note that in the method call, we are sending both the success closure and the failure closure. In this example, we will see the `Success: 8 is greater than 6` message. If we reversed the numbers, we would see the `Failure: 6 is not greater than 8` message. This use case is really good when we call asynchronous methods, such as loading data from a web service. If the web service call was successful, the success closure is called; otherwise, the failure closure is called.

One big advantage of using closures like this is that the UI does not freeze while we wait for the asynchronous call to complete. This also involves a concurrency piece, which we will be covering in *Chapter 16, Concurrency and Parallelism in Swift*. As an example, imagine we tried to retrieve data from a web service as follows:

```
var data = myWebClass.myWebServiceCall(someParameter)
```

Our UI would freeze while we waited for the response, or we would have to make the call in a separate thread so that the UI would not hang. With closures, we pass the closures to the networking framework and rely on the framework to execute the appropriate closure when it is done. This relies on the framework to implement concurrency correctly, to make the calls asynchronously, but a decent framework should handle that for us.

Summary

In this chapter, we saw that we can define a closure just like we can define an integer or string type. We can assign closures to a variable, pass them as an argument to functions, and return them from functions. Closures capture strong references to any constants or variables from the context in which the closure was defined. We do have to be careful with this functionality, to make sure that we do not create a strong reference cycle, which would lead to memory leaks in our applications.

Swift closures are very similar to blocks in Objective-C, but they have a much cleaner and more eloquent syntax. This makes them a lot easier to use and understand. Having a good understanding of closures is vital to mastering the Swift programming language and will make it easier to develop great applications that are easy to maintain. They are also essential for creating first-class frameworks that are easy both to use and to maintain.

The use cases that we looked at in this chapter are by no means the only useful use cases for closures. I can promise you that the more you use closures in Swift, the more uses you will find for them. Closures are definitely one of the most powerful and useful features of the Swift language, and Apple did a great job by implementing them.

In the next chapter, we will look at how we can use the advanced bitwise operators provided by Swift and how we can create our own custom operators.

15
Advanced and Custom Operators

When I started learning how to program computers, one of the first things I learned was how to use operators. These include basic operators like assignment and arithmetic operators, which were covered in *Chapter 3, Learning about Variables, Constants, Strings, and Operators*. It wasn't until much later, when I learned how to program in the C language, that I learned about advanced operators such as bitwise operators. While the advanced operators are not as popular as the basic operators, they can be very powerful when used correctly. Advanced operators are especially useful if you are planning on writing applications that use low-level C-based libraries.

In this chapter, you will learn:

- How to use bitwise operators
- What overflow operators are for
- How to write operator methods
- How to create your own custom operator

In *Chapter 3, Learning about Variables, Constants, Strings, and Operators*, we looked at the most common operators, like assignment, comparison, and arithmetic operators. While these operators are used in virtually every useful application, there are some additional operators that aren't used as often but can be very powerful when you know how to use them. We will look at some of these more advanced operators in this chapter, starting with bitwise operators, but first, we need to understand what bits and bytes are.

Bits and bytes

A computer thinks in terms of binary digits. These digits are called **bits** and can have only two values: *0* or *1*, which represent *on* or *off* in electrical terms. Bits are very small and have limited usefulness on their own outside of using them for true/false flags. They are grouped together into groups of 4, 8, 16, 32, or 64 to form data that a computer can use.

A **byte** in computer terms is a group of 8 bits. If we think in terms of a byte, the number 42 is represented like this, where the least significant bit is to the right and the most significant bit is to the left:

Number 42	0	0	1	0	1	0	1	0
Bit Values	128	64	32	16	8	4	2	1

Figure 15.1: The number 42 represented in bits

The top row in *Figure 15.1* shows the value, on or off, of each bit for an 8-bit byte that equals the number **42**. The second row shows you the value represented by each bit in the byte. We can see that for the number **42**, the bits for the values of **32**, **8**, and **2** are set. We can then add up those values and see that they equal 42: 32+8+2 = 42. This means that the value of the 8-bit byte is 42.

By default, Swift uses 64-bit numbers; as an example, the standard Int type is 64 bits. In this chapter we will mostly use the UInt8 type, which is an unsigned integer that has only 8 bits or 1 byte. Keep in mind that the 64-bit types store bits in the same way as a byte; they just contain more bits.

In the previous example, the least significant bit is to the right while the most significant is to the left. This is the way that bits are usually represented when shown in diagrams. However, in real-world computer architectures, the bits may be stored in memory, where either the most significant bit or the least significant bit is stored in the lowest memory address. Let's take a look at what this means.

Endianness

In computer terms, the **endianness** of an architecture is the order in which bits are stored in the memory. Endianness is expressed as big-endian or little-endian. In an architecture that is considered little-endian, the least significant bit is stored in the lowest memory address, while in architectures that are considered big-endian, the most significant bit is stored in the lowest memory address.

When working with the Swift standard library, and for the most part when working solely within the Swift language itself, you do not need to worry about how the bits are stored. If you need to work with low-level C libraries, across multiple architectures, then you may need to understand how information is stored within the system because you may be dealing with pointers to memory locations.

For the times when you need to worry about the endianness of the architecture, like when we need to interact with low-level C libraries, Swift does have built-in instance properties for integers named `littleEndian` and `bigEndian`. The following example shows how to use these properties:

```
let en = 42
en.littleEndian
en.bigEndian
```

The `en.littleEndian` line would return the little-endian representation of the number 42, while the `en.bigEndian` line would return the big-endian representation of the number 42.

The endianness of both Intel processors and Apple's own A processors is little-endian; therefore, in this chapter, we will assume that everything is little-endian.

Let's look at what bitwise operators are and how we can use them.

Bitwise operators

Bitwise operators enable us to manipulate the individual bits of a value. One of the advantages of bitwise operators is that they are directly supported by the processor and so can be significantly faster than basic arithmetic operations like multiplication and division. We will see how to do basic multiplication and division using bitwise shift operators later in this chapter.

Before we look at what we can do with bitwise operators, we will need to have the ability to show the binary representation of our variables in order to see what the operators are doing. Let's take a look at a couple of ways that we can do this.

Printing binary numbers

Apple provides us with a generic initializer for the String type that will provide us with the string representation of a given value. This initializer is init(_:radix:uppercase:). By default uppercase is set to false and radix is set to 10. The radix defines the number base that will be displayed, where the 10 stands for base 10. In order to see the binary representation, we will need to set that to 2. We can use this initializer to show the binary representation of a value like this:

```
let en = 42
print(String(en, radix:2))
print(String(53, radix:2))
```

The previous code would display the following results:

```
101010
110101
```

Here, 101010 is the binary representation of the number 42 and 110101 is the binary representation of the number 53. This works really well; however, it does not show leading zeros. For example, if we are comparing the binary representation of 53 and 123456, like the following code shows:

```
print(String(53, radix:2))
print(String(123456, radix:2))
```

We end up with results that look like this:

```
110101
11110001001000000
```

This can be a lot harder to compare. When I need to easily see the binary representation of a number, I usually drop the following extension into my code base:

```
extension BinaryInteger {
    func binaryFormat(_ nibbles: Int) -> String {
        var number = self
        var binaryString = ""
        var counter = 0
```

```
        let totalBits = nibbles*4

        for _ in (1...totalBits).reversed() {
            binaryString.insert(contentsOf: "\(number & 1)", at:
 binaryString.startIndex)
            number >>= 1
            counter += 1
            if counter % 4 == 0 && counter < totalBits {
                binaryString.insert(contentsOf: " ", at: binaryString.
 startIndex)
            }
        }
        return binaryString
    }
}
```

 It is OK if you do not understand how this code works at this time since bitwise shift operators have not been explained yet. Once they have been explained later in this chapter, you will be able to understand how it works.

This extension will take an integer and return the binary representation of the number, with the appropriate number of nibbles. Earlier in the chapter we mentioned that a byte has 8 bits; a nibble is half a byte or 4 bits. Within the string that is returned, this code will put a space between each nibble to make it easier to read. We can use this extension as shown in the following code:

```
print(53.binaryFormat(2))
print(230.binaryFormat(2))
```

With this code we are displaying the binary representation of the numbers 53 and 230 in two nibbles. The following results show what would be printed to the console:

```
0011 0101
1110 0110
```

Now that we have a very basic idea of what bits, bytes, nibbles, and endianness are, and we are able to display numbers in binary format, let's look at bitwise operators, starting with the bitwise AND operator.

The bitwise AND operator

The bitwise AND operator (&) takes two values and returns a new value where the bits in the new value are set to 1 only if the corresponding bits of both input values are set to 1. The AND operator can be read as: if the bit from the first value AND the bit of the second value are both 1, then set the corresponding bit of the resultant value to 1. Let's see how this works by seeing how we would do a bitwise AND operation on the numbers 42 and 11:

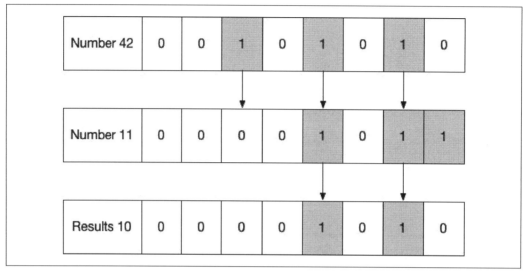

Figure 15.2: The AND operator

As this diagram shows, the second and fourth bit from the right are both set to **1**, therefore the results of the AND operation has those bits set, resulting in an output value of **10**. Now let's see how this works in code:

```
let numberOne: Int8 = 42
let numberTwo: Int8 = 11

print("\(numberOne) = \(numberOne.binaryFormat(2))")
print("\(numberTwo) = \(numberTwo.binaryFormat(2))")
let andResults = numberOne & numberTwo
print("\(andResults) = \(andResults.binaryFormat(2))")
```

The previous code sets two integers to 42 and 11. It then prints the binary representation of the numbers, in two nibbles, using the `binaryFormat` extension to the console. It then performs a bitwise AND operation on the integers and prints the binary representation of the results to the console. The following results will be printed to the console:

```
42 = 0010 1010
11 = 0000 1011
10 = 0000 1010
```

As we can see, the result from the code is the same as shown in the diagram, which has a result of 10. Now let's look at the bitwise OR operator.

The bitwise OR operator

The bitwise OR operator (|) takes two values and returns a new value where the bits of the results are set to 1 only if the corresponding bits of either or both values are set to 1. The OR operation reads as: if the bit from the first value OR the bit of the second value is 1, then set the bit in the results to 1. Let's see how this works by seeing how we would do a bitwise OR operation on the numbers 42 and 11:

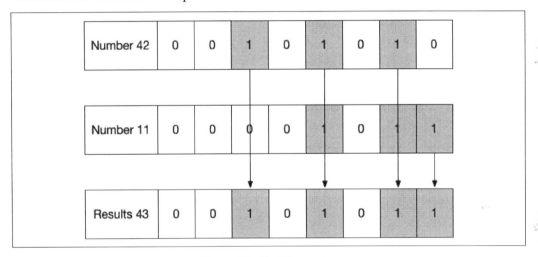

Figure 15.3: The OR operator

As this diagram shows, the first, second, fourth, and sixth bits from the right are set in one or both of the values, therefore the results of the OR operation have all of those bits set. Now let's see how this works in code:

```
let numberOne: Int8 = 42
let numberTwo: Int8 = 11

print("\(numberOne) = \(numberOne.binaryFormat(2))")
print("\(numberTwo) = \(numberTwo.binaryFormat(2))")
let orResults = numberOne | numberTwo
print("\(orResults) = \(orResults.binaryFormat(2))")
```

The previous code sets two integers to 42 and 11. It then prints the binary representation of the numbers, in two nibbles, using the `binaryFormat` extension to the console. It then performs a bitwise OR operation on the integers and prints the binary representation of the results. The following results will be printed to the console:

```
42 = 0010 1010
11 = 0000 1011
43 = 0010 1011
```

As we can see, the result from the code is the same as shown in *Figure 15.3*, which has a result of 43. Now let's look at the bitwise XOR operator.

The bitwise XOR operator

The bitwise XOR operator (^) takes two values and returns a new value where the bits of the new value are set to 1 only if the corresponding bits of either but not both input values are set to 1. The XOR operator reads: if the bit from the first value OR the bit of the second value is 1, but not both, then set the bit of the results to 1. Let's see how this works by seeing how we would do a bitwise OR operation on the numbers 42 and 11:

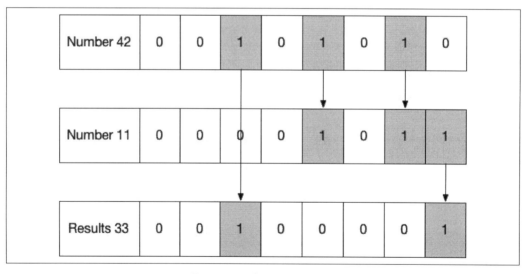

Figure 15.4: The XOR operator

As this diagram shows, the second and fourth bits from the right are set to **1** for both numbers, therefore in the results those bits are not set. However, the sixth bit in the number **42** is set to **1** and the first bit in the number **11** is set to **1**, therefore in the results those bits are set. Now let's see how this works in code:

```
let numberOne: Int8 = 42
let numberTwo: Int8 = 11

print("\(numberOne) = \(numberOne.binaryFormat(2))")
print("\(numberTwo) = \(numberTwo.binaryFormat(2))")
let xorResults = numberOne ^ numberTwo
print("\(xorResults) = \(xorResults.binaryFormat(2))")
```

The previous code sets two integers to 42 and 11. It then prints the binary representation of the numbers to two nibbles using the `binaryFormat` extension. It then performs a bitwise XOR operation on the integers and prints the binary representation of the results. The following results will be printed to the console:

```
42 = 0010 1010
11 = 0000 1011
33 = 0010 0001
```

As we can see, the result from the code is the same as shown in the diagram, which has a result of 33. Now let's look at the bitwise NOT operator.

The bitwise NOT operator

The bitwise NOT operator (~) is different from the other logical operators because it only takes one value. The bitwise NOT operator will return a value where all of the bits are reversed. What this means is that any bit on the input value that is set to 1 will be set to 0 on the resulting value, and any bit that is set to 0 on the input value will be set to 1 on the resulting value. Let's see how this would work given a value of 42:

Number 42	0	0	1	0	1	0	1	0
Results 213	1	1	0	1	0	1	0	1

Figure 15.5: The NOT operator

The diagram illustrates that when we perform the bitwise NOT operation, all of the bits in the result's value will be the opposite of what they were in the original value. Let's see what this looks like in code:

```
let numberOne: Int8 = 42

let notResults = ~numberOne
print("\(notResults) = \(notResults.binaryFormat(2))")
```

The previous code performs the NOT operation on the value of the numberOne variable. The following results will be printed to the console:

```
-43 = 1101 0101
```

Notice the results are a negative number. The reason for this is an integer is a signed number. With signed numbers, the most significant bit designates whether the number is a positive number or a negative number. With all bits being reversed, with the NOT operation, a negative number will always turn into a positive number and a positive number will always turn into a negative number.

Now that we have looked at the logical bitwise operators, let's look at the bitwise shifting operators.

Bitwise shift operators

Swift provides two bitwise shift operators, the bitwise left shift operator (<<) and the bitwise right shift operator (>>). These operators shift all bits to the left or right by the number of places specified. The shift operators have the effect of multiplying (left shift operator) or dividing (right shift operator) by factors of two. By shifting the bits to the left by one, you are doubling the value, and shifting them to the right by one will halve the value. Let's see how these operators work, starting with the left shift operator:

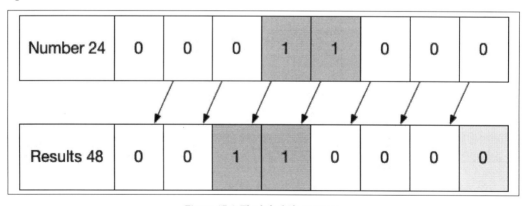

Figure 15.6: The left shift operator

With the left shift operator, all bits in the original value are shifted to the left by one, with the most significant bit falling off and not factoring into the final result. The least significant bit in the result will always be set to zero. Now let's look at the right shift operation:

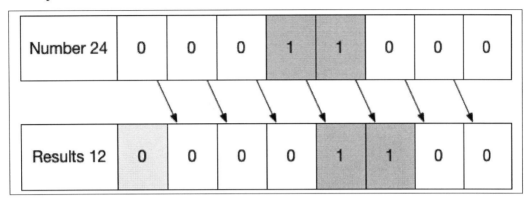

Figure 15.7: The right shift operator

With the right shift operator, all bits in the original value are shifted to the right one spot, with the least significant digit falling off. The most significant digit in the result will always be set to zero.

Now let's see what this looks like in code:

```
let numberOne: UInt8 = 24

let resultsLeft = numberOne << 1
let resultsRight = numberOne >> 1

let resultsLeft3 = numberOne << 3
let resultsRight4 = numberOne >> 4

print("24  \(numberOne.binaryFormat(2))")
print("<<1 \(resultsLeft.binaryFormat(2))")
print(">>1 \(resultsRight.binaryFormat(2))")
print("<<3 \(resultsLeft3.binaryFormat(2))")
print(">>4 \(resultsRight4.binaryFormat(2))")
```

In this code, we start off by setting a variable to the number 24. We then use the left shift operator to shift the bits one spot to the left. The number after the shift operator defines how many spots to shift the numbers. The next line shifts the bits one spot to the right, then the next line shifts the bits three spots to the left, and the next line shifts the bits four spots to the right. The final five lines print out the results to the console. If you run this code, you should see the following results:

```
24  0001 1000
<<1 0011 0000
>>1 0000 1100
<<3 1100 0000
>>4 0000 0001
```

Looking at the results, we can see that the bits are shifted to the left or right depending on the shifting operator used. In the last line, we can see that when we shifted to the right four spaces, only one bit was set to 1 rather than two. This is because the bit in the fourth spot from the right in the original number actually fell off. If we would have shifted to the right five spots, both bits that were set to one in the original number would have fallen off and we would have been left with all zeros.

Now let's look at overflow operators.

Overflow operators

Swift, at its core, is designed for safety. One of these safety mechanisms is the inability to insert a number into a variable when the variable type is too small to hold it. As an example, the following code will throw the following error: `arithmetic operation '255 + 1' (on type 'UInt8') results in an overflow`:

```
let b: UInt8 = UInt8.max +1
```

The reason an error is thrown is we are trying to add one to the maximum number that a `UInt8` can hold. This error checking can help prevent unexpected and hard-to-trace issues in our applications. Let's take a second and look at what would happen if Swift did not throw an error when an overflow occurs. In a `UInt8` variable, which is an 8-bit unsigned integer, the number 255 is stored like this, where all of the bits are set to 1:

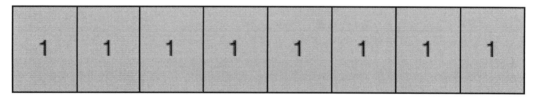

Figure 15.8: The binary representation of 255

Now if we add 1 to this number, the new number will be stored like this:

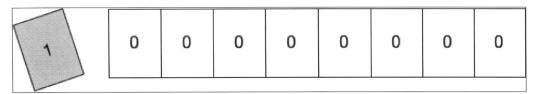

Figure 15.9: Overflow when trying to represent 256

Notice that the 8 bits that represent the UInt8 number are all zeros, while the leading one falls off or overflows because we can only store 8 bits. In this case, when we add one to the number 255, the number stored in the results would be 0 if we did not have overflow error checking. This could lead to very unexpected behavior in our code that would be hard to track down.

If this is the behavior that we want, Swift does offer three overflow operators that will allow us to opt into this behavior. These are the overflow addition operator (&+), the overflow subtraction operator (&-), and the overflow multiplication operator (&*). The following code shows how these operators work:

```
let add: UInt8 = UInt8.max &+ 1
let sub: UInt8 = UInt8.min &- 1
let mul: UInt8 = 42 &* 10

print("add: \(add): \(add.binaryFormat(2))")
print("sub: \(sub): \(sub.binaryFormat(2))")
print("mul: \(mul): \(mul.binaryFormat(2))")
```

In this code, we add one to the maximum value of the UInt8 type, which is 255, subtract one from the UInt8 type minimum value, which is 0, and then multiply 42 by 10, which has a result greater than the 255 maximum value of the UInt8 type. The results that are printed to the console are:

```
add: 0: 0000 0000
sub: 255: 1111 1111
mul: 164: 1010 0100
```

As we can see from the results, when we add 1 to the maximum value of the UInt8 type, the result is 0. When we subtract 1 from the minimum value of the UInt8 type, the result is 255 (the maximum value of the UInt8 type). Finally, when we multiply 42 by 10, which our arithmetic teachers would tell us is 420, we actually end up with 164 because of the overflow.

Now let's look at how we can use operator methods to add operators to our custom types.

Operator methods

Operator methods enable us to add implementations of standard Swift operators to classes and structures. This is also known as overloading operators. This is a very useful feature because it enables us to provide common functionality to our custom types using known operators. We'll take a look at how to do this, but first, let's create a custom type called `MyPoint`:

```swift
struct MyPoint {
    var x = 0
    var y = 0
}
```

The `MyPoint` structure defines a two-dimensional point on a graph. Now let's add three operator methods to this type. The operators that we will add are the addition operator (+), the addition assignment operator (+=), and the inverse operator (-). The addition operator and the addition assignment operator are infix operators because there is a left and right operand (value) to the operation, while the inverse operator is a prefix operator because it is used before a single value. We also have postfix operators, which are used at the end of a single value:

```swift
extension MyPoint {
    static func + (left: MyPoint, right: MyPoint) -> MyPoint {
        return MyPoint(x: left.x + right.x, y: left.y + right.y)
    }
    static func += (left: inout MyPoint, right: MyPoint) {
        left.x += right.x
        left.y += right.y
    }
    static prefix func -(point: MyPoint) -> MyPoint {
        return MyPoint(x: -point.x, y: -point.y)
    }
}
```

When we add operator methods to our types, we add them as static functions using the operator symbols as the method names. When we add prefix or postfix operators, we also include the `prefix` or `postfix` keyword before the function declaration.

The addition operator is an infix operator; therefore, it takes two input parameters of the `MyPoint` type. One parameter is for the `MyPoint` instance that is to the left side of the addition operator and the other parameter is for the `MyPoint` instance that is to the right of the addition operator.

The addition assignment operator is also an infix operator; therefore, it also takes two input parameters of the MyPoint type. The main difference from the addition operator is that the resulting value of the addition operation is assigned to the MyPoint instance that is to the left side of the addition assignment operator. Therefore, this parameter is designated as an inout parameter so the results can be returned within that instance.

The final operator method that we added is the inverse operator. This operator is a prefix operator and is used before an instance of the MyPoint type; therefore, it only takes a single parameter of the MyPoint type. Let's see how these operators work:

```
let firstPoint = MyPoint(x: 1, y: 4)
let secondPoint = MyPoint(x: 5, y: 10)
var combined = firstPoint + secondPoint
print("\(combined.x), \(combined.y)")

combined += firstPoint
print("\(combined.x), \(combined.y)")

let inverse = -combined
print("\(inverse.x), \(inverse.y)")
```

In this code, we begin by defining two points and then adding them together using the addition operator that we created. The results of this operator are put in the new combined instance of the MyPoint type. The combined instance will contain the values of x as 6 and y as 14.

We then use the addition assignment operator that we created to add the values in the firstPoint instance to the values in the combined instance. The result of this operation is put in the combined instance of the MyPoint type. The combined instance now contains the values of x as 7 and y as 14.

Finally, we use the inverse operator on the combined instance of the MyPoint type to reverse the values and save the new values in the inverse instance of the MyPoint type. The inverse instance contains the values of x as -7 and y as -18.

We are not limited to using only current operators but can also create our own custom operators as well. Let's see how we can do this.

Custom operators

Custom operators enable us to declare and implement our own operators outside of the standard operators provided by the Swift language. New operators must be declared globally using the operator keyword. They must also be defined with the infix, prefix, or postfix keywords. Once an operator is defined globally, we are then able to add it to our types using the operator methods as shown in the previous section. Let's take a look at this by adding two new operators: •, which we will use to multiply two points together, and ••, which will be used to square a value. We will add these operators to the MyPoint type that we created in the last section.

 The • symbol can be typed by holding down the *option* key and pressing the number *8* on a computer running macOS.

The first thing we need to do is to declare the operators globally. This can be done with the following code:

```
infix operator •
prefix operator ••
```

Notice that we define what type of operator it is (infix, prefix, or postfix) followed by the operator keyword and then the symbol(s) that will be used for the operator. Now we can use them exactly like we do normal operators with our MyPoint type:

```
extension MyPoint {
    static func • (left: MyPoint, right: MyPoint) -> MyPoint {
        return MyPoint(x: left.x * right.x, y: left.y * right.y)
    }

    static prefix func •• (point: MyPoint) -> MyPoint {
        return MyPoint(x: point.x * point.x, y: point.y * point.y)
    }
}
```

These new custom operators are added to the MyPoint type exactly as we added standard operators, using static functions. We are now able to use these operators exactly like we would use standard operators:

```
let firstPoint = MyPoint(x: 1, y: 4)
let secondPoint = MyPoint(x: 5, y: 10)
let multiplied = firstPoint • secondPoint
```

```
print("\(multiplied.x), \(multiplied.y)")

let squared = ••secondPoint
print("\(squared.x), \(squared.y)")
```

In the first line we use the • operator to multiply two instances of the MyPoint type together. The results are put in the multiplied instance of the MyPoint type. The multiplied instance will now contain the values of x as 5 and y as 40.

We then use the •• operator to square the value of the secondPoint instance and put the new value in the squared instance. The squared instance will now contain the values of x as 25 and y as 100.

Summary

In this chapter we looked at how we can use the advanced bitwise AND, OR, XOR, and NOT operators to manipulate the bits of values stored in variables. We also looked at how we can use the left and right shift operators to shift bits to the left and right. We then saw how we can use overflow operators to change the default behavior for addition, subtraction, and multiplication so errors are not thrown if operations return values above the maximum or below the minimum values for a type.

In the second half of the chapter, we saw how we can add operator methods to types, which enables us to use the standard operators provided by Swift with our custom types. We also saw how we can create our own custom operators as well.

In the next chapter, we will look at how we can use grand central dispatch and operation queues to add concurrency and parallelism to our applications' code.

16

Concurrency and Parallelism in Swift

When I first started learning Objective-C, I already had a good understanding of concurrency and multitasking with my background in other languages, such as C and Java. This background made it very easy for me to create multithreaded applications using threads. Then, Apple changed everything when they released **Grand Central Dispatch** (**GCD**) with OS X 10.6 and iOS 4. At first, I went into denial; there was no way GCD could manage my application's threads better than I could. Then, I entered the anger phase; GCD was hard to use and understand. Next was the bargaining phase; maybe I could use GCD with my threading code, so I could still control how the threading worked. Then, there was the depression phase; maybe GCD does handle threading better than I could. Finally, I entered the wow phase; this GCD thing is really easy to use and works amazingly well.

After using GCD and operation queues with Objective-C, I do not see a reason for using manual threads with Swift.

In this chapter, we will learn about the following topics:

- The basics of concurrency and parallelism
- How to use GCD to create and manage concurrent dispatch queues
- How to use GCD to create and manage serial dispatch queues
- How to use various GCD functions to add tasks to the dispatch queues
- How to use Operation and OperationQueues to add concurrency to our applications

We have not seen a lot of improvement with regards to concurrency in the Swift language over the course of Swift 5.x. It does appear that this will change in the future as concurrency improvements are one of the main goals of Swift 6. Let's start off by looking at the difference between concurrency and parallelism, one that is important to understand.

Concurrency and parallelism

Concurrency is the concept of multiple tasks starting, running, and completing within the same time period. This does not necessarily mean that the tasks are executing simultaneously. In fact, in order for tasks to be run simultaneously, our application needs to be running on a multicore or multiprocessor system. Concurrency allows us to share the processor or cores for multiple tasks; however, a single core can only execute one task at a given time.

Parallelism is the concept of two or more tasks running simultaneously. Since each core of our processor can only execute one task at a time, the number of tasks executing simultaneously is limited to the number of cores within our processors and the number of processors that we have. As an example, if we have a four-core processor, then we are limited to running four tasks simultaneously. Today's processors can execute tasks so quickly that it may appear that larger tasks are executing simultaneously. However, within the system, the larger tasks are actually taking turns executing subtasks on the cores.

In order to understand the difference between concurrency and parallelism, let's look at how a juggler juggles balls. If you watch a juggler, it seems they are catching and throwing multiple balls at any given time; however, a closer look reveals that they are, in fact, only catching and throwing one ball at a time. The other balls are in the air waiting to be caught and thrown. If we want to be able to catch and throw multiple balls simultaneously, we need to have multiple jugglers.

This example is really good because we can think of jugglers as the cores of a processor. A system with a single-core processor (one juggler), regardless of how it seems, can only execute one task (catch or throw one ball) at a time. If we want to execute more than one task at a time, we need to use a multicore processor (more than one juggler).

Back in the days when all of the processors were single-core, the only way to have a system that executed tasks simultaneously was to have multiple processors in the system. This also required specialized software to take advantage of the multiple processors. In today's world, just about every device has a processor that has multiple cores, and both iOS and macOS are designed to take advantage of these multiple cores to run tasks simultaneously.

Traditionally, the way applications added concurrency was to create multiple threads; however, this model does not scale well to an arbitrary number of cores. The biggest problem with using threads was that our applications ran on a variety of systems (and processors), and in order to optimize our code, we needed to know how many cores/processors could be efficiently used at a given time, which is usually not known at the time of development.

To solve this problem, many operating systems, including iOS and macOS, started relying on asynchronous functions. These functions are often used to initiate tasks that could possibly take a long time to complete, such as making an HTTP request or writing data to disk. An asynchronous function typically starts a long-running task and then returns prior to the task's completion. Usually, this task runs in the background and uses a callback function (such as a closure in Swift) when the task completes.

These asynchronous functions work great for the tasks that the operating system provides them for, but what if we need to create our own asynchronous functions and do not want to manage the threads ourselves? For this, Apple provides a couple of technologies. In this chapter, we will be covering two of these: GCD and operation queues.

GCD is a low-level, C-based API that allows specific tasks to be queued up for execution and schedules the execution on any of the available processor cores. Operation queues are similar to GCD; however, they are Foundation objects and are internally implemented using GCD.

Let's begin by looking at GCD.

Grand Central Dispatch (GCD)

Prior to Swift 3, using GCD felt like writing low-level C code. The API was a little cumbersome and sometimes hard to understand because it did not use any of the Swift language design features. This all changed with Swift 3 because Apple took up the task of rewriting the API so it would meet the Swift 3 API guidelines.

GCD provides what is known as dispatch queues to manage submitted tasks. The queues manage these submitted tasks and execute them in a **First-In, First-Out (FIFO)** order. This ensures that the tasks are started in the order they were submitted.

A task is simply some work that our application needs to perform. For example, we can create tasks that perform simple calculations, read/write data to disk, make an HTTP request, or anything else that our application needs to do. We define these tasks by placing the code inside either a function or a closure and adding it to a dispatch queue.

GCD provides three types of dispatch queues:

- **Serial queues**: Tasks in a serial queue (also known as a **private queue**) are executed one at a time in the order they were submitted. Each task is started only after the preceding task is completed. Serial queues are often used to synchronize access to specific resources because we are guaranteed that no two tasks in a serial queue will ever run simultaneously. Therefore, if the only way to access the specific resource is through the tasks in the serial queue, then no two tasks will attempt to access the resource at the same time or out of order.

- **Concurrent queues**: Tasks in a concurrent queue (also known as a **global dispatch queue**) execute concurrently; however, the tasks are still started in the order that they were added to the queue. The exact number of tasks that can be executed at any given instance is variable and is dependent on the system's current conditions and resources. The decision of when to start a task is up to GCD and is not something that we can control within our application.

- **Main dispatch queue**: The main dispatch queue is a globally available serial queue that executes tasks on the application's main thread. Since tasks put into the main dispatch queue run on the main thread, it is usually called from a background queue when some background processing has finished and the user interface needs to be updated.

Dispatch queues offer several advantages over traditional threads. The first and foremost advantage is that, with dispatch queues, the system handles the creation and management of threads rather than the application itself. The system can scale the number of threads dynamically, based on the overall available resources of the system and the current system conditions. This means that dispatch queues can manage the threads with greater efficiency than we could.

Another advantage of dispatch queues is that we are able to control the order in which the tasks are started. With serial queues, not only do we control the order in which tasks are started, but we also ensure that one task does not start before the preceding one is complete. With traditional threads, this can be very cumbersome and brittle to implement, but with dispatch queues, as we will see later in this chapter, it is quite easy.

Calculation types

Before we look at how to use dispatch queues, let's create a class that will help us to demonstrate how the various types of queues work. This class will contain two basic functions and we will name the class DoCalculations. The first function will simply perform some basic calculations and then return a value. Here is the code for this function, which is named doCalc():

```
func doCalc() {
    let x = 100
    let y = x*x
    _ = y/x
}
```

The other function, which we will name performCalculation(), accepts two parameters. One is an integer named iterations and the other is a string named tag. The performCalculation() function calls the doCalc() function repeatedly until it calls the function the same number of times as defined by the iterations parameter. We also use the CFAbsoluteTimeGetCurrent() function to calculate the elapsed time it took to perform all of the iterations, and then we print the elapsed time with the tag string to the console. This will let us know when the function completes and how long it took to complete it. Here is the code for this function:

```
func performCalculation(_ iterations: Int, tag: String) {
    let start = CFAbsoluteTimeGetCurrent()
    for _ in 0 ..< iterations {
        self.doCalc()
    }
    let end = CFAbsoluteTimeGetCurrent()
    print("time for \(tag):\(end-start)")
}
```

These functions will be used together to keep our queues busy, so we can see how they work. Let's begin by looking at how we would create a dispatch queue.

Creating queues

We use the DispatchQueue initializer to create a new dispatch queue. The following code shows how we would create a new dispatch queue:

```
let concurrentQueue = DispatchQueue(label: "cqueue.hoffman.jon",
                      attributes: .concurrent)
let serialQueue = DispatchQueue(label: "squeue.hoffman.jon")
```

The first line would create a concurrent queue with a label of `cqueue.hoffman.jon`, while the second line would create a serial queue with a label of `squeue.hoffman.jon`. The `ispatchQueue` initializer takes the following parameters:

- `label`: This is a string label that is attached to the queue to uniquely identify it in debugging tools, such as instruments and crash reports. It is recommended that we use a reverse DNS naming convention. This parameter is optional and can be `nil`.

- `attributes`: This specifies the type of queue to make. This can be `DispatchQueue.Attributes.serial`, `DispatchQueue.Attributes.concurrent`, or `nil`. If this parameter is `nil`, a serial queue is created. You can use `.serial` or `.concurrent` as we showed in the sample code.

 Some programming languages use the reverse DNS naming convention to name certain components. This convention is based on a registered domain name that is reversed. As an example, if we worked for a company that had a domain name of `mycompany.com` with a product called widget, the reverse DNS name would be `com.mycompany.widget`.

Let's now look at how we can create and use concurrent queues.

Creating and using a concurrent queue

A concurrent queue will execute tasks in a FIFO order; however, the tasks will execute concurrently and finish in any order. Let's see how we would create and use a concurrent queue. The following line will create the concurrent queue that we will be using for this section and will also create an instance of the `DoCalculations` type that will be used to test the queue:

```
let cqueue = DispatchQueue(label: "cqueue.hoffman.jon",
            attributes:.concurrent)
let calculation = DoCalculations()
```

The first line will create a new dispatch queue that we will name `cqueue`, and the second line creates an instance of the `DoCalculations` type. Now, let's see how we would use our concurrent queue by using the `performCalculation()` method from the `DoCalculations` type to perform some calculations:

```
let c = {calculation.performCalculation(1000, tag: "async1")}
cqueue.async(execute: c)
```

In the preceding code, we created a closure, which represents our task and simply calls the `performCalculation()` function of the `DoCalculation` instance, requesting that it runs through 1,000 iterations of the `doCalc()` function. Finally, we use the `async(execute:)` method of our queue to execute it. This code will execute the task in a concurrent dispatch queue, which is separate from the main thread.

While the preceding example works perfectly, we can actually shorten the code a little bit. The next example shows that we do not need to create a separate closure as we did in the preceding example. We can also submit the task to execute, as follows:

```
cqueue.async {
    calculation.performCalculation(1000, tag: "async1")
}
```

This shorthand version is how we usually submit small code blocks to our queues. If we have larger tasks or tasks that we need to submit multiple times, we will generally want to create a closure and submit the closure to the queue as we showed in the first example.

Let's see how a concurrent queue works by adding several items to the queue and looking at the order and time that they return. The following code will add three tasks to the queue. Each task will call the `performCalculation()` function with various iteration counts.

Remember that the `performCalculation()` function will execute the calculation routine continuously until it is executed the number of times defined by the iteration count passed in. Therefore, the larger the iteration count we pass into the function, the longer it should take to execute. Let's look at the following code:

```
cqueue.async {
    calculation.performCalculation(10_000_000, tag: "async1")
}

cqueue.async {
    calculation.performCalculation(1000, tag: "async2")
}

cqueue.async {
    calculation.performCalculation(100_000, tag: "async3")
}
```

Note that each of the functions is called with a different value in the `tag` parameter. Since the `performCalculation()` function prints out the `tag` variable with the elapsed time, we can see the order in which the tasks complete and the time they took to execute. If we execute the preceding code, we should see results similar to this:

```
time for async2: 0.000200986862182617
time for async3: 0.00800204277038574
time for async1: 0.461670994758606
```

 The elapsed time will vary from one run to the next and from system to system.

Since the queues function in a FIFO order, the task that had the tag of `async1` was executed first. However, as we can see from the results, it was the last task to finish. Since this is a concurrent queue, if it is possible (if the system has the available resources), the blocks of code will execute concurrently. This is why tasks with the tags of `async2` and `async3` completed prior to the task that had the `async1` tag, even though the execution of the `async1` task began before the other two.

Now, let's see how a serial queue executes tasks.

Creating and using a serial queue

A serial queue functions a little differently to a concurrent queue. A serial queue will only execute one task at a time and will wait for one task to complete before starting the next one. This queue, like the concurrent dispatch queue, follows the FIFO order. The following line of code will create a serial queue that we will be using for this section and will create an instance of the `DoCalculations` type:

```
let squeue = DispatchQueue(label: "squeue.hoffman.jon")
let calculation = DoCalculations()
```

The first line will create a new serial dispatch queue that we name `squeue`, and the second line creates an instance of the `DoCalculations` type. Now, let's see how we would use our serial queue by using the `performCalculation()` method from the `DoCalculations` type to perform some calculations:

```
let s = {calculation.performCalculation(1000, tag: "async1")}
squeue.async (execute: s)
```

In the preceding code, we created a closure, which represents our task, that simply calls the performCalculation() function of the DoCalculation instance, requesting that it runs through 1,000 iterations of the doCalc() function. Finally, we use the async(execute:) method of our queue to execute it. This code will execute the task in a serial dispatch queue, which is separate from the main thread. As we can see from this code, we use the serial queue exactly like we use the concurrent queue.

We can shorten this code a little bit, just like we did with the concurrent queue. The following example shows how we would do this with a serial queue:

```
squeue.async {
    calculation.performCalculation(1000, tag: "async2")
}
```

Let's see how the serial queue works by adding several items to the queue and looking at the order in which they complete. The following code will add three tasks, which will call the performCalculation() function with various iteration counts to the queue:

```
squeue.async {
    calculation.performCalculation(100000, tag: "async1")
}

squeue.async {
    calculation.performCalculation(1000, tag: "async2")
}

squeue.async {
    calculation.performCalculation(100000, tag: "async3")
}
```

Just as we did in the concurrent queue example, we call the performCalculation() function with various iteration counts and different values in the tag parameter. Since the performCalculation() function prints out the tag string with the elapsed time, we can see the order in which the tasks complete and the time it takes to execute. If we execute this code, we should see the following results:

```
time for async1: 0.00648999214172363
time for async2: 0.00009602308273315
time for async3: 0.0051580071449279
```

The elapsed time will vary from one run to the next and from system to system.

Unlike the concurrent queues, we can see that the tasks completed in the same order that they were submitted in, even though the sync2 and sync3 tasks took considerably less time to complete. This demonstrates that a serial queue only executes one task at a time and that the queue waits for each task to complete before starting the next one.

In the previous examples, we used the async method to execute the code blocks. We could also use the sync method.

async versus sync

In the previous examples, we used the async method to execute the code blocks. When we use the async method, the call will not block the current thread. This means that the method returns and the code block is executed asynchronously.

Rather than using the async method, we could use the sync method to execute the code blocks. The sync method will block the current thread, which means it will not return until the execution of the code has completed. Generally, we use the async method, but there are use cases where the sync method is useful. These use cases are usually when we have a separate thread and we want that thread to wait for some work to finish.

Executing code on the main queue function

The DispatchQueue.main.async(execute:) function will execute code on the application's main queue. We generally use this function when we want to update our code from another thread or queue.

The main queue is automatically created for the main thread when the application starts. This main queue is a serial queue; therefore, items in this queue are executed one at a time, in the order that they were submitted. We will generally want to avoid using this queue unless we have a need to update the user interface from a background thread.

The following code example shows how we would use this function:

```
let squeue = DispatchQueue(label: "squeue.hoffman.jon")
squeue.async {
    let resizedImage = image.resize(to: rect)
    DispatchQueue.main.async {
        picView.image = resizedImage
    }
}
```

In the previous code, we assume that we have added a method to the UIImage type that will resize the image. In this code, we create a new serial queue and, in that queue, we resize an image. This is a good example of how to use a dispatch queue because we would not want to resize an image on the main queue since it would freeze the UI while the image is being resized. Once the image is resized, we then need to update UIImageView with the new image; however, all updates to the UI need to occur on the main thread. Therefore, we will use the DispatchQueue.main.async function to perform the update on the main queue.

There will be times when we need to execute tasks after a delay. If we were using a threading model, we would need to create a new thread, perform some sort of delay or sleep function, and execute our task. With GCD, we can use the asyncAfter function.

Using asyncAfter

The asyncAfter function will execute a block of code asynchronously after a given delay. This is very useful when we need to pause the execution of our code. The following code sample shows how we would use the asyncAfter function:

```
let queue2 = DispatchQueue(label: "squeue.hoffman.jon")
let delayInSeconds = 2.0
let pTime = DispatchTime.now() + Double(delayInSeconds * Double(NSEC_
PER_SEC)) / Double(NSEC_PER_SEC)
queue2.asyncAfter(deadline: pTime) {
    print("Time's Up")
}
```

In this code, we begin by creating a serial dispatch queue. We then create an instance of the DispatchTime type and calculate the time to execute the block of code based on the current time. We then use the asyncAfter function to execute the code block after the delay.

Now, that we have looked at GCD, let's look at operation queues.

Using the Operation and OperationQueue types

The Operation and OperationQueue types, working together, provide us with an alternative to GCD for adding concurrency to our applications. Operation queues are part of the Foundation framework and function like dispatch queues as they are a higher level of abstraction over GCD.

We define the tasks (operations) that we wish to execute and then add the tasks to the operation queue. The operation queue will then handle the scheduling and execution of tasks. Operation queues are instances of the OperationQueue class and operations are instances of the Operation class.

An operation represents a single unit of work or a task. The Operation type is an abstract class that provides a thread-safe structure for modeling the state, priority, and dependencies. This class must be subclassed to perform any useful work; we will look at how to subclass this class in the *Subclassing the Operation class* section of this chapter.

Apple provides a concrete implementation of the Operation type that we can use as-is for situations where it does not make sense to build a custom subclass. This subclass is BlockOperation.

More than one operation queue can exist at the same time, and, in fact, there is always at least one operation queue running. This operation queue is known as the **main queue**. The main queue is automatically created for the main thread when the application starts and is where all of the UI operations are performed.

One thing to keep in mind with operation queues is that they add additional overhead because they are Foundation objects. For the large majority of applications, this little extra overhead should not be an issue or even noticed; however, for some projects, such as games that need every last resource that they can get, this extra overhead might very well be an issue.

There are several ways that we can use the Operation and OperationQueue classes to add concurrency to our application. In this chapter, we will look at three of these ways. The first one we will look at is the use of the BlockOperation implementation of the Operation abstract class.

Using BlockOperation

In this section, we will be using the same `DoCalculation` class that we used in the *Grand Central Dispatch (GCD)* section to keep our queues busy with work so that we can see how the `OperationQueue` class works.

The `BlockOperation` class is a concrete implementation of the `Operation` type that can manage the execution of one or more blocks. This class can be used to execute several tasks at once without the need to create separate operations for each task.

Let's see how we can use the `BlockOperation` class to add concurrency to our application. The following code shows how to add three tasks to an operation queue using a single `BlockOperation` instance:

```
let calculation = DoCalculations()
let blockOperation1: BlockOperation = BlockOperation.init(
    block: {
        calculation.performCalculation(10000000, tag: "Operation 1")
    }
)
blockOperation1.addExecutionBlock({
        calculation.performCalculation(10000, tag: "Operation 2")
    }
)
blockOperation1.addExecutionBlock({
        calculation.performCalculation(1000000, tag: "Operation 3")
    }
)
let operationQueue = OperationQueue()
operationQueue.addOperation(blockOperation1)
```

In this code, we begin by creating an instance of the `DoCalculation` class and an instance of the `OperationQueue` class. Next, we create an instance of the `BlockOperation` class using the init constructor. This constructor takes a single parameter, which is a block of code that represents one of the tasks we want to execute in the queue. Next, we add two additional tasks using the `addExecutionBlock()` method.

One of the differences between dispatch queues and operations is that, with dispatch queues, if resources are available, the tasks are executed as they are added to the queue. With operations, the individual tasks are not executed until the operation itself is submitted to an operation queue. This allows us to initiate all of the operations into a single block operation prior to executing them.

Once we add all of the tasks to the BlockOperation instance, we then add the operation to the OperationQueue instance that we created at the beginning of the code. At this point, the individual tasks within the operation start to execute.

This example shows how to use BlockOperation to queue up multiple tasks and then pass the tasks to the operation queue. The tasks are executed in a FIFO order; therefore, the first task that is added will be the first task executed. However, the tasks can be executed concurrently if we have the available resources.

The output from this code should look similar to this:

```
time for Operation 2: 0.00546294450759888
time for Operation 3: 0.0800899863243103
time for Operation 1: 0.484337985515594
```

What if we do not want the tasks to run concurrently? What if we wanted them to run serially like the serial dispatch queue? We can set a property in the operation queue that defines the number of tasks that can be run concurrently in the queue. The property is named maxConcurrentOperationCount, and is used like this:

```
operationQueue.maxConcurrentOperationCount = 1
```

However, if we add this line to our previous example, it will not work as expected. To see why this is, we need to understand what the property actually defines. If we look at Apple's OperationQueue class reference, the definition of the property is *the maximum number of queued operations that can execute at the same time*.

What this tells us is that this property defines the number of operations (this is the keyword) that can be executed at the same time. The BlockOperation instance, which we added all of the tasks to, represents a single operation; therefore, no other BlockOperation added to the queue will execute until the first one is complete, but the individual tasks within the operation will execute concurrently. To run the tasks serially, we would need to create a separate instance of BlockOperation for each task.

Using an instance of the BlockOperation class is good if we have several tasks that we want to execute concurrently, but they will not start executing until we add the operation to an operation queue. Let's look at a simpler way of adding tasks to an operation queue using the addOperationWithBlock() method.

Using the addOperation() method of the operation queue

The OperationQueue class has a method named addOperation(), which makes it easy to add a block of code to the queue. This method automatically wraps the block of code in an operation object and then passes that operation to the queue. Let's see how to use this method to add tasks to a queue:

```
let operationQueue = OperationQueue()
let calculation = DoCalculations()
operationQueue.addOperation() {
    calculation.performCalculation(10000000, tag: "Operation1")
}
operationQueue.addOperation() {
    calculation.performCalculation(10000, tag: "Operation2")
}
operationQueue.addOperation() {
    calculation.performCalculation(1000000, tag: "Operation3")
}
```

In the BlockOperation example earlier in this chapter, we added the tasks that we wished to execute into a BlockOperation instance. In this example, we are adding the tasks directly to the operation queue, and each task represents one complete operation. Once we create the instance of the operation queue, we then use the addOperation() method to add the tasks to the queue.

Also, in the BlockOperation example, the individual tasks did not execute until all of the tasks were added, and then that operation was added to the queue. This example is similar to the GCD example where the tasks began executing as soon as they were added to the operation queue.

If we run the preceding code, the output should be similar to this:

```
time for Operation2: 0.0115870237350464
time for Operation3: 0.0790849924087524
time for Operation1: 0.520610988140106
```

You will notice that the operations are executed concurrently. With this example, we can execute the tasks serially by using the `maxConcurrentOperationCount` property that we mentioned earlier. Let's try this by initializing the `OperationQueue` instance as follows:

```
var operationQueue = OperationQueue()
operationQueue.maxConcurrentOperationCount = 1
```

Now, if we run the example, the output should be similar to this:

```
time for Operation1: 0.418763995170593
time for Operation2: 0.000427007675170898
time for Operation3: 0.0441589951515198
```

In this example, we can see that each task waited for the previous task to complete before starting.

Using the `addOperation()` method to add tasks to the operation queue is generally easier than using the `BlockOperation` method; however, the tasks will begin as soon as they are added to the queue. This is usually the desired behavior, although there are use cases where we do not want the tasks executing until all operations are added to the queue, as we saw in the `BlockOperation` example.

Now, let's look at how we can subclass the `Operation` class to create an operation that we can add directly to an operation queue.

Subclassing the Operation class

The previous two examples showed how to add small blocks of code to our operation queues. In these examples, we called the `performCalculations` method in the `DoCalculation` class to perform our tasks. These examples illustrate two really good ways to add concurrency for functionality that is already written, but what if, at design time, we want to design our `DoCalculation` class itself for concurrency? For this, we can subclass the `Operation` class.

The `Operation` abstract class provides a significant amount of infrastructure. This allows us to very easily create a subclass without a lot of work. We will need to provide at least an initialization method and a `main` method. The `main` method will be called when the queue begins executing the operation.

Let's see how to implement the `DoCalculation` class as a subclass of the `Operation` class; we will call this new class `MyOperation`:

```swift
class MyOperation: Operation {
    let iterations: Int
    let tag: String
    init(iterations: Int, tag: String) {
        self.iterations = iterations
        self.tag = tag
    }

    override func main() {
        performCalculation()
    }

    func performCalculation() {
        let start = CFAbsoluteTimeGetCurrent()
        for _ in 0 ..< iterations {
            self.doCalc()
        }
        let end = CFAbsoluteTimeGetCurrent()
        print("time for \(tag):\(end-start)")
    }

    func doCalc() {
        let x=100
        let y = x*x
        _ = y/x
    }
}
```

We begin by defining that the MyOperation class is a subclass of the Operation class. Within the implementation of the class, we define two class constants, which represent the iteration count and the tag that the performCalculations() method uses. Keep in mind that when the operation queue begins executing the operation, it will call the main() method with no parameters; therefore, any parameters that we need to pass it must be passed through initializers.

In this example, our initializer takes two parameters that are used to set the iterations and tag class constants. Then, the main() method, which the operation queue is going to call to begin the execution of the operation, simply calls the performCalculation() method.

We can now very easily add instances of our `MyOperation` class to an operation queue, as follows:

```
let operationQueue = NSOperationQueue()
    operationQueue.addOperation( MyOperation(iterations: 10000000,
tag:"Operation 1")
)
operationQueue.addOperation(
    MyOperation(iterations: 10000, tag:"Operation 2")
)
operationQueue.addOperation(
    MyOperation(iterations: 1000000, tag:"Operation 3")
)
```

If we run this code, we will see the following results:

```
time for Operation 2: 0.00187397003173828
time for Operation 3: 0.104826986789703
time for Operation 1: 0.866684019565582
```

As we saw earlier, we can also execute the tasks serially by setting the `maxConcurrentOperationCount` property of the operation queue to 1.

If we know that we need to execute some functionality concurrently prior to writing the code, I would recommend subclassing the `Operation` class, as shown in this example, rather than using the previous examples. This gives us the cleanest implementation; however, there is nothing wrong with using the `BlockOperation` class or the `addOperation()` methods described earlier in this section.

 Before we consider adding concurrency to our application, we should make sure that we understand why we are adding it and ask ourselves whether it is necessary. While concurrency can make our application more responsive by offloading work from our main application thread to a background thread, it also adds extra overhead and complexity to our code. I have even seen numerous applications, in various languages, which actually ran better after we pulled out some of the concurrency code. This is because the concurrency was not well thought out or planned.

Summary

At the start of this chapter, we had a discussion about running tasks concurrently compared to running tasks in parallel. We also discussed the hardware limitations that restrict how many tasks can run in parallel on a given device. Having a good understanding of these concepts is very important to understanding how and when to add concurrency to our projects.

We learned about GCD and operation queues, two different ways of implementing concurrency. While GCD is not limited to system-level applications, before we use it in our application, we should consider whether operation queues would be easier and more appropriate for our needs. In general, we should use the highest level of abstraction that meets our needs. This will usually point us to using operation queues; however, there really is nothing preventing us from using GCD, and it may be more appropriate for our needs.

We should always consider whether it is necessary to add concurrency to our applications. It is a good idea to think and talk about concurrency when we are discussing an application's expected behavior.

In the next chapter, we will look at some advanced topics and things to consider when we are creating our own custom types.

17
Custom Value Types

In most traditional object-oriented programming languages, we create classes (which are reference types) as blueprints for our objects. In Swift, unlike other object-oriented languages, structures have much of the same functionality as classes, however, they are value types. Apple has said that we should prefer value types, such as structures, to reference types, but what are the differences between a reference type and a value type?

In this chapter, you will explore the following topics:

- The differences between value types and reference types
- Why recursive data types cannot be created as a value type
- How to implement copy-on-write in your custom type
- How to conform to the Equatable protocol

As we saw in *Chapter 8*, *Classes, Structures, and Protocols*, we have the ability to create our custom types as either a reference type (or class) or a value type (or structure). Let's review the differences between these two types because it is important to understand these differences when determining what type to use for our custom types.

Value types and reference types

Structures are value types; when we pass instances of a structure in our application, we pass a copy of the structure and not the original structure. Classes are reference types; therefore, when we pass an instance of a class within our application, a reference to the original instance is passed. It is very important to understand this difference. We will discuss a very high-level view here but will provide additional details in *Chapter 18*, *Memory Management*.

When we pass structures within our application, we are passing copies of the structures and not the original structures. This means that the function gets its own copy of the structure, which it can change as needed without affecting the original instance of the structure.

When we pass an instance of a class within our application, we are passing a reference to the original instance of the class, therefore, any changes made to the instance of the class will persist.

To illustrate the difference between value types and reference types, let's examine a real-world object: a book. If we have a friend who wants to read *Mastering Swift 5.3, Sixth Edition*, we could either buy them their own copy or share ours.

If we bought our friend their own copy of the book, then any notes they made in the book would remain in their copy of the book and would not be reflected in our copy. This is how passing by value works with structures and variables. Any changes that are made to the structure or variable within the function are not reflected back to the original instance of the structure or variable.

If we share our copy of the book, then any notes that were made in the book will stay in the book when it is returned to us. This is how passing by reference works. Any changes that are made to the instance of the class remain when the function exits.

When we pass an instance of a value type, we are actually passing a copy of the instance. You may be wondering about the performance of large value types when they are passed from one part of our code to another. For structures that have the possibility of becoming very large, we can use copy-on-write.

The explanation in the previous paragraphs is pretty straightforward; however, it is a very important concept that we must understand. In this section, we are going to examine the differences between value types and reference types so that we know when to use each type.

Let's begin by creating two types; one is going to be a structure (or value type) and the other is going to be a class (or reference type). We will be using these types in this section to demonstrate the differences between value types and reference types. The first type that we will examine is named MyValueType. We will implement MyValueType using a structure, which means that it is a value type, as its name suggests:

```
struct MyValueType {
    var name: String
    var assignment: String
    var grade: Int
}
```

In `MyValueType`, we define three properties. Two of the properties are of the `String` type (`name` and `assignment`) and one is of the `Integer` type (`grade`). Now, let's take a look at how we can implement this as a class:

```
class MyReferenceType {
    var name: String
    var assignment: String
    var grade: Int

    init(name: String, assignment: String, grade: Int) {
        self.name = name
        self.assignment = assignment
        self.grade = grade
    }
}
```

The `MyReferenceType` type defines the same three properties as in the `MyValueType` type, however, we need to define an initializer in the `MyReferenceType` type that we did not need to define in the `MyValueType` type. The reason for this is that structures provide us with a default initializer that will initialize all the properties that need to be initialized if we do not provide a default initializer.

Let's take a look at how we can use each of these types. The following code shows how we can create instances of each of these types:

```
var ref = MyReferenceType(name: "Jon", assignment: "Math Test 1",
grade: 90)
var val = MyValueType(name: "Jon", assignment: "Math Test 1", grade:
90)
```

As you can see in this code, instances of structures are created in exactly the same way as the instances of classes. Being able to use the same format to create instances of structures and classes is good because it makes our lives easier; however, we do need to bear in mind that value types behave in a different manner to reference types. Let's explore this; the first thing we need to do is create two functions that will change the grades for the instances of the two types:

```
func extraCreditReferenceType(ref: MyReferenceType, extraCredit: Int) {
    ref.grade += extraCredit
}

func extraCreditValueType(val: MyValueType, extraCredit: Int) {
    val.grade += extraCredit
}
```

Each of these functions takes an instance of one of our types and an extra credit amount. Within the function, we will add the extra credit amount to the grade. If we try to use this code we will receive an error in the `extraCreditValueType()` function telling us that the left side of the mutable operation is not mutable. The reason for this is that a value type parameter, by default, is immutable because the function is receiving an immutable copy of the parameter.

Using a value type like this protects us from making accidental changes to the instances; this is because the instances are scoped to the function or type in which they are created. Value types also protect us from having multiple references to the same instance. Therefore, they are, by default, thread (concurrency) safe because each thread will have its own version of the value type. If we absolutely need to change an instance of a value type outside of its scope, we could use an `inout` parameter.

We define an `inout` parameter by placing the `inout` keyword at the start of the parameter's definition. An `inout` parameter has a value that is passed into the function. This value is then modified by the function and is passed back out of the function to replace the original value.

Let's explore how we can use an `inout` parameter. We will begin by creating a function that is designed to retrieve the grade for an assignment from a data store. However, to simplify our example, we will simply generate a random score. The following code demonstrates how we can write this function.

Let's take a look at how we can use value types with the `inout` keyword to create a version of the previous example that will work correctly. The first thing we need to do is modify the `getGradesForAssignment()` function to use an instance of `MyValueType` that it can modify:

```
func getGradeForAssignment(assignment: inout MyValueType) {
    // Code to get grade from DB
    // Random code here to illustrate issue
    let num = Int.random(in: 80..<100)
    assignment.grade = num
    print("Grade for \(assignment.name) is \(num)")
}
```

This function is designed to retrieve the grade for the assignment that is defined in the `MyValueType` instance and is then passed into the function. Once the grade is retrieved, we will use it to set the grade property of the `MyValueType` instance. We will also print the grade out to the console so that we can see what grade it is. Now let's explore how to use this function:

```
var mathGrades = [MyValueType]()
var students = ["Jon", "Kailey", "Kara"]
var mathAssignment = MyValueType(name: "", assignment: "Math
Assignment", grade: 0)
for student in students {
    mathAssignment.name = student
    getGradeForAssignment(assignment: &mathAssignment)
    mathGrades.append(mathAssignment)
}

for assignment in mathGrades {
    print("\(assignment.name): grade \(assignment.grade)")
}
```

In the previous code, we created a `mathGrades` array that will store the grades for our assignment and a `students` array that will contain the names of the students that we wish to retrieve the grades for. We then created an instance of the `MyValueType` structure that contains the name for the assignment. We will use this instance to request the grades from the `getGradeForAssignment()` function. Notice that when we pass in the `mathAssignment` instance, we prefix the name of the instance with the & symbol. This lets us know that we are passing the reference to the original instance and not a copy. Now that everything is defined, we will loop through the list of students to retrieve the grades. The output of this code will look similar to the following snippet:

```
Grade for Jon is 87
Grade for Kailey is 90
Grade for Kara is 83
Jon: grade 87
Kailey: grade 90
Kara: grade 83
```

The output from this code is what we expected to see, where each instance in the `mathGrades` array represents the correct grade. The reason this code works correctly is that we are passing a reference from the `mathAssignment` instance to the `getGradeForAssignment()` function, and not a copy.

There are some things we cannot do with value types that we can do with reference (or class) types. The first thing that we will look at is the recursive data type.

Recursive data types for reference types

A recursive data type is a type that contains values of the same type as a property for the type. Recursive data types are used when we want to define dynamic data structures, such as lists and trees. The size of these dynamic data structures can grow or shrink depending on our runtime requirements.

Linked lists are perfect examples of a dynamic data structure that we can implement using a recursive data type. A linked list is a group of nodes that are linked together and where, in its simplest form, each node maintains a link to the next node in the list. *Figure 17.1* shows how a very basic linked list works:

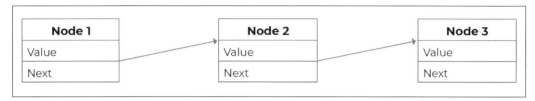

Figure 17.1: A basic linked list

Each node in the list contains a value or data, and it also contains the link to the next node in the list. If one of the nodes in the list loses the reference to the next node, then the remainder of the list will be lost because each node is only aware of the next node. Some linked lists maintain a link to both the previous nodes and the following nodes to allow us to move both forward and backward through the list.

The following code shows how we can create a linked list using a reference type:

```
class LinkedListReferenceType {
    var value: String
    var next: LinkedListReferenceType?
    init(value: String) {
        self.value = value
    }
}
```

In the `LinkedListReferenceType` class, we have two properties. The first property is named `value` and it contains the data for this instance. The second property is named `next`, which points to the next item in the linked list. If the `next` property is `nil`, then this instance will be the last node in the list. If we try to implement this linked list as a value type, the code will be similar to the following:

```
struct LinkedListValueType {
    var value: String
    var next: LinkedListValueType?
}
```

When we add this code to a playground, we receive the following error: `Recursive value type LinkedListValueType is not allowed`. This tells us that Swift does not allow recursive value types. However, we can implement them as a reference type, which we discussed earlier.

If you think about it, recursive value types are a really bad idea because of how value types function. Let's examine this for a minute, because it will really stress the difference between value types and reference types. It will also help you to understand *why* we need reference types.

Let's say that we are able to create the `LinkedListValueType` structure without any errors. Now let's create three nodes for our list, as shown in the following code:

```
var one = LinkedListValueType(value: "One",next: nil)
var two = LinkedListValueType(value: "Two",next: nil)
var three = LinkedListValueType(value: "Three",next: nil)
```

Now we will link these nodes together using the following code:

```
one.next = two
two.next = three
```

Do you see the problem with this code? If not, think about how a value type is passed. In the first line, `one.next = two`, we are not actually setting the `next` property to the original `two` instance; in fact, we are actually setting it to a copy of the `two` instance, because by implementing the `LinkedListValueType` as a value type, we are passing the value and not the actual instance. This means that in the next line, `two.next = three`, we are setting the `next` property of the original `two` instance to the `three` instance.

However, this change is not reflected back in the copy that was made for the `next` property of the one instance. Sounds a little confusing? Let's clear it up a little by looking at a diagram that shows the state of our three `LinkedListValueType` instances if we were able to run this code:

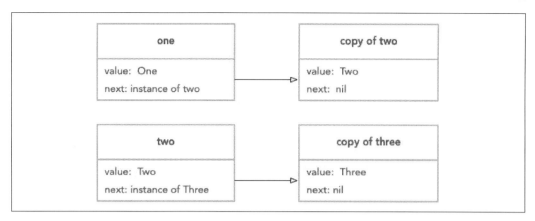

Figure 17.2: A linked list structure example

As you can see from the diagram, the next property of the one instance is pointing to a copy of the two instance whose next property is still `nil`. The next property of the original two instance, however, is pointing to the three instance. This means that, if we try to go through the list by starting at the one instance, we will not reach the three instance because the copy of the two instance will still have a next property that is `nil`.

Another thing that we can only do with reference (or class) types is class inheritance.

Inheritance for reference types

In object-oriented programming, inheritance refers to one class (known as a **sub** or **child class**) being derived from another class (known as a **super** or **parent class**). The subclass will inherit methods, properties, and other characteristics from the superclass. With inheritance, we can also create a class hierarchy where we can have multiple layers of inheritance.

Let's take a look at how we can create a class hierarchy with classes in Swift. We will start off by creating a base class named `Animal`:

```swift
class Animal {
    var numberOfLegs = 0
    func sleeps() {
        print("zzzzz")
    }
    func walking() {
        print("Walking on \(numberOfLegs) legs")
    }
```

```
    func speaking() {
        print("No sound")
    }
}
```

In the `Animal` class, we defined one property (`numberOfLegs`) and three methods (`sleeps()`, `walking()`, and `speaking()`). Now, any class that is a subclass of the `Animal` class will also have these properties and methods. Let's examine how this works by creating two classes that are subclasses of the `Animal` class. These two classes will be named `Biped` (an animal with two legs) and `Quadruped` (an animal with four legs):

```
class Biped: Animal {
    override init() {
        super.init() numberOfLegs =2
    }
}

class Quadruped: Animal {
    override init() {
        super.init() numberOfLegs = 4
    }
}
```

Since these two classes inherit all the properties and methods from the `Animal` class, all we need to do is create an initializer that sets the `numberOfLegs` property to the correct number of legs. Now, let's add another layer of inheritance by creating a `Dog` class that will be a subclass of the `Quadruped` class:

```
class Dog: Quadruped {
    override func speaking() {
        print("Barking")
    }
}
```

In the `Dog` class, we inherit from the `Quadruped` class, which, in turn, inherits from the `Animal` class. Therefore, the `Dog` class will have all the properties, methods, and characteristics of both the `Animal` and `Quadruped` classes. If the `Quadruped` class overrides anything from the `Animal` class, then the `Dog` class will inherit the version from the `Quadruped` class.

We can create very complex class hierarchies in this manner; for example, *Figure 17.3* expands on the class hierarchy that we just created to add several other animal classes:

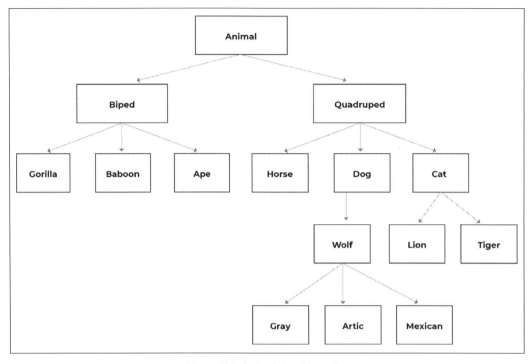

Figure 17.3: Animal class hierarchy

Class hierarchies can get very complex. However, as you just saw, they can eliminate a lot of duplicate code because our subclasses inherit methods, properties, and other characteristics from their superclasses. Therefore, we do not need to recreate them in all of the subclasses.

The biggest drawback of a class hierarchy is the complexity. When we have a complex hierarchy (as shown in the preceding diagram), it is easy to make a change and not realize how it is going to affect all of the subclasses. If you consider the Dog and Cat classes, for example, we may want to add a furColor property to our Quadruped class so that we can set the color of the animal's fur. However, horses do not have fur; they have hair. So, before we can make any changes to a class in our hierarchy, we need to understand how it will affect all the subclasses in the hierarchy.

In Swift, it is best to avoid using complex class hierarchies (as shown in this example), and instead use a protocol-oriented design, unless, of course, there are specific reasons to use them. Now that we have a good understanding of reference and value types, let's explore dynamic dispatch.

Dynamic dispatch

In the previous section, we learned how to use inheritance with classes in order to inherit and override the functionality defined in a superclass. You may be wondering how and when the appropriate implementation is chosen. The process of choosing which implementation to call is performed at runtime and is known as **dynamic dispatch**.

One of the key points to understand from the last paragraph is that the implementation is chosen at runtime. What this means is that a certain amount of runtime overhead is associated with using class inheritance, as shown in the *Inheritance for reference types* section. For most applications, this overhead is not a concern; however, for performance-sensitive applications such as games, this overhead can be costly.

One of the ways that we can reduce the overhead associated with dynamic dispatch is to use the final keyword. The final keyword puts a restriction on the class, method, or function to indicate that it cannot be overridden, in the case of a method or function, or subclasses, in the case of a class.

To use the final keyword, you put it prior to the class, method, or function declaration, as shown in the following code:

```
final func myFunc() {}
final var myProperty = 0
final class MyClass {}
```

In the *Inheritance for reference types* section, we defined a class hierarchy that started with the Animal superclass. If we want to restrict subclasses from overriding the walking() method and the numberOfLegs property, we can change the Animal implementation, as shown in the next example:

```
class Animal {
    final var numberOfLegs = 0

    func sleeps() {
        print("zzzzz")
    }

    final func walking() {
        print("Walking on \(numberOfLegs) legs")
    }
    func speaking() {
        print("No  sound")
    }
}
```

This change allows the application, at runtime, to make a direct call to the `walking()` method rather than an indirect call that gives the application a slight performance increase. If you must use a class hierarchy, it is good practice to use the `final` keyword wherever possible; however, it is better to use a protocol-oriented design, with value types, to avoid this.

Now, let's take a look at something that can help with the performance of our custom value types: copy-on-write.

Copy-on-write

Normally, when we pass an instance of a value type, such as a structure, a new copy of the instance is created. This means that if we have a large data structure that contains 100,000 elements, then every time we pass that instance, we will have to copy all 100,000 elements. This can have a detrimental impact on the performance of our applications, especially if we pass the instance to numerous functions.

To solve this issue, Apple has implemented the copy-on-write feature for all the data structures (such as `Array`, `Dictionary`, and `Set`) in the Swift standard library. With copy-on-write, Swift does not make a second copy of the data structure until a change is made to that data structure. Therefore, if we pass an array of 50,000 elements to another part of our code, and that code does not make any changes to the array, we will avoid the runtime overhead of copying all the elements.

This is a very useful feature and can greatly increase the performance of our applications. However, our custom value types do not automatically get this feature by default. In this section, we will explore how we can use reference types and value types together to implement the copy-on-write feature for our custom value types. To do this, we will create a very basic queue type that will demonstrate how you can add copy-on-write functionality to your custom value types.

We will start off by creating a backend storage type called `BackendQueue` and will implement it as a reference type. The following code gives our `BackendQueue` type the basic functionality of a queue type:

```
fileprivate class BackendQueue<T> {
    private var items = [T]()

    public func addItem(item: T) {
        items.append(item)
    }
```

```
public func getItem() -> T? {
    if items.count > 0 {
        return items.remove(at: 0)
    } else {
        return nil
    }
}

public func count() -> Int {
    return items.count
}
```

The BackendQueue type is a generic type that uses an array to store the data. This type contains three methods, which enables us to add items to the queue, retrieve an item from the queue, and return the number of items in the queue. We use the fileprivate access level to prevent the use of this type outside of the defining source file, because it should only be used to implement the copy-on-write feature for our main queue type.

We now need to add a couple of extra items to the BackendQueue type so that we can use it to implement the copy-on-write feature for the main queue type. The first thing that we will add is a public default initializer and a private initializer that can be used to create a new instance of the BackendQueue type; the following code shows the two initializers:

```
public init() {}
private init(_ items: [T]) {
    self.items = items
}
```

The public initializer will be used to create an instance of the BackendQueue type without any items in the queue. The private initializer will be used internally to create a copy of itself that contains any items that are currently in the queue. Now we will need to create a method that will use the private initializer to create a copy of itself when required:

```
public func copy() -> BackendQueue<T> {
    return BackendQueue<T>(items)
}
```

It could be very easy to make the private initializer public and then let the main queue type call that initializer to create the copy; however, it is good practice to keep the logic needed to create the new copy within the type itself. The reason why you should do this is that if you need to make changes to the type, that may affect how the type is copied. Instead, the logic that you need to change the type is embedded within the type itself and is easy to find. Additionally, if you use the BackendQueue type as the backend storage for multiple types, you will only need to make the changes to the copy logic in one place if it changes.

Here is the final code for the BackendQueue type:

```swift
fileprivate class BackendQueue<T> {
    private var items = [T]()

    public init() {}
    private init(_ items: [T]) {
        self.items = items
    }

    public func addItem(item: T) {
        items.append(item)
    }

    public func getItem() -> T? {
        if items.count > 0 {
            return items.remove(at: 0)
        } else {
            return nil
        }
    }

    public func count() -> Int {
        return items.count
    }

    public func copy() -> BackendQueue<T> {
        return BackendQueue<T>(items)
    }
}
```

Now let's create our Queue type, which will use the BackendQueue type to implement the copy-on-write feature. The following code adds the basic queue functionality to our Queue type:

```swift
struct Queue {
    private var internalQueue = BackendQueue<Int>()

    public mutating func addItem(item: Int) {
        internalQueue.addItem(item: item)
    }
    public mutating func getItem() -> Int? {
        return internalQueue.getItem()
    }
    public func count() -> Int {
        return internalQueue.count()
    }
}
```

The Queue type is implemented as a value type. This type has one private property of the BackendQueue type, which will be used to store the data. This type contains three methods to add items to the queue, retrieve an item from the queue, and return the number of items in the queue. Now let's explore how we can add the copy-on-write feature to the Queue type.

Swift has a global function named isKnownUniquelyReferenced(). This function will return true if there is only one reference to an instance of a reference type, or false if there is more than one reference.

We will begin by adding a function to check whether there is a unique reference to the internalQueue instance. This will be a private function named checkUniquelyReferencedInternalQueue. The following code shows how we can implement this method:

```swift
mutating private func checkUniquelyReferencedInternalQueue() {
    if !isKnownUniquelyReferenced(&internalQueue) {
        internalQueue = internalQueue.copy()
        print("Making a copy of internalQueue")
    } else {
        print("Not making a copy of internalQueue")
    }
}
```

In this method, we check to see whether there are multiple references to the internalQueue instances. If there are multiple references, then we know that we have multiple copies of the Queue instance and, therefore, we can create a new copy.

The Queue type itself is a value type; therefore, when we pass an instance of the Queue type within our code, the code that we pass the instance to receives a new copy of that instance. The BackendQueue type, which the Queue type is using, is a reference type. Therefore, when a copy is made of a Queue instance, then that new copy receives a reference to the original Queue's BackendQueue instance and not a new copy. This means that each instance of the Queue type has a reference to the same internalQueue instance. Consider the following code as an example; both queue1 and queue2 have references to the same internalQueue instance:

```
var queue1 = Queue()
var queue2 = queue1
```

In the Queue type, we know that both the addItem() and getItem() methods change the internalQueue instance. Therefore, before we make these changes, we will want to call the checkUniquelyReferencedInternalQueue() method to create a new copy of the internalQueue instance. These two methods will now have the following code:

```
public mutating func addItem(item: Int) {
    checkUniquelyReferencedInternalQueue()
    internalQueue.addItem(item: item)
}
public mutating func getItem() -> Int? {
    checkUniquelyReferencedInternalQueue()
    return internalQueue.getItem()
}
```

With this code, when either the addItem() or getItem() methods are called – which will change the data in the internalQueue instance – we use the checkUniquelyReferencedInternalQueue() method to create a new instance of the data structure.

Let's add one additional method to the Queue type, which will allow us to see whether there is a unique reference to the internalQueue instance or not. Here is the code for this method:

```
mutating public func uniquelyReferenced() -> Bool {
    return isKnownUniquelyReferenced(&internalQueue)
}
```

Here is the full code listing for the `Queue` type:

```
struct Queue {
    private var internalQueue = BackendQueue<Int>()

    mutating private func checkUniquelyReferencedInternalQueue() {
        if !isKnownUniquelyReferenced(&internalQueue) {
            print("Making a copy of internalQueue")
            internalQueue = internalQueue.copy()
        } else {
            print("Not making a copy of internalQueue")
        }
    }

    public mutating func addItem(item: Int) {
        checkUniquelyReferencedInternalQueue()
        internalQueue.addItem(item: item)
    }

    public mutating func getItem() -> Int? {
        checkUniquelyReferencedInternalQueue();
        return internalQueue.getItem()
    }

    public func count() -> Int {
        return internalQueue.count()
    }

    mutating public func uniquelyReferenced() -> Bool {
        return isKnownUniquelyReferenced(&internalQueue)
    }
}
```

Now let's examine how the copy-on-write functionality works with the `Queue` type. We will start off by creating a new instance of the `Queue` type, adding an item to the queue, and then checking whether we have a unique reference to the `internalQueue` instance. The following code demonstrates how to do this:

```
var queue3 = Queue()
queue3.addItem(item: 1)

print(queue3.uniquelyReferenced())
```

When we add the item to the queue, the following message will be printed to the console. This tells us that within the `checkUniquelyReferencedInternalQueue()` method, it was determined that there was only one reference to the `internalQueue` instance:

```
Not making a copy of internalQueue
```

We can verify this by printing the results of the `uniquelyReference()` method to the console. Now let's make a copy of the `queue3` instance by passing it to a new variable, as follows:

```
var queue4 = queue3
```

Now let's check whether we have a unique reference to the `internalQueue` instances of either the `queue3` or `queue4` instance. The following code will do this:

```
print(queue3.uniquelyReferenced())
print(queue4.uniquelyReferenced())
```

This code will print two `false` messages to the console, letting us know that neither instance has a unique reference to their `internalQueue` instances. Now let's add an item to either one of the queues. The following code will add another item to the `queue3` instance:

```
queue3.addItem(item: 2)
```

When we add the item to the queue, we will see the following message printed to the console:

```
Making a copy of internalQueue
```

This message tells us that when we add the new item to the queue, a new copy of the `internalQueue` instance is created. In order to verify this, we can print the results of the `uniquelyReferenced()` methods to the console again. If you do check this, you will see two `true` messages printed to the console this time rather than two `false` methods. We can now add additional items to the queues and we will see that we are not creating new instances of the `internalQueue` instance because each instance of the Queue type now has its own copy.

 If you are planning on creating your own data structure that may contain a large number of items, it is recommended that you implement it with the copy-on-write feature as described here.

If you are comparing your custom types, it is also recommended that you implement the Equatable protocol within these custom types. This will enable you to compare two instances of the type using the equal-to (==) and not-equal-to (!=) operators.

Implementing the Equatable protocol

In this section, we will demonstrate how we can conform to the Equatable protocol using extensions. When a type conforms to the Equatable protocol, we can use the equal-to (==) operator to compare for equality and the not-equal-to (!=) operator to compare for inequality.

 If you will be comparing instances of a custom type, then it is a good idea to have that type conform to the Equatable protocol because it makes comparing instances very easy.

Let's start off by creating the type that we will compare. We will name this type Place:

```
struct Place {
    let id: String
    let latitude: Double
    let longitude: Double
}
```

In the Place type, we have three properties that represent the ID of the place and the latitude and longitude coordinates for its location. If there are two instances of the Place type that have the same ID and coordinates, then they will be considered the same place.

To implement the Equatable protocol, we can create a global function; however, that is not the recommended solution for protocol-oriented programming. We could also add a static function to the Place type itself, but sometimes it is better to pull the functionality needed to conform to a protocol out of the implementation itself. The following code will make the Place type conform to the Equatable protocol:

```
extension Place: Equatable {
    static func ==(lhs: Place, rhs: Place) -> Bool {
        return lhs.id == rhs.id &&
            lhs.latitude == rhs.latitude &&
            lhs.longitude == rhs.longitude
    }
}
```

We can now compare the instances of the `Place` type as follows:

```
var placeOne = Place(id: "Fenway Park", latitude: 42.3467, longitude:
-71.0972)
var placeTwo = Place(id: "Wrigley Field", latitude: 41.9484, longitude:
-87.6553)
print(placeOne == placeTwo)
```

This will print `false` because `Fenway Park` and `Wrigley Field` are two different baseball stadiums.

You may be wondering why we said that it may be better to pull the functionality needed to conform to a protocol out of the implementation itself. Well, think about some of the larger types that you have created in the past. Personally speaking, I have seen types that had several hundred lines of code and conformed to numerous protocols. By pulling the code that is needed to conform to a protocol out of the type's implementation and putting it in its own extension, we are making our code much easier to read and maintain in the future because the implementation code is isolated in its own extension.

Starting with Swift 5.2, if all of the properties conform to the `Equatable` protocol and you want to compare all of the properties, as shown in the previous examples, we actually do not need to implement the `==` function. All we really need to do is to implement the code as shown in the following example:

```
struct Place: Equatable {
    let id: String
    let latitude: Double
    let longitude: Double
}
```

In the previous code, Swift will add all of the boilerplate code to make the `Place` structure conform to the `Equatable` protocol for us; however, it is good to know how to implement this ourselves if all of the properties do not conform to the `Equatable` protocol or we do not want to compare all of the properties.

Summary

In this chapter, we looked at the differences between value types and reference types. We also looked at how to implement copy-on-write and the `Equatable` protocol with our custom types. We can implement the copy-on-write feature with value types that become very large. We can implement the `Equatable` protocol for any custom type, including reference types, when we need to compare two instances.

While Swift takes care of managing the memory for us, it is still a good idea to understand how this memory management works so that we can avoid the pitfalls that may cause it to fail. In the next chapter, we will look at how memory management in Swift works and demonstrate how it can fail.

18
Memory Management

For many years, the primary languages that I used were C and C-based object-oriented languages. These languages required a good handle on managing memory and knowing when to release memory. Luckily, modern languages like Swift take care of managing memory for us. However, it is a good idea to understand how this memory management works so we can avoid the pitfalls that cause this memory management to fail.

In this chapter, we will learn:

- How ARC works
- What a strong reference cycle is
- How to use weak and unowned references to prevent strong reference cycles

As we saw in *Chapter 17, Custom Value Types*, structures are value types and classes are reference types. What this means is that when we pass an instance of a structure within our application, such as a parameter of a method, we create a new instance of the structure in the memory. This new instance of the structure is only valid while the application is in the scope where the structure was created. Once the structure goes out of scope, the new instance of the structure is automatically destroyed, and the memory is released. This makes the memory management of structures very easy and painless.

Classes, on the other hand, are reference types. This means that we allocate memory for the instance of the class only once, which is when it is initially created. When we pass an instance of the class within our application, either as a function argument or by assigning it to a variable, we are really passing a reference to where the instance is stored in memory. Since the instance of a class may be referenced in multiple scopes (unlike a structure), it cannot be automatically destroyed, and memory is not released when it goes out of scope because it may be referenced in another scope. Therefore, Swift needs some form of memory management to track and release the memory used by instances of classes when the class is no longer needed. Swift uses **Automatic Reference Counting** (**ARC**) to track and manage memory usage.

With ARC, for the most part, memory management in Swift simply works. ARC will automatically track the references to instances of classes, and when an instance is no longer needed (when there are no references pointing to it), ARC will automatically destroy the instance and release the memory. There are a few instances where ARC requires additional information about relationships to properly manage memory. Before we look at the instances where ARC needs help, let's look at how ARC itself works.

How ARC works

Whenever we create a new instance of a class, **ARC** allocates the memory needed to store that instance. This ensures that there is enough memory to store the information associated with that instance of the class, and also locks the memory so that nothing overwrites it.

When the instance of the class is no longer needed, ARC will release the memory allocated for the instance so that it can be used for other purposes. This ensures that we are not tying up memory that is no longer needed. It is known as a **memory leak** when memory is reserved for instances that are no longer needed.

If ARC were to release the memory for an instance of a class that is still needed, it would not be possible to retrieve the class information from memory. If we did try to access the instance of the class after the memory was released, there is a possibility that the application would crash or the data would be corrupted. To ensure memory is not released for an instance of a class that is still needed, ARC counts how many times the instance is referenced; that is, how many active properties, variables, or constants are pointing to the instance of the class. Once the reference count for an instance of a class equals zero (that is, nothing is referencing the instance), the memory is marked for release.

All the previous examples run properly in a playground; however, the following examples will not. When we run sample code in a playground, ARC does not release objects that we create; this is by design so that we can see how the application runs and also the state of the objects at each step. Therefore, we will need to run these samples as an iOS or macOS project. Let's look at an example of how ARC works. We begin by creating a MyClass class with the following code:

```
class MyClass {
    var name = ""
    init(name: String) {
        self.name = name
        print("Initializing class with name \(self.name)")
    }
    deinit {
        print("Releasing class with name \(self.name)")
    }
}
```

In this class, we have a name property that will be set by an initiator accepting a string value. This class also has a deinitializer that is called just before an instance of the class is destroyed and removed from memory. This deinitializer prints out a message to the console that lets us know that the instance of the class is about to be removed.

Now, let's look at the code that shows how ARC creates and destroys instances of a class:

```
var class1ref1: MyClass? = MyClass(name: "One")
var class2ref1: MyClass? = MyClass(name: "Two")
var class2ref2: MyClass? = class2ref1

print("Setting class1ref1 to nil")
class1ref1 = nil
print("Setting class2ref1 to nil")
class2ref1 = nil
print("Setting class2ref2 to nil")
class2ref2 = nil
```

In the example, we begin by creating two instances of the MyClass class named class1ref1 (which stands for class 1 reference 1) and class2ref1 (which stands for class 2 reference 1). We then create a second reference to class2ref1 named class2ref2.

Now, in order to see how ARC works, we need to begin setting the references to nil. We start out by setting `class1ref1` to `nil`. Since there is only one reference to `class1ref1`, the deinitializer will be called. Once the deinitializer completes its task, in our case it prints a message to the console letting us know that the instance of the class has been destroyed and the memory has been released.

We then set `class2ref1` to `nil`, but there is a second reference to this class (`class2ref2`) that prevents ARC from destroying the instance so that the deinitializer is not called.

Finally, we set `class2ref2` to `nil`, which allows ARC to destroy this instance of the `MyClass` class.

If we run this code, we will see the following output, which illustrates how ARC works:

```
Initializing class with name One
Initializing class with name Two
Setting class1ref1 to nil
Releasing class with name One
Setting class2ref1 to nil
Setting class2ref2 to nil
Releasing class with name Two
```

From the example, it seems that ARC handles memory management very well. However, it is possible to write code that will prevent ARC from working properly.

Strong reference cycles

A **strong reference cycle**, or **strong retain cycle**, is where the instances of two classes hold a strong reference to each other, preventing ARC from releasing either instance. Once again, we are not able to use a playground for this example, so we need to create an Xcode project. In this project, we start off by creating two classes named `MyClass1_Strong` and `MyClass2_Strong` with the following code:

```
class MyClass1_Strong {
    var name = ""
    var class2: MyClass2_Strong?
    init(name: String) {
        self.name = name
        print("Initializing class1_Strong with name \(self.name)")
    }
    deinit {
```

```
            print("Releasing class1_Strong with name \(self.name)")
    }
}

class MyClass2_Strong {
    var name = ""
    var class1: MyClass1_Strong?
    init(name: String) {
        self.name = name
        print("Initializing class1_Strong with name \(self.name)")
    }
    deinit {
        print("Releasing class1_Strong with name \(self.name)")
    }
}
```

As we can see from the code, MyClass1_Strong contains an instance of MyClass2_
Strong, therefore the instance of MyClass2_Strong cannot be released until MyClass1_
Strong is destroyed. We can also see from the code that MyClass2_Strong contains an
instance of MyClass1_Strong, therefore, the instance of MyClass1_Strong cannot be
released until MyClass2_Strong is destroyed. This creates a cycle of dependency in
which neither instance can be destroyed until the other one is destroyed.

Let's see how this works by running the following code:

```
var class1: MyClass1_Strong? = MyClass1_Strong(name: "Class1_Strong")
var class2: MyClass2_Strong? = MyClass2_Strong(name: "Class2_Strong")

class1?.class2 = class2
class2?.class1 = class1

print("Setting classes to nil")
class2 = nil
class1 = nil
```

In this example, we create instances of both the MyClass1_Strong and MyClass2_
Strong classes. We then set the class2 property of the class1 instance to the
MyClass2_Strong instance. We also set the class1 property of the class2 instance to
the MyClass1_Strong instance. This means that the MyClass1_Strong instance cannot
be destroyed until the MyClass2_Strong instance is destroyed. This means that the
reference counters for each instance will never reach zero, therefore, ARC cannot
destroy the instances, producing the following output in this case:

```
Initializing class1_Strong with name Class1_Strong
Initializing class1_Strong with name Class2_Strong
Setting classes to nil
```

This inability to destroy instances creates a memory leak, where an application continues to use memory and does not properly release it. This can cause an application to eventually crash.

To resolve a strong reference cycle, we need to prevent one of the classes from keeping a strong hold on the instance of the other class, thereby allowing ARC to destroy them both. Swift provides two ways of doing this by letting us define the properties as either a weak or an unowned reference.

The difference between a weak reference and an unowned reference is that the instance that a weak reference refers to can be `nil`, whereas the instance that an unowned reference is referring to cannot be `nil`. This means that when we use a weak reference, the property must be an optional property. Let's see how we would use unowned and weak references to resolve a strong reference cycle. Let's start by looking at the unowned reference.

Unowned references

We begin by creating two more classes, `MyClass1_Unowned` and `MyClass2_Unowned`:

```
class MyClass1_Unowned {
    var name = ""
    unowned let class2: MyClass2_Unowned
    init(name: String, class2: MyClass2_Unowned) {
        self.name = name
        self.class2 = class2
        print("Initializing class1_Unowned with name \(self.name)")
    }
    deinit {
        print("Releasing class1_Unowned with name \(self.name)")
    }
}

class MyClass2_Unowned {
    var name = ""
    var class1: MyClass1_Unowned?
    init(name: String) {
        self.name = name
        print("Initializing class2_Unowned with name \(self.name)")
```

```
    }
    deinit {
        print("Releasing class2_Unowned with name \(self.name)")
    }
}
```

The MyClass1_Unowned class looks pretty similar to the MyClass1_Strong and MyClass2_Strong classes in the preceding example. The difference here is the MyClass1_Unowned class — we set the class2 property to unowned, which means it cannot be nil and it does not keep a strong reference to the instance that it is referring to. Since the class2 property cannot be nil, we also need to set it when the class is initialized.

Let's see how we can initialize and deinitialize the instances of these classes with the following code:

```
let class2 = MyClass2_Unowned(name: "Class2_Unowned")
let class1: MyClass1_Unowned? = MyClass1_Unowned(name: "class1_
Unowned",class2: class2)

class2.class1 = class1
print("Classes going out of scope")
```

In the preceding code, we create an instance of the MyClass_Unowned class and then use that instance to create an instance of the MyClass1_Unowned class. We then set the class1 property of the MyClass2 instance to the MyClass1_Unowned instance we just created.

This creates a reference cycle of dependency between the two classes again, but this time, the MyClass1_Unowned instance is not keeping a strong hold on the MyClass2_Unowned instance, allowing ARC to release both instances when they are no longer needed.

If we run this code, we see the following output, showing that both the class1 and class2 instances are released, and the memory is freed:

```
Initializing class2_Unowned with name Class2_Unowned
Initializing class1_Unowned with name class1_Unowned
Classes going out of scope
Releasing class2_Unowned with name Class2_Unowned
Releasing class1_Unowned with name class1_Unowned
```

As we can see, both instances are properly released. Now let's look at how we would use a weak reference to prevent a strong reference cycle.

Weak references

Once again, we begin by creating two new classes:

```
class MyClass1_Weak {
    var name = ""
    var class2: MyClass2_Weak?
    init(name: String) {
        self.name = name
        print("Initializing class1_Weak with name \(self.name)")
    }
    deinit {
        print("Releasing class1_Weak with name \(self.name)")
    }
}

class MyClass2_Weak {
    var name = ""
    weak var class1: MyClass1_Weak?
    init(name: String) {
        self.name = name
        print("Initializing class2_Weak with name \(self.name)")
    }
    deinit {
        print("Releasing class2_Weak with name \(self.name)")
    }
}
```

The `MyClass1_Weak` and `MyClass2_Weak` classes look very similar to the previous classes we created that showed how a strong reference cycle works. The difference is that we define the `class1` property in the `MyClass2_Weak` class as a weak reference.

Now, let's see how we can initialize and deinitialize instances of these classes with the following code:

```
let class1: MyClass1_Weak? = MyClass1_Weak(name: "Class1_Weak")
let class2: MyClass2_Weak? = MyClass2_Weak(name: "Class2_Weak")

class1?.class2 = class2
class2?.class1 = class1
print("Classes going out of scope")
```

In the preceding code, we create instances of the MyClass1_Weak and MyClass2_Weak classes and then set the properties of those classes to point to the instance of the other class. Once again, this creates a cycle of dependency, but since we set the class1 property of the MyClass2_Weak class to weak, it does not create a strong reference, allowing both instances to be released.

If we run the code, we will see the following output, showing that both the class1_Weak and class2_Weak instances are released and the memory is freed:

```
Initializing class1_Weak with name Class1_Weak
Initializing class2_Weak with name Class2_Weak
Classes going out of scope
Releasing class1_Weak with name Class1_Weak
Releasing class2_Weak with name Class2_Weak
```

On an additional note, a retain cycle for a closure is exactly the same as a strong reference cycle; a closure actually is a strong reference by default. We would use weak and unowned references to prevent this exactly as explained in this chapter, simply by changing the variable that holds an instance of a class to hold an instance of a closure.

It is recommended that you avoid creating circular dependencies, as shown in this section, but there are times when you may need them. For those times, remember that ARC needs some help to release them.

Summary

In this chapter, we explained how ARC works to give you an understanding of how memory is managed in your application. We showed what a strong reference cycle is and explained how it can cause ARC to fail. We concluded the chapter by showing how we can use weak and unowned references to prevent strong reference cycles.

In the next chapter, we will look at how to properly format our Swift code for consistency and readability.

19
Swift Formatting and Style Guide

Throughout my development experience, every time I learned a new programming language, there was usually some mention of how the code for that language should be written and formatted. Early in my development career (which was a long time ago), these recommendations were very basic formatting recommendations, being about things such as how to indent your code, or having one statement per line. It really wasn't until the last 10-12 years that I started to see complex and detailed formatting and style guides for different programming languages. Today, you would be hard-pressed to find a development shop with more than two or three developers that does not have a style/formatting guide for each language that they use. Even companies that do not create their own style guides generally refer back to some standard guide published by other companies, such as Google, Oracle, or Microsoft. These style guides help teams to write consistent and easy-to-maintain code.

In this chapter, you will learn the following:

- What a style guide is
- What makes a good style guide
- Why it is important to use a style guide
- How to create a sample style guide

What is a programming style guide?

Coding styles are very personal, and every developer has their own preferred style. These styles can vary from language to language, from person to person, and over time. The personal nature of coding styles can make it difficult to have a consistent and readable code base when numerous individuals are contributing to the code.

While most developers might have their own preferred styles, the recommended or preferred style between languages can vary. As an example, in C#, when we name a method or function, it is preferred that we use Pascal case, which is similar to camel case except the first letter is capitalized. In most other languages, such as C, Objective-C, and Java, it is also recommended that we use camel case, where the first letter is lowercase.

The best applications are coded so they are easy to maintain and the code is easy to read. It is hard for large projects and companies with many developers to have code that is easy to maintain and read if every developer uses their own coding style. This is why companies and projects with multiple developers usually adopt programming style guidelines for each language that they use.

A programming style guide defines a set of rules and guidelines that a developer should follow while writing applications with a specific language within a project or company. These style guides can differ greatly between companies or projects and reflect how a company or project expects code to be written. These guides can also change over time. It is important to follow these style guides to maintain a consistent code base.

A lot of developers do not like the idea of being told how they should write code, and claim that as long as their code functions correctly, it shouldn't matter how they format it. This type of philosophy doesn't work in a coding team for the same reason it doesn't work in a sports team. What do you think would happen if all the players on a basketball team believed that they could all play the way they wanted to play and the team was better when they did their own thing? That team would probably lose a lot of games. It is impossible for a basketball team (or any sports team, for that matter) to win consistently unless all team members are working together. It is up to the coach to make sure that everyone is working together and executing the same game plan, just as it is up to the team leader of a development project to make sure all the developers are writing code according to the adopted style guide.

API Design Guide

Apple has released API Design Guidelines for Swift. This defines how APIs should be designed and is different from a language style guide. A language style guide defines how code should be written for a particular language; an API design guide defines how APIs should be designed. If you are creating an API that will be used by other Swift developers, you should become familiar with Apple's API Design Guidelines, which can be found here: `https://swift.org/documentation/api-design-guidelines/`.

Your style guide

The style guide that we define in this book is just a guide. It reflects the author's opinion on how Swift code should be written and is meant to be a good starting point for creating your own style guide. If you really like this guide and adopt it as it is, great. If there are parts that you do not agree with and you change them within your guide, that is great as well.

The appropriate style for you and your team is the one that you and your team feel comfortable with, and it may or may not be different from the guide in this book. Don't be afraid to adjust your style guide as needed. One thing that is noticeable in the style guide within this chapter, and most good style guides, is that there is very little explanation about why each item is preferred or not preferred. Style guides should give enough details so that the reader understands the preferred and non-preferred methods for each item but should also be small and compact to make them easy and quick to read. If a developer has questions about why a particular method is preferred, they should bring that concern up with the development group. With that in mind, let's get started with the guide.

Do not use semicolons at the end of statements

Unlike a lot of languages, Swift does not require semicolons at the end of statements. Therefore, we should not use them. Let's look at the following code:

```
//Preferred Method
var name = "Jon"
print(name)

//Non-preferred Method
var name = "Jon";
print(name);
```

Do not use parentheses for conditional statements

Unlike a lot of languages, parentheses are not required around conditional statements; therefore, we should avoid using them unless they are needed for clarification. Let's look at the following code:

```
//Preferred Method
if speed == 300_000_000 {
    print("Speed of light")
}
//Non-Preferred Method
if (speed == 300_000_000) {
    print("Speed of light")
}
```

Naming

We should always use descriptive names with camel case for custom types, methods, variables, constants, and so on. Let's look at some general naming rules.

Custom types

Custom types should have a descriptive name that describes what the type is for. The name should be in Pascal case. Here are examples of proper names and non-proper names based on our style guide:

```
//Proper Naming Convention
BaseballTeam
LaptopComputer

//Non-Proper Naming Convention
baseballTeam  //Starts with a lowercase letter
Laptop_Computer  //Uses an underscore
```

Functions and methods

Function names should be descriptive, describing the function or method. They should be in camel case. Here are some examples of proper and non-proper names:

```
//Proper Naming Convention
getCityName
playSound

//Non-Proper Naming Convention
get_city_name  //All lowercase and has an underscore
PlaySound  //Begins with an uppercase letter
```

Constants and variables

Constants and variables should have a descriptive name. They should begin with a lowercase letter and be in camel case. The only exception is when the constant is global; in that case, the name of the constant should contain all uppercase characters with the words separated by underscores. I have seen numerous guides that frown upon having all-uppercase names, but I personally like them for constants in the global scope, because it stands out that they are globally, not locally, scoped.

Here are some examples of proper and non-proper names:

```
//Proper Names
playerName
driveSize

//Non-Proper Names
PlayerName  //Starts with uppercase letter
drive_size  //Has underscore in name
```

Indenting

Indenting width in Xcode, by default, is defined as four spaces, and tab width is also defined as four spaces. We should leave this as the default. The following screenshot shows the indentation setting in Xcode:

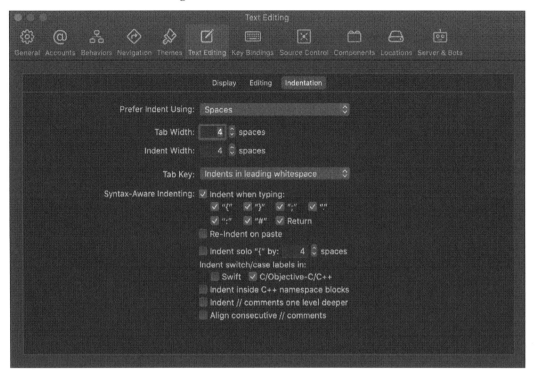

Figure 19.1: Indentations

We should add an extra blank line between functions/methods. We should also use a blank line to separate functionality within a function or method. That being said, using many blank lines within a function or method might indicate that we should break the function into multiple functions.

Comments

We should use comments as needed to explain how and why our code is written. We should use block comments before custom types and functions. We should use double slashes to comment our code in one line. Here is an example of how comments should be written:

```
/**
This is a block comment that should be used to explain a class or
```

```
function
**/
public class EmployeeClass {
    // This is an inline comment with double slashes
    var firstName = ""
    var lastName = ""
/**
    Use Block comments for functions
        parameter paramName: use this tag for parameters
        returns: explain what is returned
        throws: Error thrown
**/
    func getFullName() -> String {
        return firstName + " " + lastName
    }
}
```

When we are commenting methods, we should also use documentation tags, which will generate documentation in Xcode, as shown in the preceding example. At a minimum, we should use the following tags if they apply to our method:

- **Parameter**: This is used for parameters
- **Returns**: This is used for what is returned
- **Throws**: This is used to document errors that may be thrown

Using the self keyword

Since Swift does not require us to use the self keyword when accessing properties or invoking methods of an object, we should avoid using it unless we need to distinguish between an instance property and local variables. Here is an example of when you should use the self keyword:

```
public class EmployeeClass {
    var firstName = ""
    var lastName = ""

    func setName(firstName: String, lastName: String) {
        self.firstName = firstName
        self.lastName = lastName
    }
}
```

Here is an example of when not to use the `self` keyword:

```swift
public class EmployeeClass {
    var firstName = ""
    var lastName = ""

    func getFullName() -> String {
        return self.firstName + " " + self.lastName
    }
}
```

Constants and variables

The difference between constants and variables is that the value of a constant never changes, whereas the value of a variable may change. Wherever possible, we should define constants rather than variables.

One of the easiest ways of doing this is by defining everything as a constant by default, and then changing the definition to a variable only after you reach a point in your code that requires you to change it. In Swift, you will get a warning if you define a variable and then never change the value within your code.

Optional types

Only use optional types when absolutely necessary. If there is no absolute need for a nil value to be assigned to a variable, we should not define it as an optional.

Using optional binding

We should avoid forced unwrapping of optionals, as there is rarely any need to do this. We should preferably use optional binding or optional chaining rather than forced unwrapping.

The following examples show the preferred and non-preferred methods where the `myOptional` variable is defined as an optional:

```swift
//Preferred Method Optional Binding
if let value = myOptional {
    // code if myOptional is not nil
} else {
    // code if myOptional is nil
```

```
}

//Non-Preferred Method
if myOptional != nil {
    // code if myOptional is not nil
} else {
    // code if myOptional is nil
}
```

If there are several optionals that we need to unwrap, we should include them in the same if-let or guard statement, rather than unwrapping them on separate lines. There are times, however, when our business logic may require us to handle nil values differently, and this may require us to unwrap the optionals on separate lines. The following examples show the preferred and non-preferred methods:

```
//Preferred Method Optional Binding
if let value1 = myOptional1, let value2 = myOptional2 {
// code if myOptional1 and myOptional2 is not nil
} else {
// code if myOptional1 and myOptional2 is nil
}

//Non-Preferred Method Optional Binding
if let value1 = myOptional1 {
    if let value2 = myOptional2 {
        // code if myOptional is not nil
    } else {
        // code if myOptional2 is nil
    } else {
    // code if myOptional1 is nil
}
```

Using optional chaining

When we need to unwrap multiple layers, we should use optional chaining over multiple optional binding statements. The following example shows the preferred and non-preferred methods:

```
//Preferred Method
if let color = jon.pet?.collar?.color {
    print("The color of the collar is \(color)")
} else {
```

```
        print("Cannot retrieve color")
}


//Non-Preferred Method
if let tmpPet = jon.pet, let tmpCollar = tmpPet.collar{
    print("The color of the collar is \(tmpCollar.color)")
} else {
    print("Cannot retrieve color")
}
```

Using type inference

Rather than defining variable types, we should let Swift infer the type. The only time we should define the variable or constant type is when we are not giving it a value while defining it. Let's look at the following code:

```
//Preferred method
var myVar = "String Type" //Infers a String type
var myNum = 2.25 //Infers a Double type


//Non-Preferred method
var myVar: String = "String Type"
var myNum: Double = 2.25
```

Using shorthand declarations for collections

When declaring native Swift collection types, we should use the shorthand syntax, and, unless absolutely necessary, we should initialize the collection. The following example shows the preferred and non-preferred methods:

```
//Preferred Method
var myDictionary: [String: String] = [:]
var strArray: [String] = []
var strOptional: String?


//Non-Preferred Method
var myDictionary: Dictionary<String,String>
var strArray: Array<String>
var strOptional: Optional<String>
```

Using switch rather than multiple if statements

Wherever possible, we should prefer to use a single switch statement over multiple if statements. The following example shows the preferred and non-preferred methods:

```
//Preferred Method
let speed = 300_000_000
switch speed {
    case 300_000_000:
        print("Speed of light")
    case 340:
        print("Speed of sound")
    default:
        print("Unknown speed")
}

//Non-preferred Method
let speed = 300_000_000 if speed == 300_000_000 {
        print("Speed of light")
} else if speed == 340 {
        print("Speed of sound")
} else {
        print("Unknown speed")
}
```

Don't leave commented-out code in your application

If we comment out a block of code while we attempt to replace it, once we are comfortable with the changes we should remove the code that we commented out. Having large blocks of code commented out can make the code base look messy and make it harder to follow.

Summary

When we are developing an application in a team environment, it is important to have a well-defined coding style that is adhered to by everyone on the team. This allows us to have a code base that is easy to read and maintain.

If a style guide remains static for too long, it means that it is probably not keeping up with the latest changes within the language. What is considered "too long" is different for each language. For example, with the C language, too long will be defined in years, since the language is very stable; however, with Swift, the language is relatively new, and changes come pretty often, so "too long" can probably be defined as a couple of months.

It is recommended that we keep our style guides in a version control system so that we can refer to older versions if need be. This allows us to pull older versions of the style guide and refer back to them when we are looking at older code.

It is recommended, not only with Swift but other languages as well, that you use a lint tool to check and enforce good coding practices. For Swift, there is a great tool called SwiftLint (`https://github.com/realm/SwiftLint`), which has a command-line tool.

As you work on a style guide for your organization, you may want to keep an eye on Swift Evolution Proposal SE-0250 (`https://github.com/apple/swift-evolution/blob/master/ proposals/0250-swift-style-guide-and-formatter.md`). This proposal is to create an official Swift style guide and formatter. If this proposal is accepted and an official style guide is released, then you should adopt those guidelines.

20

Adopting Design Patterns in Swift

Although the first publication of the *Gang of Four's Design Patterns: Elements of Reusable Object-Oriented Software* was released in October 1994, I have only been paying attention to design patterns for the last 14 years. Like most experienced developers, when I first started reading about design patterns, I recognized a lot of the patterns because I had already been using them without realizing what they were. I would have to say that since I first read about design patterns, I have not written a serious application without using at least one of them. I will tell you that I am definitely not a design pattern zealot, and if I get into a conversation about design patterns, there are usually only a couple of them that I can name without having to look them up. But one thing that I do remember is the concepts behind the major patterns and the problems they are designed to solve. This way, when I encounter one of these problems, I can look up the appropriate pattern and apply it. So, remember, as you go through this chapter, to take the time to understand the major concepts behind design patterns rather than trying to memorize the patterns themselves.

In this chapter, you will learn about the following topics:

- What are design patterns?
- What types of patterns make up the creational, structural, and behavioral categories of design patterns?
- How to implement the singleton and builder creational patterns in Swift
- How to implement the bridge, facade, and proxy structural patterns in Swift
- How to implement the command and strategy behavioral patterns in Swift

What are design patterns?

Every experienced developer has a set of informal strategies that shape how they design and write applications. These strategies are shaped by their past experiences and the obstacles that they have had to overcome in previous projects. While these developers might swear by their own strategies, it does not mean that their strategies have been fully vetted. The use of these strategies can also introduce inconsistent implementations between different projects and developers.

While the concept of design patterns dates back to the mid-1980s, they did not gain popularity until the Gang of Four released *Elements of Reusable Object-Oriented Software*, published in 1994. The book's authors, Erich Gamma, Richard Helm, Ralph Johnson, and John Vlissides (also known as the Gang of Four), discuss the pitfalls of object-oriented programming and describe 23 classic software design patterns. These patterns are broken up into three categories: *creational*, *structural*, and *behavioral*.

A design pattern identifies common software development problems and provides a strategy to deal with them. These strategies have been proven, over the years, to be an effective solution for the problems they are intended to solve. Using these patterns can greatly speed up the development process because they provide us with solutions that have been proven to solve common software development problems.

Another advantage that we get when using design patterns is consistent code that is easy to maintain because months or years from now when we look at the code, we will recognize the patterns and understand what the code does. If we properly document the code and document the design pattern we are implementing, it will also help other developers to understand what the code is doing.

The two main philosophies behind design patterns are code reuse and flexibility. As a software architect, it is essential that we build reusability and flexibility into the code. This allows us to easily maintain the code in the future and also makes it easier for the applications to expand to meet future requirements, because we all know how quickly requirements change.

While there is a lot to like about design patterns, and they are extremely beneficial for developers and architects, they are not the solution to world hunger that some developers make them out to be. Sometime in your development career, you will probably meet a developer or an architect who thinks that design patterns are immutable laws. These developers usually try to force the use of design patterns even when they are not necessary. A good rule of thumb is to make sure that you have a problem that needs to be fixed before you try to fix it.

Design patterns are starting points for avoiding and solving common programming problems. We can think of each design pattern as a recipe. Just like a good recipe, we can tinker and adjust it to meet particular tastes. But we usually do not want to stray too far from the original recipe because we may mess it up.

There are also times when we do not have a recipe for a certain dish that we want to make, just like there are times when there isn't a design pattern to solve the problem we face. In cases like this, we can use our knowledge of design patterns and their underlying philosophy to come up with an effective solution for the problem.

Design patterns are generally split into three categories. These are as follows:

- **Creational patterns**: Creational patterns support the creation of objects
- **Structural patterns**: Structural patterns concern types and object compositions
- **Behavioral patterns**: Behavioral patterns communicate between types

While the Gang of Four defined over 20 design patterns, we are only going to look at examples of some of the more popular patterns in this chapter. Let's start off by looking at creational patterns.

Design patterns were originally defined for object-oriented programming. In this chapter, where possible, we will focus on implementing patterns in a more protocol-oriented way. Therefore, the examples in this chapter may look a little different from examples in other design pattern books, but the underlying philosophy of the solutions will be the same.

Creational design patterns

Creational patterns are design patterns that deal with how an object is created. These patterns create objects in a manner suitable for a particular situation.

There are two basic ideas behind creational patterns. The first is encapsulating the knowledge of *which* concrete types should be created and the second is hiding *how* the instances of these types are created.

There are five well-known patterns that are a part of the creational pattern category. They are as follows:

- **The abstract factory pattern**: This provides an interface for creating related objects without specifying the concrete type
- **The builder pattern**: This separates the construction of a complex object from its representation, so the same process can be used to create similar types
- **The factory method pattern**: This creates objects without exposing the underlying logic of how the object (or which type of object) is created
- **The prototype pattern**: This creates an object by cloning an existing one
- **The singleton pattern**: This allows one (and only one) instance of a class for the lifetime of an application

In this chapter, we are going to show examples of how to implement the singleton and builder patterns in Swift. Let's start off by looking at one of the most controversial and possibly overused design patterns, the singleton pattern.

The singleton pattern

The use of the **singleton pattern** is a fairly controversial subject among certain corners of the development community. One of the main reasons for this is that the singleton pattern is probably the most overused and misused pattern. Another reason this pattern is controversial is that it introduces a global state into an application, which provides the ability to change the object at any point within the application. The singleton pattern can also introduce hidden dependencies and tight compiling. My personal opinion is that, if the singleton pattern is used correctly, there is nothing wrong with using it. However, we do need to be careful not to misuse it.

The singleton pattern restricts the instantiation of a class to a single instance for the lifetime of an application. This pattern is very effective when we need exactly one object to coordinate actions within the application. An example of a good use of a singleton is if the application communicates with a remote device over Bluetooth and we also want to maintain that connection throughout the application. Some would say that we could pass the instance of the connection class from one page to the next, which is essentially what a singleton is. In my opinion, the singleton pattern, in this instance, is a much cleaner solution, because with the singleton pattern any page that needs the connection can get it without forcing every page to maintain the instance. This also allows us to maintain the connection without having to reconnect each time we go to another page.

Understanding the problem

The problem that the singleton pattern is designed to address is when we need one and only one instance of a type for the lifetime of the application. The singleton pattern is usually used when we need centralized management of an internal or external resource, and a single global point of access. Another popular use of the singleton pattern is when we want to consolidate a set of related activities needed throughout the application that do not maintain a state in one place.

In *Chapter 9, Protocols and Protocol Extensions*, we used the singleton pattern in the text validation example. In that example, we used the singleton pattern because we wanted to create a single instance of the types that could then be used by all the components of the application without requiring us to create new instances of the types. These text validation types did not have a state that could be changed. They only had methods that performed the validation on the text and constants that defined how to validate the text. While some may disagree with me, I believe types like these are excellent candidates for the singleton pattern because there is no reason to create multiple instances of these types.

 In that example, we implemented it using structures, which isn't a true singleton because a structure is a value type. A true singleton is implemented using a reference (class) type.

When using the singleton pattern, one of the biggest concerns is multi-threaded applications with race conditions. The issue occurs when one thread changes the state of the singleton while another thread is accessing it, producing unexpected results. As an example, if the TextValidation classes stored the text to be validated and then we called a method to do the validation, one thread could change the stored text before the original thread did the validation. It is advisable to understand how a singleton will be used in your application, before implementing this pattern.

Understanding the solution

There are several ways to implement the singleton pattern in Swift. In the method that we use here, a single instance of the class is created the first time the class constant is accessed. We will then use the class constant to gain access to this instance throughout the lifetime of the application. We will also create a private initializer that will prevent external code from creating additional instances of the class.

Note that we use the word *class* in this description and not *type*. The reason for this is that the singleton pattern can only truly be implemented using a reference type.

Implementing the singleton pattern

Let's look at how we implement the singleton pattern with Swift. The following code example shows how to create a singleton class:

```
class MySingleton {
    static let sharedInstance = MySingleton()
    var number = 0
    private init() {}
}
```

We can see that, within the MySingleton class, we created a static constant named sharedInstance, which contains an instance of the MySingleton class. A static constant can be called without having to instantiate the class. Since we declared the sharedInstance constant static, only one instance will exist throughout the lifecycle of the application, thereby creating the singleton pattern.

We also created the private initiator, which cannot be accessed outside of the class, which will restrict other code from creating additional instances of the MySingleton class.

Now, let's see how this pattern works. The MySingleton pattern has another property, named number, which is an integer. We will monitor how this property changes as we use the sharedInstance property to create multiple variables of the MySingleton type, as shown in the following code:

```
var singleA = MySingleton.sharedInstance
var singleB = MySingleton.sharedInstance
var singleC = MySingleton.sharedInstance

singleB.number = 2
print(singleA.number)
print(singleB.number)
print(singleC.number)

singleC.number = 3
print(singleA.number)
print(singleB.number)
print(singleC.number)
```

In this example, we used the `sharedInstance` property to create three variables of the `MySingleton` type. We initially set the `number` property of the second `MySingleton` variable (`singleB`) to the number 2. When we printed out the value of the `number` property for the `singleA`, `singleB`, and `singleC` instances, we saw that the `number` property for all three equaled 2.

We then changed the value of the `number` property of the third `MySingleton` instance (`singleC`) to the number 3. When we printed out the value of the `number` property again, we saw that all three now have a value of 3. Therefore, when we change the value of the `number` property in any of the instances, the values of all three change because each variable is pointed to the same instance.

In this example, we implemented the singleton pattern using a reference (class) type because we wanted to ensure that only one instance of the type existed throughout the application. If we implemented this pattern with a value type, such as a structure or an enumeration, we would run the risk of there being multiple instances of the type.

If you recall, each time we pass an instance of a value type, we are actually passing a copy of that instance, which means that, if we implemented the singleton pattern with a value type, each time we called the `sharedInstance` property we would receive a new copy, which would effectively break the singleton pattern.

The singleton pattern can be very useful when we need to maintain the state of an object throughout the application; however, be careful not to overuse it. The singleton pattern should not be used unless there is a specific requirement (*requirement* is the keyword here) for having one, and only one, instance of the class throughout the lifecycle of the application. If we are using the singleton pattern simply for convenience, then we are probably misusing it.

Keep in mind that, while Apple generally recommends that we prefer value types to reference types, there are still plenty of examples, such as the singleton pattern, where we need to use reference types. When we continually tell ourselves to prefer value types to reference types, it can be very easy to forget that there are times when a reference type is needed. Don't forget to use reference types with this pattern.

Now, let's look at the builder design pattern.

The builder pattern

The **builder pattern** helps us with the creation of complex objects and enforces the process of how these objects are created. With this pattern, we generally separate the creation logic from the complex type and put the creation logic into another type. This allows us to use the same construction process to create different representations of the type.

Understanding the problem

The problem that the builder pattern is designed to address is when an instance of a type requires a large number of configurable values. We could set the configuration options when we create instances of the class, but that can cause issues if the options are not set correctly or we do not know the proper values for all the options. Another issue is the amount of code that may be needed to set all the configurable options each time we create an instance of the types.

Understanding the solution

The builder pattern solves this problem by introducing an intermediary known as a builder type. This builder type contains most, if not all, of the information necessary to create an instance of the original complex type.

There are two methods that we can use to implement the builder pattern. The first method is to have multiple builder types where each of the types contains the information to configure the original complex object in a specific way. In the second method, we implement the builder pattern with a single builder type that sets all the configurable options to a default value, and then we would change the values as needed.

In this section, we will look at both ways to use the builder pattern, because it is important to understand how each works.

Implementing the builder pattern

Before we show how we would use the builder pattern, let's look at how to create a complex structure without the builder pattern and the problems we run into.

The following code creates a structure named BurgerOld, and does not use the builder pattern:

```swift
struct BurgerOld {
    var name: String
    var patties: Int
    var bacon: Bool
    var cheese: Bool
    var pickles: Bool
    var ketchup: Bool
    var mustard: Bool
    var lettuce: Bool
    var tomato: Bool
```

```
    init(name: String, patties: Int, bacon: Bool, cheese: Bool,
pickles:Bool, ketchup: Bool, mustard: Bool,lettuce: Bool, tomato: Bool)
    {
        self.name = name
        self.patties = patties
        self.bacon = bacon
        self.cheese = cheese
        self.pickles = pickles
        self.ketchup = ketchup
        self.mustard = mustard
        self.lettuce = lettuce
        self.tomato = tomato
    }
}
```

In the `BurgerOld` structure, we have several properties that define which condiments are on the burger and the name of the burger. Since we need to know which items are on the burgers and which items aren't, when we create an instance of the `BurgerOld` structure, the initializer requires us to define each item. This can lead to some complex initializations throughout the application, not to mention that, if we had more than one standard burger (bacon cheeseburger, cheeseburger, hamburger, and so on), we would need to make sure that each is defined correctly. Let's see how to create instances of the `BurgerOld` class:

```
// Create Hamburger
var hamburger = BurgerOld(name: "Hamburger", patties: 1, bacon: false,
cheese: false, pickles: true, ketchup: true, mustard: true, lettuce:
false, tomato: false)

// Create Cheeseburger
var cheeseburger = BurgerOld(name: "Cheeseburger", patties: 1 , bacon:
false, cheese: true, pickles: true, ketchup: true, mustard: true,
lettuce: false, tomato: false)
```

As we can see, creating instances of the `BurgerOld` type requires a lot of code. Now, let's look at a better way to do this. In this example, we will show how to use multiple builder types where each type will define what goes on each type of burger. We will begin by creating a `BurgerBuilder` protocol that will have the following code in it:

```
protocol BurgerBuilder {
    var name: String { get }
    var patties: Int { get }
    var bacon: Bool { get }
```

```
    var cheese: Bool { get }
    var pickles: Bool { get }
    var ketchup: Bool { get }
    var mustard: Bool { get }
    var lettuce: Bool { get }
    var tomato: Bool { get }
}
```

This protocol simply defines the nine properties that will be required for any type that implements this protocol. Now, let's create two structures that implement this protocol: the HamburgerBuilder and CheeseBurgerBuilder structures:

```
struct HamburgerBuilder: BurgerBuilder {
    let name = "Burger"
    let patties = 1
    let bacon = false
    let cheese = false
    let pickles = true
    let ketchup = true
    let mustard = true
    let lettuce = false
    let tomato = false
}

struct CheeseBurgerBuilder: BurgerBuilder {
    let name = "CheeseBurger"
    let patties = 1
    let bacon = false
    let cheese = true
    let pickles = true
    let ketchup = true
    let mustard = true
    let lettuce = false
    let tomato = false
}
```

In both the HamburgerBuilder and the CheeseBurgerBuilder structures, all we are doing is defining the values for each of the required properties. In more complex types, we might need to initialize additional resources.

Now, let's look at the `Burger` structure, which will use instances of the `BurgerBuilder` protocol to create instances of itself. The following code shows this new `Burger` type:

```swift
struct Burger {
    var name: String
    var patties: Int
    var bacon: Bool
    var cheese: Bool
    var pickles: Bool
    var ketchup: Bool
    var mustard: Bool
    var lettuce: Bool
    var tomato: Bool

    init(builder: BurgerBuilder) {
        self.name = builder.name
        self.patties = builder.patties
        self.bacon = builder.bacon
        self.cheese = builder.cheese
        self.pickles = builder.pickles
        self.ketchup = builder.ketchup
        self.mustard = builder.mustard
        self.lettuce = builder.lettuce
        self.tomato = builder.tomato
    }

    func showBurger() {
        print("Name:\(name)")
        print("Patties: \(patties)")
        print("Bacon: \(bacon)")
        print("Cheese: \(cheese)")
        print("Pickles: \(pickles)")
        print("Ketchup: \(ketchup)")
        print("Mustard: \(mustard)")
        print("Lettuce: \(lettuce)")
        print("Tomato: \(tomato)")
    }
}
```

The difference between this `Burger` structure and the `BurgerOld` structure shown earlier is the initializer. In the previous `BurgerOld` structure, the initializer took nine arguments—one for each constant defined in the structure. In the new structure, the initializer takes one argument, which is an instance of a type that conforms to the `BurgerBuilder` protocol. This new initializer allows us to create instances of the `Burger` class as follows:

```
// Create Hamburger
var myBurger = Burger(builder: HamburgerBuilder())
myBurger.showBurger()

// Create Cheeseburger
var myCheeseBurger = Burger(builder: CheeseBurgerBuilder())

// Let's hold the ketchup
myCheeseBurger.ketchup = false
myCheeseBurger.showBurger()
```

If we compare how we create instances of the new `Burger` structure to the earlier `BurgerOld` structure, we can see that it is much easier to create instances of the `Burger` structure. We also know that we are correctly setting the property values for each type of burger because the values are set directly in the builder classes.

As we mentioned earlier, there is a second method that we can use to implement the builder pattern. Rather than having multiple builder types, we can have a single builder type that sets all the configurable options to a default value; then we change the values as needed. I use this implementation method a lot when I am updating older code because it is easy to integrate it with preexisting code.

For this implementation, we will create a single `BurgerBuilder` structure. This structure will be used to create instances of the `BurgerOld` structure and will, by default, set all the ingredients to their default values.

The `BurgerBuilder` structure also gives us the ability to change which ingredients will go on the burger prior to creating instances of the `BurgerOld` structure. We create the `BurgerBuilder` structure as follows:

```
struct BurgerBuilder {
    var name = "Burger"
    var patties = 1
    var bacon = false
    var cheese = false
    var pickles = true
    var ketchup = true
```

```
    var mustard = true
    var lettuce = false
    var tomato = false

mutating func setPatties(choice: Int) {
        self.patties = choice
    }
mutating func setBacon(choice: Bool) {
        self.bacon = choice
    }
mutating func setCheese(choice: Bool) {
        self.cheese = choice

    }
mutating func setPickles(choice: Bool) {
        self.pickles = choice

    }
mutating func setKetchup(choice: Bool) {
        self.ketchup = choice

    }
mutating func setMustard(choice: Bool) {
        self.mustard = choice

    }
mutating func setLettuce(choice: Bool) {
        self.lettuce = choice

    }
mutating func setTomato(choice: Bool) {
        self.tomato = choice

    }
    func buildBurgerOld(name: String) -> BurgerOld {
        return BurgerOld(name: name, patties: self.patties,bacon:
self.bacon, cheese: self.cheese,pickles: self.pickles, ketchup: self.
ketchup,mustard: self.mustard, lettuce: self.lettuce,tomato: self.
tomato)
    }
}
```

In the BurgerBuilder structure, we define the nine properties (ingredients) for the
burger and then create a setter method for each of the properties except for the name
property.

We also create one method named `buildBurgerOld()`, which will create an instance of the `BurgerOld` structure based on the values of the properties for the `BurgerBuilder` instance. We use the `BurgerBuilder` structure as follows:

```
var burgerBuilder = BurgerBuilder()
burgerBuilder.setCheese(choice: true)
burgerBuilder.setBacon(choice: true)
var jonBurger = burgerBuilder.buildBurgerOld(name: "Jon's Burger")
```

In this example, we create an instance of the `BurgerBuilder` structure. We then use the `setCheese()` and `setBacon()` methods to add cheese and bacon to the burger. Finally, we call the `buildBurgerOld()` method to create the instance of the `burgerOld` structure.

As we can see, both methods that were used to implement the builder pattern greatly simplify the creation of the complex type. Both methods also ensured that the instances were properly configured with default values. If you find yourself creating instances of types with very long and complex initialization commands, I recommend that you look at the builder pattern to see if you can use it to simplify the initialization.

Now, let's look at structural design patterns.

Structural design patterns

Structural design patterns describe how types can be combined to form larger structures. These larger structures can generally be easier to work with and hide a lot of the complexity of the individual types. Most patterns in the structural pattern category involve connections between objects.

There are seven well-known patterns that are part of the structural design pattern type. These are as follows:

- **Adapter**: This allows types with incompatible interfaces to work together
- **Bridge**: This is used to separate the abstract elements of a type from the implementation so the two can vary
- **Composite**: This allows us to treat a group of objects as a single object
- **Decorator**: This lets us add or override behavior in an existing method of an object
- **Facade**: This provides a simplified interface for a larger and more complex body of code

- **Flyweight**: This allows us to reduce the resources needed to create and use a large number of similar objects
- **Proxy**: This is a type acting as an interface for another class or classes

In this chapter, we are going to give examples of how to use the bridge, facade, and proxy patterns in Swift. Let's start off by looking at the bridge pattern.

The bridge pattern

The **bridge pattern** decouples the abstraction from the implementation so that they can both vary independently. The bridge pattern can also be thought of as a two-layer abstraction.

Understanding the problem

The bridge pattern is designed to solve a couple of problems, but the one we are going to focus on here tends to arise over time as new requirements come in with new features. At some point, as these come in, we will need to change how the features interact. Eventually, this will require us to refactor the code.

In object-oriented programming, this is known as an exploding class hierarchy, but it can also happen in protocol-oriented programming.

Understanding the solution

The bridge pattern solves this problem by taking the interacting features and separating the functionality that is specific to each feature from the functionality that is shared between them. A bridge type can then be created, which will encapsulate the shared functionality, bringing them together.

Implementing the bridge pattern

To demonstrate how we would use the bridge pattern, we will create two features. The first feature is a message feature that will store and prepare a message that we wish to send out. The second feature is the sender feature that will send the message through a specific channel, such as email or SMS messaging.

Let's start off by creating two protocols named Message and Sender. The Message protocol will define the requirements for types that are used to create messages. The Sender protocol will be used to define the requirements for types that are used to send the messages through the specific channels.

The following code shows how we define these two protocols:

```
protocol Message {
    var messageString: String { get set }
    init(messageString: String)
    func prepareMessage()
}

protocol Sender {
    func sendMessage(message: Message)
}
```

The Message protocol defines a single property named messageString of the String type. This property will contain the text of the message and cannot be nil. We also define one initiator and a method named prepareMessage(). The initializer will be used to set the messageString property and anything else required by the message type. The prepareMessage() method will be used to prepare the message prior to sending it. This method can be used to encrypt the message or add formatting.

The Sender protocol defines a method named sendMessage(). This method will send the message through the channel defined by conforming types. In this function, we will need to ensure that the prepareMessage() method from the message type is called prior to sending the message.

Now let's see how we define two types that conform to the Message protocol:

```
class PlainTextMessage: Message {
    var messageString: String
    required init(messageString: String) {
        self.messageString = messageString
    }
    func prepareMessage() {
        //Nothing to do
    }
}

class DESEncryptedMessage: Message {
    var messageString: String
    required init(messageString: String) {
        self.messageString = messageString
    }
    func prepareMessage() {
        // Encrypt message here
```

```
        self.messageString = "DES: " + self.messageString
    }
}
```

Each of these types contains the required functionality to conform to the Message protocol. The only real difference between these types is in the prepareMessage() methods. In the PlainTextMessage class, the prepareMessage() method is empty because we do not need to do anything to the message prior to sending it. The prepareMessage() method of the DESEncryptionMessage class would normally contain the logic to encrypt the message, but for this example we will just prepend a DES tag to the beginning of the message, letting us know that this method was called.

Now let's create two types that will conform to the Sender protocol. These types would typically handle sending the message through a specific channel; however, in the example, we will simply print a message to the console:

```
class EmailSender: Sender {
    func sendMessage(message: Message) {
        print("Sending through E-Mail:")
        print("\(message.messageString)")
    }
}
class SMSSender: Sender {
    func sendMessage(message: Message) {
        print("Sending through SMS:")
        print("\(message.messageString)")
    }
}
```

Both the EmailSender and the SMSSender types conform to the Sender protocol by implementing the sendMessage() function.

We can now use these two features, as shown in the following code:

```
var myMessage = PlainTextMessage(messageString: "Plain Text Message")
myMessage.prepareMessage()
var sender = SMSSender()
sender.sendMessage(message: myMessage)
```

This will work well, and we could add code similar to this anywhere we need to create and send a message. Now let's say that, one day in the near future, we get a requirement to add a new functionality to verify the message prior to sending it, to make sure it meets the requirements of the channel we are sending the message through.

To do this, we would start off by changing the Sender protocol to add the verify functionality.

The new Sender protocol would look as follows:

```
protocol Sender {
    var message: Message? { get set }
    func sendMessage()
    func verifyMessage()
}
```

To the Sender protocol, we added a method named verifyMessage() and added a property named Message. We also changed the definition of the sendMessage() method. The original Sender protocol was designed to simply send the message, but now we need to verify the message prior to calling the sendMessage() function; therefore, we couldn't simply pass the message to it, as we did in the previous definition.

Now we will need to change the types that conform to the Sender protocol to make them conform to this new protocol. The following code shows how we would make these changes:

```
class EmailSender: Sender {
    var message: Message?
    func sendMessage() {
        print("Sending through E-Mail:")
        print("\(message!.messageString)")
    }
    func verifyMessage() {
        print("Verifying E-Mail message")
    }
}
class SMSSender: Sender {
    var message: Message?
    func sendMessage() {
        print("Sending through SMS:")
        print("\(message!.messageString)")
    }
    func verifyMessage() {
        print("Verifying SMS message")
    }
}
```

With the changes that we made to the types that conform to the `Sender` protocol, we will need to change how the code uses these types. The following example shows how we can now use them:

```
var myMessage = PlainTextMessage(messageString: "Plain Text Message")
myMessage.prepareMessage()
var sender = SMSSender()
sender.message = myMessage
sender.verifyMessage()
sender.sendMessage()
```

These changes are not that hard to make; however, without the bridge pattern, we would need to refactor the entire code base and make the change everywhere that we are sending messages. The bridge pattern tells us that when we have two hierarchies that closely interact together like this, we should put this interaction logic into a bridge type that will encapsulate the logic in one spot. This way, when we receive new requirements or enhancements, we can make the change in one spot, thereby limiting the refactoring that we must do. We could make a bridge type for the message and sender hierarchies, as shown in the following example:

```
struct MessagingBridge {
    static func sendMessage(message: Message, sender: Sender) {
        var sender = sender
        message.prepareMessage()
        sender.message = message
        sender.verifyMessage()
        sender.sendMessage()
    }
}
```

The logic of how the messaging and sender hierarchies interact is now encapsulated into the `MessagingBridge` structure. Now, when the logic needs to change, we only need to make the change to this one structure rather than having to refactor the entire code base.

The bridge pattern is a very good pattern to remember and use. There have been (and still are) times that I have regretted not using the bridge pattern in my code because, as we all know, requirements change frequently, and being able to make the changes in one spot rather than throughout the code base can save us a lot of time in the future.

Now, let's look at the next pattern in the structural category: the facade pattern.

The facade pattern

The **facade pattern** provides a simplified interface to a larger and more complex body of code. This allows us to make the libraries easier to use and understand by hiding some of the complexities. It also allows us to combine multiple APIs into a single, easier-to-use API, which is what we will see in the example.

Understanding the problem

The facade pattern is often used when we have a complex system that has a large number of independent APIs that are designed to work together. Sometimes it is hard to tell where we should use the facade pattern during the initial application design. The reason for this is that we normally try to simplify the initial API design; however, over time, and as requirements change and new features are added, the APIs become more and more complex, and then it becomes evident where the facade pattern should be used.

Understanding the solution

The main idea of the facade pattern is to hide the complexity of the APIs behind a simple interface. This offers us several advantages, the most obvious being that it simplifies how we interact with the APIs. It also promotes loose coupling, which allows the APIs to change as requirements change, without the need to refactor all the code that uses them.

Implementing the facade pattern

To demonstrate the facade pattern, we will create three APIs: `HotelBooking`, `FlightBooking`, and `RentalCarBooking`. These APIs will be used to search for and book hotels, flights, and rental cars for trips. While we could very easily call each of the APIs individually in the code, we are going to create a `TravelFacade` structure that will allow us to access the functionality of the APIs in single calls.

We will begin by defining the three APIs. Each of the APIs will need a data storage class that will store the information about the hotel, flight, or rental car. We will start off by implementing the hotel API:

```
struct Hotel {
    //Information about hotel room
}

struct HotelBooking {
    static func getHotelNameForDates(to: Date, from: Date) -> [Hotel]?
```

```
{
        let hotels = [Hotel]()
        //Logic to get hotels
        return hotels
    }
    static func bookHotel(hotel: Hotel) {
        // Logic to reserve hotel room
    }
}
```

The hotel API consists of the Hotel and HotelBooking structures. The Hotel structure will be used to store the information about a hotel room, and the HotelBooking structure will be used to search for a hotel room and to book the room for the trip. The flight and rental car APIs are very similar to the hotel API. The following code shows both of these APIs:

```
struct Flight {
    //Information about flights
}

struct FlightBooking {
    static func getFlightNameForDates(to: Date, from: Date) ->[Flight]?
    {
        let flights = [Flight]()
        //Logic to get flights return flights
    }
    static func bookFlight(flight: Flight) {
        // Logic to reserve flight
    }
}

struct RentalCar {
    //Information about rental cars
}

struct RentalCarBooking {
    static func getRentalCarNameForDates(to: Date, from: Date)->
[RentalCar]?

    {
        let cars = [RentalCar]()
        //Logic to get flights return cars
    }
```

```swift
    static func bookRentalCar(rentalCar: RentalCar) {
        // logic to reserve rental car
    }
}
```

In each of these APIs, we have a structure that is used to store information and a structure that is used to provide the search/booking functionality. In the initial design, it would be very easy to call these individual APIs within the application; however, as we all know, requirements tend to change, which causes the APIs to change over time.

By using the facade pattern here, we are able to hide how we implement the APIs; therefore, if we need to change how the APIs work in the future, we will only need to update the facade type rather than refactoring all of the code. This makes the code easier to maintain and update in the future. Now let's look at how we will implement the facade pattern by creating a TravelFacade structure:

```swift
struct TravelFacade {
    var hotels: [Hotel]?
    var flights: [Flight]?
    var cars: [RentalCar]?

    init(to: Date, from: Date) {
        hotels = HotelBooking.getHotelNameForDates(to: to, from:from)
        flights = FlightBooking.getFlightNameForDates(to: to,
from:from)
        cars = RentalCarBooking.getRentalCarNameForDates(to: to,
from:from)
    }

    func bookTrip(hotel: Hotel, flight: Flight, rentalCar: RentalCar) {
        HotelBooking.bookHotel(hotel: hotel)
        FlightBooking.bookFlight(flight: flight)
        RentalCarBooking.bookRentalCar(rentalCar: rentalCar)
    }
}
```

The TravelFacade class contains the functionality to search the three APIs and book a hotel, flight, and rental car. We can now use the TravelFacade class to search for hotels, flights, and rental cars without having to directly access the individual APIs.

As we mentioned at the start of this chapter, it is not always obvious when we should use the facade pattern in the initial design.

A good rule to follow is: if we have several APIs that are working together to perform a task, we should think about using the facade pattern.

Now, let's look at the last structural pattern, which is the proxy design pattern.

The proxy pattern

In the **proxy design pattern**, there is one type acting as an interface for another type or API. This wrapper class, which is the proxy, can then add functionality to the object, make the object available over a network, or restrict access to the object.

Understanding the problem

We can use the proxy pattern to solve several problems, but I find that I mainly use this pattern to solve one of two problems.

The first problem that I use this pattern to solve is when I want to create a layer of abstraction between a single API and my code. The API could be a local or remote API, but I usually use this pattern to put an abstraction layer between my code and a remote service. This will allow changes to the remote API without the need to refactor large portions of the application code.

The second problem that I use the proxy pattern to solve is when I need to make changes to an API, but I do not have the code or there is already a dependency on the API elsewhere in the application.

Understanding the solution

To solve these problems, the proxy pattern tells us that we should create a type that will act as an interface for interacting with the other type or API. In the example, we will show how to use the proxy pattern to add functionality to an existing type.

Implementing the proxy pattern

In this section, we will demonstrate the proxy pattern by creating a house class that we can add multiple floor plans to, where each floor plan represents a different story of the house. Let's begin by creating a FloorPlan protocol:

```
protocol FloorPlan {
    var bedRooms: Int { get set }
    var utilityRooms: Int { get set }
    var bathRooms: Int { get set }
    var kitchen: Int { get set }
```

```
        var livingRooms: Int { get set }
    }
```

In the `FloorPlan` protocol, we define five properties that will represent the number of rooms contained in each floor plan. Now, let's create an implementation of the `FloorPlan` protocol named `HouseFloorPlan`, which is as follows:

```
struct HouseFloorPlan: FloorPlan {
    var bedRooms = 0
    var utilityRooms = 0
    var bathRooms = 0
    var kitchen = 0
    var livingRooms = 0
}
```

The `HouseFloorPlan` structure implements all five properties required from the `FloorPlan` protocol and assigns default values to them. Next, we will create the `House` type, which will represent a house:

```
struct House {
    var stories = [FloorPlan]()
    mutating func addStory(floorPlan: FloorPlan) {
        stories.append(floorPlan)
    }
}
```

Within the `House` structure, we have an array of instances that conforms to the `FloorPlan` protocol where each floor plan will represent one story of the house. We also have a function named `addStory()`, which accepts an instance of a type that conforms to the `FloorPlan` protocol. This function will add the floor plan to the array of `FloorPlan` protocols.

If we think about the logic of this class, there is one problem that we might encounter: we are allowed to add as many floor plans as we want, which may lead to houses that are 60 or 70 stories high. This would be great if we were building skyscrapers, but we just want to build basic single-family houses. If we want to limit the number of floor plans without changing the `House` class (either we cannot change it, or we simply do not want to), we can implement the proxy pattern. The following example shows how to implement the `HouseProxy` class, where we limit the number of floor plans we can add to the house:

```
struct HouseProxy {
    var house = House()
    mutating func addStory(floorPlan: FloorPlan) -> Bool {
```

```
        if house.stories.count < 3 {
            house.addStory(floorPlan: floorPlan)
            return true
        } else {
            return false
        }
    }
}
```

We begin the HouseProxy class by creating an instance of the House class. We then create a method named addStory(), which lets us add a new floor plan to the house. In the addStory() method, we check to see if the number of stories in the house is fewer than three; if so, we add the floor plan to the house and return true. If the number of stories is equal to or greater than three, then we do not add the floor plan to the house and return false. Let's see how we can use this proxy:

```
var ourHouse = HouseProxy()

var basement = HouseFloorPlan(bedRooms: 0, utilityRooms: 1,
bathRooms:1,kitchen: 0, livingRooms: 1)
var firstStory = HouseFloorPlan (bedRooms: 1, utilityRooms:
0,bathRooms: 2,kitchen: 1, livingRooms: 1)
var secondStory = HouseFloorPlan (bedRooms: 2, utilityRooms:
0,bathRooms: 1,kitchen: 0, livingRooms: 1)
var additionalStory = HouseFloorPlan (bedRooms: 1, utilityRooms:
0,bathRooms:1, kitchen: 1, livingRooms: 1)

ourHouse.addStory(floorPlan: basement)
ourHouse.addStory(floorPlan: firstStory)
ourHouse.addStory(floorPlan: secondStory)
ourHouse.addStory(floorPlan: additionalStory)
```

In the example code, we start off by creating an instance of the HouseProxy class named ourHouse. We then create four instances of the HouseFloorPlan type, each with a different number of rooms. Finally, we attempt to add each of the floor plans to the ourHouse instance. If we run this code, we will see that the first three instances of the floorplans class were added to the house successfully, but the last one wasn't because we are only allowed to add three floors.

The proxy pattern is very useful when we want to add some additional functionality or error checking to a type, but we do not want to change the actual type itself. We can also use it to add a layer of abstraction between a remote or local API.

Now, let's look at behavioral design patterns.

Behavioral design patterns

Behavioral design patterns explain how types interact with each other. These patterns describe how different instances of types send messages to each other to make things happen.

There are nine well-known patterns that are part of the behavioral design pattern type. They are as follows:

- **Chain of responsibility**: This is used to process a variety of requests, each of which may be delegated to a different handler.
- **Command**: This creates objects that can encapsulate actions or parameters so that they can be invoked later or by a different component.
- **Iterator**: This allows us to access the elements of an object sequentially without exposing the underlying structure.
- **Mediator**: This is used to reduce coupling between types that communicate with each other.
- **Memento**: This is used to capture the current state of an object and store it in a manner that can be restored later.
- **Observer**: This allows an object to publish changes to an object's state. Other objects can then subscribe so they can be notified of any changes.
- **State**: This is used to alter the behavior of an object when its internal state changes.
- **Strategy**: This allows one out of a family of algorithms to be chosen at runtime.
- **Visitor**: This is a way of separating an algorithm from an object structure.

In this section, we are going to give examples of how to use strategy and command patterns in Swift. Let's start off by looking at the command pattern.

The command pattern

The command design pattern lets us define actions that we can execute later. This pattern generally encapsulates all the information needed to call or trigger the actions at a later time.

Understanding the problem

There are times in applications when we need to separate the execution of a command from its invoker. Typically, this is when we have a type that needs to perform one of several actions, but the choice of which action to use needs to be made at runtime.

Understanding the solution

The command pattern tells us that we should encapsulate the logic for the actions into a type that conforms to a command protocol. We can then provide instances of the command types for use by the invoker. The invoker will use the interface provided by the protocol to invoke the necessary actions.

Implementing the command pattern

In this section, we will demonstrate how to use the command pattern by creating a Light type. In this type, we will define the lightOnCommand and lightOffCommand commands and will use the turnOnLight() and turnOffLight() methods to invoke these commands. We will begin by creating a protocol named Command, which all of the command types will conform to. Here is the Command protocol:

```
protocol Command {
    func execute()
}
```

This protocol contains a method named execute(), which will be used to execute the command. Now, let's look at the command types that the Light type will use to turn the light on and off. They are as follows:

```
struct RockerSwitchLightOnCommand: Command {
    func execute() {
        print("Rocker Switch:Turning Light On")
    }
}

struct RockerSwitchLightOffCommand: Command {
    func execute() {
        print("Rocker Switch:Turning Light Off")
    }
}
```

```swift
struct PullSwitchLightOnCommand: Command {
    func execute() {
        print("Pull Switch:Turning Light On")
    }
}

struct PullSwitchLightOffCommand: Command {
    func execute() {
        print("Pull Switch:Turning Light Off")
    }
}
```

The `RockerSwitchLightOffCommand`, `RockerSwitchLightOnCommand`, `PullSwitchLightOnCommand`, and `PullSwitchLightOffCommand` commands all conform to the `Command` protocol by implementing the `execute()` method; therefore, we will be able to use them in the `Light` type. Now, let's look at how to implement the `Light` type:

```swift
struct Light {
    var lightOnCommand: Command
    var lightOffCommand: Command

    func turnOnLight() {
        self.lightOnCommand.execute()
    }

    func turnOffLight() {
        self.lightOffCommand.execute()
    }
}
```

In the `Light` type, we start off by creating two variables, named `lightOnCommand` and `lightOffCommand`, which will contain instances of types that conform to the `Command` protocol. Then we create the `turnOnLight()` and `turnOffLight()` methods that we will use to turn the light on and off. In these methods, we call the appropriate command to turn the light on or off.

We would then use the `Light` type as follows:

```swift
var on = PullSwitchLightOnCommand()
var off = PullSwitchLightOffCommand()
var light = Light(lightOnCommand: on, lightOffCommand: off)
light.turnOnLight()
```

```
light.turnOffLight()

light.lightOnCommand = RockerSwitchLightOnCommand()
light.turnOnLight()
```

In this example, we begin by creating an instance of the `PullSwitchLightOnCommand` type named on and an instance of the `PullSwitchLightOffCommand` type named off. We then create an instance of the `Light` type using the two commands that we just created and call the `turnOnLight()` and `turnOffLight()` methods of the `Light` instance to turn the light on and off. In the last two lines, we change the `lightOnCommand` method, which was originally set to an instance of the `PullSwitchLightOnCommand` class, to an instance of the `RockerSwitchLightOnCommand` type. The `Light` instance will now use the `RockerSwitchLightOnCommand` type whenever we turn the light on. This allows us to change the functionality of the `Light` type during runtime.

There are several benefits of using the command pattern. One of the main benefits is that we are able to set which command to invoke at runtime, which also lets us swap the commands out with different implementations that conform to the `Command` protocol as needed throughout the life of the application. Another advantage of the command pattern is that we encapsulate the details of command implementations within the command types themselves rather than in the container type.

Now, let's look at the last design pattern, the strategy pattern.

The strategy pattern

The strategy pattern is pretty similar to the command pattern in that they both allow us to decouple implementation details from the calling type, and also allow us to switch the implementation out at runtime. The big difference is that the strategy pattern is intended to encapsulate algorithms. By swapping out an algorithm, we are expecting the object to perform the same functionality, but in a different way. In the command pattern, when we swap out the commands, we are expecting the object to change the functionality.

Understanding the problem

There are times in applications when we need to change the backend algorithm that is used to perform an operation. Typically, this is when we have a type that has several different algorithms that can be used to perform the same task, but the choice of which algorithm to use needs to be made at runtime.

Understanding the solution

The strategy pattern tells us that we should encapsulate the algorithm in a type that conforms to a strategy protocol. We can then provide instances of the strategy types for use by the invoker. The invoker will use the interface provided by the protocol to invoke the algorithm.

Implementing the strategy pattern

In this section, we will demonstrate the strategy pattern by showing you how we could swap out compression algorithms at runtime. Let's begin this example by creating a CompressionStrategy protocol that each one of the compression types will conform to. Let's look at the following code:

```swift
protocol CompressionStrategy {
    func compressFiles(filePaths: [String])
}
```

This protocol defines a method named compressFiles() that accepts a single parameter, which is an array of strings that contains the paths to the files we want to compress. We will now create two structures that conform to this protocol. These are the ZipCompressionStrategy and RarCompressionStrategy structures, which are as follows:

```swift
struct ZipCompressionStrategy: CompressionStrategy {
    func compressFiles(filePaths: [String]) {
        print("Using Zip Compression")
    }
}

struct RarCompressionStrategy: CompressionStrategy {
    func compressFiles(filePaths: [String]) {
        print("Using RAR Compression")
    }
}
```

Both of these structures implement the CompressionStrategy protocol by using a method named compressFiles(), which accepts an array of strings. Within these methods, we simply print out the name of the compression that we are using. Normally, we would implement the compression logic in these methods.

Now, let's look at the `CompressContent` class, which will be used to compress the files:

```
struct CompressContent {
    var strategy: CompressionStrategy
    func compressFiles(filePaths: [String]) {
        self.strategy.compressFiles(filePaths: filePaths)
    }
}
```

In this class, we start off by defining a variable, named `strategy`, which will contain an instance of a type that conforms to the `CompressionStrategy` protocol. Then we create a method named `compressFiles()`, which accepts an array of strings that contains the paths to the list of files that we wish to compress. In this method, we compress the files using the compression strategy that is set in the `strategy` variable.

We will use the `CompressContent` class as follows:

```
var filePaths = ["file1.txt", "file2.txt"]
var zip = ZipCompressionStrategy()
var rar = RarCompressionStrategy()

var compress = CompressContent(strategy: zip)
compress.compressFiles(filePaths: filePaths)

compress.strategy = rar
compress.compressFiles(filePaths: filePaths)
```

We begin by creating an array of strings that contains the files we wish to compress. We also create an instance of both the `ZipCompressionStrategy` and `RarCompressionStrategy` types. We then create an instance of the `CompressContent` class, setting the compression strategy to the `ZipCompressionStrategy` instance, and call the `compressFiles()` method, which will print the `Using zip compression` message to the console. We then set the compression strategy to the `RarCompressionStrategy` instance and call the `compressFiles()` method again, which will print the `Using rar compression` message to the console.

The strategy pattern is really good for setting the algorithms to use at runtime, which also lets us swap the algorithms out with different implementations as needed by the application. Another advantage of the strategy pattern is that we encapsulate the details of the algorithm within the strategy types themselves and not in the main implementation type.

This concludes the tour of design patterns in Swift.

Summary

Design patterns are solutions to software design problems that we tend to see over and over again in real-world application design. These patterns are designed to help us create reusable and flexible code. Design patterns can also make code easier to read and understand for other developers and also for ourselves when we look back at the code months or years later.

If we look at the examples in this chapter carefully, we will notice that one of the backbones of design patterns is the protocol. Almost all design patterns (the singleton design pattern is an exception) use protocols to help us create very flexible and reusable code.

If this was the first time that you really looked at design patterns, you probably noticed some strategies that you have used in the past in your own code. This is expected when experienced developers are first introduced to design patterns. I would also encourage you to read more about design patterns because they will definitely help you to create more flexible and reusable code.

Swift is a language that is rapidly changing and it is important to keep up to date with it. Since Swift is an open source project, there are plenty of resources that will help you. I would definitely recommend bookmarking `http://swiftdoc.org` in your favorite browser. It has auto-generated documentation for the Swift language and is a great resource.

Another site to bookmark is `https://swift.org`. This is the main open source Swift site. On this site, you will find links to the Swift source code, blog posts, getting started pages, and information on how to install Swift.

I would also recommend signing up for some of the mailing lists on the swift. org site. The lists are located in the community section. The `Swift-users` mailing list is an excellent place to ask questions and is the list that Apple monitors. If you want to stay up to date with changes to Swift, then I would recommend the `swift-evolution-announce` list.

I hope you have enjoyed reading this book as much as I have enjoyed writing it.

Other Books You May Enjoy

If you enjoyed this book, you may be interested in these other books by Packt:

Extreme C

Kamran Amini

ISBN: 978-1-78934-362-5

- Build advanced C knowledge on strong foundations, rooted in first principles
- Understand memory structures and compilation pipeline and how they work, and how to make most out of them
- Apply object-oriented design principles to your procedural C code
- Write low-level code that's close to the hardware and squeezes maximum performance out of a computer system
- Master concurrency, multithreading, multi-processing, and integration with other languages
- Unit Testing and debugging, build systems, and inter-process communication for C programming

Responsive Web Design with HTML5 and CSS

Benjamin Frain

ISBN: 978-1-83921-156-0

- Integrate CSS media queries into your designs; apply different styles to different devices
- Load different sets of images depending upon screen size or resolution
- Leverage the speed, semantics, and clean markup of accessible HTML patterns
- Implement SVGs into your designs to provide resolution-independent images
- Apply the latest features of CSS like custom properties, variable fonts, and CSS Grid
- Add validation and interface elements like date and color pickers to HTML forms
- Understand the multitude of ways to enhance interface elements with filters, shadows, animations, and more

Leave a review - let other readers know what you think

Please share your thoughts on this book with others by leaving a review on the site that you bought it from. If you purchased the book from Amazon, please leave us an honest review on this book's Amazon page. This is vital so that other potential readers can see and use your unbiased opinion to make purchasing decisions, we can understand what our customers think about our products, and our authors can see your feedback on the title that they have worked with Packt to create. It will only take a few minutes of your time, but is valuable to other potential customers, our authors, and Packt. Thank you!

Index

X

Made in the USA
Monee, IL
16 March 2023

29997823R00230